SURF IS WHERE YOU FIND IT

Gerry Lopez

→2   →2A   →3   →3A   →4

KODAK PLUS X PAN FILM

→8   →8A   →9   →9A   →10

→3   →3A   →4   →4A   →5

LUS X PAN FILM   KODAK S

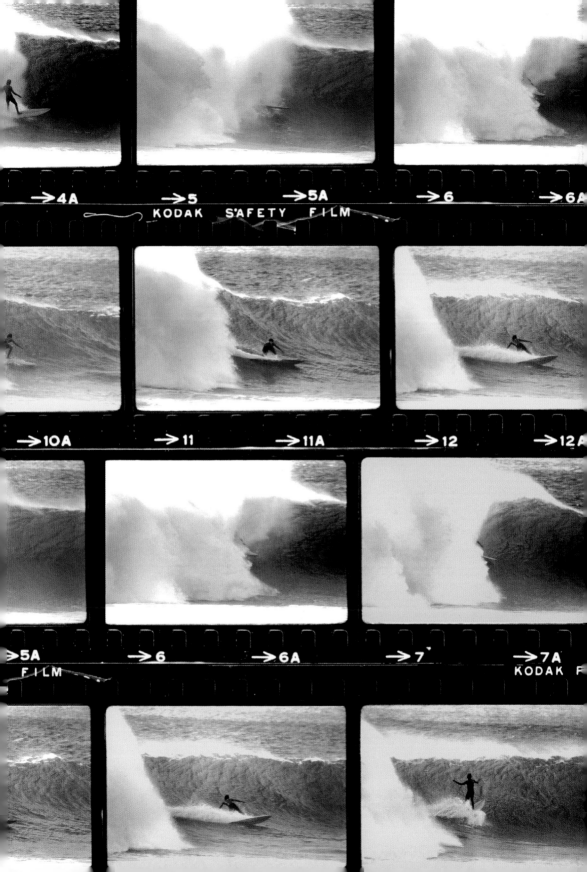

KODAK S'AFETY FILM

→4A →5 →5A →6 →6A

→10A →11 →11A →12 →12A

→5A →6 →6A →7 →7A

FILM KODAK F

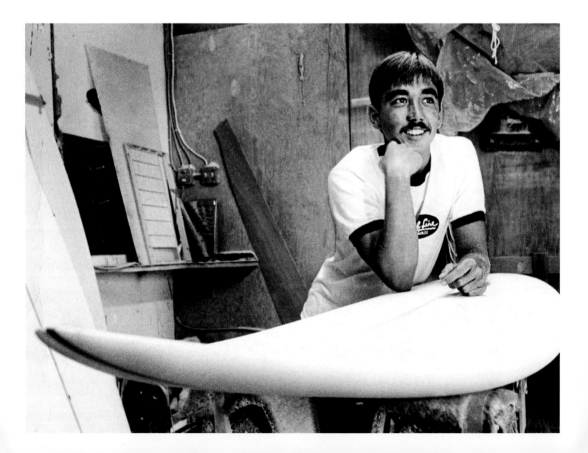

Jock Sutherland, an early master of the
Pipeline, was a great help to me when I was
starting out there. Photo: Art Brewer

Above   Buffalo and Teddy Bear headed
out for another day at the office at Makaha
Beach. Photo: Jeff Divine

Right   RB, Reno, and I posed this shot at the
Makiki Pumping Station as a tribute to our new
shortboard shapes. Photo: David Darling

Previous spread   Another routine drop at
the Pipeline that ended up as a poster
for *Surfer* magazine. Photo: Jeff Divine

Above   A slight stall at the bottom of a sweet Pipeline
wave to let the tube set up ahead. Photo: Jeff Hornbaker

Right   The tube at the Pipeline had enough room to
stand straight up inside it. Photo: Jeff Hornbaker

Above   A bottom turn at the Pipeline on the Coral Cruiser marks the beginning of some success at surfing this difficult and dangerous break. Photo: James Cassimus

Next page   The Coral Cruiser, an eight-foot pintail gun, made surfing the Pipeline, more or less, a cakewalk. Photo: Art Brewer

15

SURF IS WHERE YOU FIND IT

—

Gerry Lopez

patagonia®

SURF IS WHERE YOU FIND IT

At Patagonia, we publish a collection of books that reflect our pursuits and our values—books on wilderness, outdoor sports, innovation, and a commitment to environmental activism.

REVISED EDITION

Editor: John Dutton
Photo Editor: Jane Sievert
Design: Scott Massey
Production: Rafael Dunn

Printed in China on 100% recycled paper
Front Cover: Art Brewer

Library of Congress Control Number 2014954048
Hardcover ISBN 978-1-938340-43-7
Softcover ISBN 978-1-938340-26-0
E-Book ISBN 978-1-938340-25-3

Versions of "Sweet Candy Days," "Pakala," "A First Time at the Pipeline," "Dr. Surf," "RB," "A Giant Among Men," "Herbie," "The Fastest Wave in the World," "Flippy," "Momentary Entertainment," "Jan's Board," "Everything Bad Happens in Parking Lots," "Caught Inside Again," "The Money Motive," "Incident at Eke Moku," "The Mother of All Pipeline Swells," "The Edge of Panic," "A Good Day to Die," "Tales of Indonesia," "Jungle Love," "Treasure Islands," "The Mile-Long Rides," "Chile," "Get It While You Can," "The Country," "Whitey and the Duke," "The Last Laugh," "A Good Deal," "Cannons," and "The Coral Cruiser" were previously published in *Surf 1st* magazine.

Versions of "The Track of the Cat," "No Prisoners," "The Big Swim," and "The Best Surfer in the Flesh" were previously published in *Free & Easy* magazine.

Versions of "Caught Inside Again," "G-Land," and "The Best Surfer in the Flesh" were previously published in *Water* magazine.

A version of "Incident at Eke Moku" was previously published in a Patagonia catalog.

Versions of "A Giant Among Men," "Big Wally," and "The Country" were previously published in *The Surfer's Journal*.

A version of "Pakala" was previously published in *Bamboo Ridge: Journal of Hawai'i Literature and Arts*.

A version of "Jungle Love" was previously published in *The Surfer's Path* magazine.

Versions of "Comin' Down," "Big Wally," "The Demise of the Ditch," "A Big Score," "The Gorge," and "A Saturday at Ala Moana" were previously published in *Nalu, The Longboarder's Magazine*.

To my wife, Toni, and son, Alex.

Special thanks to these fine photographers: Erik Aeder, Branden Aroyan, Art Brewer, James Cassimus, Sylvain Cazenave, David Darling, Kirk Devoll, Jeff Divine, Dana Edmunds, Gordinho, Leroy Grannis, Jeff Hornbaker, Don James, Jeff Johnson, Don King, Kimiro Kondo, Don Marsh, Tim McCullough, Dan Merkel, Ben Moon, Bev Morgan, Joe Quigg, John Russell, Denjiro Sato, John Schwirtlich, Tom Servais, John Severson, Craig Stecyk, Ron Stoner, Andy Tullis, Mike Waggoner, Steve Wilkings, and John Wrenn.

I wish to thank my mother and father, both avid readers and writers, for instilling in me their love of books. To Michael McPherson, a surfer friend from the old days and accomplished author; mahalo for providing much needed motivation, patience, and understanding. To good friends—Gordon Clark, Roy Mesker, Bruce Bailey, Tomoko Okabe, my brother Victor Lopez, George Kam, Dale Hope, Michael Cassidy, Dave Chun, Yvon and Malinda Chouinard, Rick Ridgeway, John Dutton, Jane Sievert, Tom Adler, Casey Bevington, Takashi Isobe, Yoshinori Ueda, Steve Pezman, Jeff Divine, Drew Kampion, Alex Dick-Reed, and Steve Zelden—thanks for all the encouragement and support. To George Downing, a very special person to me and the world of surfing. And most of all, thanks to surfing and all the great surfers who made these stories happen.

It was sometime in the summer of 2004. I had been invited on a boat trip to the Mentawai Islands with a stellar cast. Laird Hamilton was the leader of the pack; he was working on a movie project and invited a crew of people to join him for an adventure. For some reason I don't remember I was arriving a day late for the trip, and I would have to jump on a different boat to catch up with the mother ship, which was already well on its way.

I landed in Padang late in the evening, was taken to a room to sleep, and was told that I would be woken up at 4:00 am to leave for the eight-hour boat ride to meet up with the crew. Sure enough, the phone rang at 4:00 am sharp, I grabbed my stuff and headed out. As I loaded my gear into our little boat I recognized a familiar face through the darkness. It was Gerry Lopez.

I have obviously known about Gerry Lopez for as long as I can remember. His poster held the prime spot on my wall directly across from my bed. He was the last image I saw before I closed my eyes at night and the first image I saw when I woke up. It was a beautiful poster of Gerry dropping in on a twelve-foot wave at the Banzai Pipeline. The sun glistening on the face of the wave. His board well positioned with his line set for what was destined to be something special. His style was flawless. So much poise. Even his hair blowing in the wind seemed surreal.

I remember staring at the poster and thinking that I would never ride a wave like that. I didn't like big waves. I was scared of them and the sight of a wave like that made my stomach turn. But I was always mesmerized by this image for some reason. Other posters came and went, but this one was always treasured and protected.

When I hit my midteens, I began to make the yearly pilgrimage to the North Shore hoping to catch a few waves here and there. By now I had learned a lot more about Mr. Lopez. I had discovered old movies of him surfing all over the world. The most memorable of those being the waves he rode at the Pipeline and, of course, his adventures through the islands of Indonesia. I remember catching the occasional glimpse of him on the North Shore. He was a god to us, a messiah. The amount of respect Gerry received was amazing. He paddled out at the Pipeline a few times and it was always such a treat to watch him navigate his way through the lineup, sit and wait patiently for the wave he wanted, and then do what he does best: glide effortlessly down the face, slide into the tube, and get spit out the other end.

I had the opportunity to meet Gerry a few times here and there over the next few years, but it was never for more than a few minutes and it always seemed to happen in those overpopulated situations like surfer poll awards, trade shows, and the like. But no matter the situation, Gerry always made time for me. He looked me in the eye and listened. He connected with people, even if it was only for a brief moment. His demeanor was always so impressive even amongst such chaos.

Back on our boat in the Padang harbor we were all loaded up and headed out for our eight-hour ride with the sun starting to peak over the hills. Our boat wasn't the biggest boat and there were only a few good seats on board. As the sun got higher in the sky and the wind started to blow, it became clear that the best and most comfortable seat on the boat was a bench seat that sat two at the front of the boat. So I took my seat and settled in. It wasn't long before Gerry was sitting right next to me. For the next six hours I sat side by side with my hero. I asked him every question that I ever wanted to ask and then some. We covered just about his entire life from growing up in Hawai'i, the shortboard revolution, the early years at the Banzai Pipeline, the golden years at the Banzai Pipeline, the Uluwatu, Padang Padang years, the discovery of G-land, shaping and surfboard design, yoga, food, the power of the mind....

Time flew by, and before we knew it we had pulled up to a perfect three- to four-foot reef pass with no one out. All of a sudden we were like two little kids scrambling to get our boards out of our bags. We each grabbed our favorite, waxed it up, and paddled out. I will never forget that session. The conditions were flawless, and wave after wave poured through the lineup. I remember one wave particularly well. It was a beautiful little four footer that was doubling up and bending around the reef. Gerry had just ridden the wave before me and was paddling back out. I slid straight into the tube and as I surfed I heard a hoot from the channel. It was right then that Gerry's big grin came into view. I've gotten bigger and better tubes in my life, but that one wave will stay with me for the rest of my life.

Thank you Gerry for being you and inspiring generations of surfers to stay true to the real feeling of surfing.

Gerry Lopez and I have been acquaintances since the 1970s. Over decades of proximity and mutual friends, a sense of familiarity and affection is created. As a surf magazine editor, it was my job to pay attention to him and what he did. Over the years I've had the pleasure of publishing his writings, beginning with "Attitude Dancing" for *Surfer* magazine in the mid-1970s, which became an anthem for the surfing of that period.

Observing Lopez from a distance: Even as a young, relatively immature surfer, Gerry Lopez had something special going on inside his brain that set him apart from the 1960s masses of teenaged gremmies, so aptly described by Phil Edwards as "legions of the stoked." Gerry's DNA is part Spanish-German newspaper-journalist father, part lifelong-teacher Japanese mother. Both parents read and wrote extensively. His sharp intellect is instinctual, with a Zen spin, inhabiting a slight frame that articulates a well-coordinated physical presence, one that somehow survives the seemingly impossible by dint of grace and savvy rather than brute power. He has none of the latter other than his mind force. However, it has been the awesome brute power of the ocean that provides the contrasting frame of reference in which he plays his game. There, Gerry operates glibly, with such panache amidst the mayhem that he has become a surfer icon, a living symbol for man surviving huge natural forces, exhibiting grace under pressure, in a game that has taken on much meaning for our society.

Along the road, for forty-some years' worth, Lopez has proven himself a keen observer of human nature encountered while living through experiences quite extraordinary. In his later years, now grown even wiser and reflective though not yet shut down in his own physicality, Gerry has taken to writing more and more about what he has seen. His is a rare slice for us to have access to, worth sharing, well told, much like his style on a wave, reflecting his hereditary roots, wry and wily, carefully considered, perceptive and clever, drawing artful lines through life.

Steve made the camera and I made the board; this first-of-its-kind inside-the-tube photo was the result. Today anyone with a GoPro can have the same picture. Photo: Steve Wilkings

A life devoted to surfing has been a splendid way to live. From the beginning, the adventures have been memorable: growing up in the extraordinary place that was Hawai'i in the 1950s and 1960s. Playing a part in the shortboard revolution of the late 1960s and early 1970s. Living the dream in the Country before it was ever called the North Shore. Experiencing the awe, fear, and ultimate satisfaction of finding the tube in the early days at the Pipeline. Traveling for surf throughout the world: to the original surf camp at G-Land, the exotic islands off Sumatra, and especially to the magic island of Bali, Indonesia—before it became a popular surf destination. Experiencing the beginnings of windsurfing on Maui, the rebirth in Hawai'i of prone paddleboarding, the early years of snowboarding and tow-in surfing at Jaws. Finding and falling in deep to the new sport of standup paddle surfing and downwind running. And through it all, designing and building the equipment, the boards, and accessories that make each new evolution of the surf game more inviting, more challenging, and more satisfying.

But it is the people who surfing molds into unique individuals, each with his own special story, who stand out. Many of these surfers who helped create the surfing world of today are unknown for their contributions, or are already forgotten.

It is said that the best thing about surfing is talking about it afterward. This is true, and, while surfing is an intimately personal endeavor, the stories can be enjoyed by anyone. My father, a career newspaperman, instilled in me a desire to put these stories into written form. There was more encouragement, help, and support given by family and friends. I've felt a duty to record some of the events and people I have had the pleasure of being involved with; they are the history of this fine sport.

These stories are for those surfers who helped shape surfing and for the younger surfers who may be interested in the way things were before their time. They are also for anyone who has never been on a surfboard or ridden a wave but finds the idea of it intriguing.

Surfing is a deeply wonderful thing—anytime, anywhere, and any way.

Bon Ching, Rell Sunn, and me at the 1965 Ala Moana Hawai'i
State Surfing Championships. Photo: David Darling

i. BEGIN—NINGS

A reflective moment on the beach about something …
a wave, a surfboard, a girl? Photo: Art Brewer

Sweet

Candy

Days

The 1950s and early 1960s were a great time to grow up in Hawai'i. I lived in Honolulu, and the days of my youth were spent on the beach at Waikiki. My parents loved the ocean, and this love rubbed off on me and my older sister, Lola, and younger brother, Victor. We passed many afternoons on weekdays and full days on weekends and holidays at Queens Surf, our favorite beach.

From Queen Kapi'olani Park looking seaward, a surf break known as the Wall was just to the right, further on were the famous Waikiki surf breaks of Queens and Canoes. Just across the street was the Honolulu Zoo, which we also visited regularly. My brother, sister, and I were familiar with all the animal exhibits and every tree to climb, especially the sprawling banyan tree at the entrance. To the left was the War Memorial Natatorium, a seawater pool built in the 1920s to honor Hawaiian soldiers lost in World War I.

Eventually the Waikiki Aquarium was constructed next to the Natatorium. Like the zoo, there was no price of admission. We walked in free as the breeze. I loved all the exhibits and came to know every single fish on display there. Not long after that, an outdoor amphitheater called the Waikiki Shell was put up in the park next to the zoo. The entire area was our playground, but we passed most of our time in the ocean and on the beach.

The water and air temperature of Waikiki Beach are the most pleasant and refreshing of any beach I've ever visited the world over. For Hawai'i old-timers Waikiki is simply 'The Beach,' as if there is no other.

As kids, we could spend hours and hours frolicking in the surge that washed upon the golden sand. I remember the water being clear and the sand sparkling clean. We would dig big holes for our father to lie in and cover him back up. We thought if we piled enough sand on top, he wouldn't be able to get out. But every time, with a strength that always amazed us, no matter how much sand was heaped on, he would flex his big hands first, then lift his knees and emerge from the mound. Soon the wave action would smooth over any digging, and the beach would be returned to its normal smooth surface.

Late in the day, after all the swimming and playing, my father would fire up the hibachi and Mom would cook something for dinner. We would eat as the sun set over

My Dad, my sister, Lola, and me enjoying a
day at the beach. Photo: Lopez collection

'Ewa Beach to our west, lighting up the whole sky in brilliant red, orange, and gold colors. Tired, sunburned, and sleepy, we would pack up and head home, our day of fun at the beach complete. The next day we would return, none of us ever bored by this natural playground and place of peace and joy. The beach was our second home.

On occasion, when the surf was up, a small wave would break alongside the rock jetty. My father showed us how to bodysurf the wave. We could ride right up onto the sand. It was very tame, but the gentle waves had enough energy to carry a small boy's body in their surge.

This was our first experience with riding the surf. Sometimes we would walk down to the Wall and watch the paipo boarders and bodysurfers ride the more serious surf there. From above, they looked like sea creatures as they shot the curl of the waves. Each rider seemed to be a part of his wave. Directly out in front of our swimming beach was an expert surf break named Public Baths, where the better surfers would ride on their long surfboards. When the waves were just right, they would glide on the face of the waves for very long distances. I would sit on the end of the stone jetty and watch them swoop across the walls of water. At some point it must have entered my mind that I wanted to try it.

I pestered my mother and father to go surfboarding but neither had any experience at it. My father had tried it once years before. He rented a solid wood board but somehow managed to drop it on his toe before he ever got in the water. The eighty-pound board smashed his toe and ended his surf session in one bloody squish.

My mother and her younger sister, my auntie Betty (Michiko), were teachers at Kaimuki High School and had some students who were not only accomplished surfers but also ran a surfboard rental concession. Probably in exchange for some relief from homework, they offered to lend their teachers the surfboards.

My brother Victor and me at Queens Surf, not long before we pestered Mom into taking us surfing for the first time. Photo: Lopez collection

Mom gave us the good news, and we could hardly go to sleep that night thinking about the next day. I was ten years old and Victor was eight. Mom's students had their concession set up on the beach in front of the Royal Hawaiian Hotel. We got to pick from a whole rack of surfboards that the beach boys made good money on renting to tourists. I chose a bright red one and my brother took a blue one. Holding the noses, we dragged the boards down to the water's edge and waited there for my mother. We were tiny and the boards seemed huge. Mom swam out next to us in the warm water while we paddled the boards. Later, I would learn that we were at a spot called Baby Queens, an inside break perfect for beginners.

We learned how to turn the big boards around so they pointed toward shore. A wave came and my mother told me to get ready. She pushed the tail and the next thing I knew, I was gliding along on a wave. I didn't have to do a thing; the wave did all the work. I remember the sound was a slight hiss as the board cut through the water and the breaking wave made a crackling sound. I was overwhelmed with a sensation that took my breath away. It seemed like I was as free as a bird in flight. I had never felt anything so good before, and the corners of my mouth curled up into a big smile. I was sailing along at a good clip, as fast as on a bicycle going down a steep hill. Soon the wave petered out and the board slowed down. I wanted to do it again. As I turned the board around, I saw my brother coming in on the next wave. He had a big smile too.

When I paddled the board out to where my mother waited, she asked how it went. When I told her I wanted to keep doing it, she smiled and suggested that maybe I should try to stand up the next time. The next wave came, she gave a shove, and I felt it again. I was gliding, as free as a bird. I carefully got to my knees and the sensation of speed seemed to increase. Gradually I pushed myself up until I could let go with my hands and stand on my feet. This was like riding a bike with no hands, only a lot faster and without any effort. The wave did everything. I knew then that this was the best thing I had ever done.

It's incredible that after almost fifty years of surfing, I can still remember those first few waves like they were yesterday. What's even more amazing is that riding them is still the only thing I want to do: keep surfing.

Pakala

Just off the narrow two-lane highway, sitting incongruously alone, is a tiny, one-room building. Lush, green sugarcane fields, their stalks billowing in the gentle trade winds, fill the rich land on either side of the road. The building is a post office and the sign reads Makaweli, Kaua'i. It sits on an intersection where the crossing road is dirt of an astonishing shade of red.

Across the paved highway, the road heads straight *mauka*, toward the mountains. However, these mountains aren't really mountains but rather low, rolling hills planted in more sugarcane. *Makai*, or toward the sea, the road runs straight, and on the left beyond a small field of cane is a large, open equipment shed. Scattered around the yard lies the machinery used to plant, maintain, and harvest sugarcane.

Much of the equipment is dilapidated, obsolete, and permanently parked. The machines that work are well used. Everything is coated with a layer of red dust. Mechanics work on trucks and other obscure farming machines under the hot sun. From the machine shop, the flash and sparks of welding can be seen, and the sounds of grinding and pounding echo off the high tin roof. On the right side of the road, a rough, rock wall and an irrigation ditch border another cane field.

Past the shed and equipment yard, a fork in the road splits and goes off to the right. There are small board and batten houses of rough sawn one-inch by twelve-inch

The summer wave still spins perfectly around its arc of shallow reef. Photo: Denjiro Sato

pine and built up off the ground; all are in the same traditional plantation labor camp design, varying slightly in size and age. The homes are set apart by small yards surrounding them and occasional wooden fences. Many have large mango trees, some citrus, a few lychee, banana, and papaya. Well-tended vegetable gardens or noisy chicken coops fill others. Some have neatly trimmed lawns with flowering shrubs, while a few are only dirt resting grounds for automobiles in varied stages of high mileage or final, slow decay.

The little community, affectionately known as Pakala by its residents, is housing for Gay & Robinson Sugar Plantation workers. The residents are a mix of Japanese, Chinese, Portuguese, Puerto Rican, Korean, and Filipino immigrants. Many are the second generation—sometimes the third generation—of their families and are lifetime employees of the plantation. Their skills vary: some are field workers, others mechanics. All work outdoors every day, their hours controlled by the morning, lunchtime, and *pau hana* whistles.

Pakala, depending on how it is pronounced, means "the shining of the sun" or "a money field." It is where Sinclair Robinson, the eldest son of the plantation family, lived. His home overlooked the sea and Niʻihau, the westernmost inhabited island in the Hawaiian chain.

In the late 1800s, Sinclair Robinson's grandmother, Elizabeth Sinclair, relocated her family from New Zealand. She spent $10,000 to purchase a rich agricultural Kauaʻi *ahupuaʻa*, a traditional Hawaiian land division consisting of a pie-shaped section beginning at a point in the middle of the island and extending out to the shoreline. She chose this in lieu of a hot, flat, and barren piece of property in Honolulu that was available for a similar price. This Oʻahu land would soon become the most valuable industrial real estate in Hawaiʻi. The Makaweli land, although fertile and beautiful to look upon, would prove to require years and generations of backbreaking work to farm.

Sinclair, who may have possessed the most vision of any of his family, was determined to work with what he had. He set about making something of his land. He built the home he named Pakala and turned his attention to growing a new crop that was putting Hawaiʻi on the U.S. and world maps, making millionaires of its growers.

Still, the sugar business offered no guarantee of success. Owning the most fertile growing land in Hawaiʻi was not enough for the Robinson Plantation. Finally, Sinclair made a deal with C. Brewer & Company to lease his land and farm the sugarcane. The new company, called Olokele Sugar Company, was more successful. The Makaweli plantation became the richest-yielding fields per acre in the islands.

My grandfather worked for the plantation, and my mother and her siblings were raised in Pakala. My grandpa, K. K. Itakura, was gifted with intellect. He won the admiration and trust of Sinclair who did a startling thing: Sinclair took my grandfather out of the fields and made him the bookkeeper for the plantation. My grandfather did so well in this position, it opened another door and he was installed as vice president of the local First National Bank in Waimea. These were unheard-of events, as plantation workers in the U.S. Territory of Hawaiʻi in 1940 were still second-class citizens, unable to vote and without the same rights as white citizens.

My mother attended the University of Hawaiʻi where she met my father, and another unusual event occurred: They married. For a Japanese girl to marry my *haole* father, an upstate New Yorker of Spanish-German descent, was shocking to the closed ranks of Hawai'i's Japanese community. It did come as a shock to my grandfather, but over a period of time that shock wore off. K.K. Itakura must have realized that the world was moving into a new era. Being on the leading edge of social change in west Kaua'i, he and his family welcomed my haole father with open arms.

In December of 1941, war came to Hawai'i with the bombing of Pearl Harbor. It must have been a trying time for my father, married to a "local Japonee" while fighting "Japan Japonees" on the island of Saipan. None of my mother's family, nor anyone they knew, suffered the resentment, or worse, the internment to which the "Katonks," or West Coast Japanese, were subjected. It was a difficult endeavor in Hawai'i, where the Japanese community made up a majority within the working-class population.

After World War II, both my uncles Hiroshi and Saburo returned from Europe, where they and the other Hawai'i Japanese boys served with great distinction in the 100th Battalion of the 442nd Regiment. Real changes began to happen in post-World War II Hawai'i. The veterans made use of the GI Bill college entitlement, and many graduated as lawyers, using their new knowledge to bring about the change from second-class to first-class citizenship.

I was born in 1948 and had the great fortune to be the first grandson. I spent a lot of my youth at my grandparents' home in Pakala and came to love that place more than any other. My grandfather died of a heart attack when I was eight years old and I will miss him always. My grandmother, my Uncle Sab, and Auntie Betty still lived in the Pakala house, and during my childhood I spent as much time there as I could.

The house was spotlessly clean inside and out. I was hustled out in the morning so my sister and female cousins could help my grandmother and aunt clean it again. I never had shoes, never wore a pair until I went to the seventh grade. Once outside, my feet were dirty, and I wasn't allowed back into the house unless I washed and dried my feet. This was too big a task for a little boy, and I preferred the outdoors anyway. There were big mango trees to climb in the front yard and kiawe trees across the road. The beach in front was a vast playground in itself.

With my uncle's dog Rusty, I scoured the beach for sand crabs, carefully following the twisting holes down in the soft sand, digging until the crab was exposed and would attempt its escape back to the water. Rusty would pounce on the scuttling crab and bite it once before spitting it out. I would throw the remains into the water and watch the shoreline fish rush in for a meal.

There was an old Filipino man named Juanito who sometimes caught the crabs, chewed them up, and spit into the water, driving the fish into a feeding frenzy, where he hooked them one after another with his bamboo pole. Sometimes he put on a pair of small, homemade bamboo goggles, one over each eye, and with a small metal hook he dove the shallow water near shore for *tako*, or octopus.

This was even more fascinating to me. I recall watching as he surfaced for air and then disappeared underwater for long periods. Sitting on the beach, I tried to hold my breath until I saw him again. I needed to breathe four or five times during the time he was underwater. When he was done, he came ashore with octopuses stuck all over his body. The heads were turned inside out and the guts cleaned. He peeled them off in front of me, then gave me the biggest one to take home to my grandmother. I ran home to the back door and yelled for Gramma. She came out, smiled, and commented about the fresh tako, then took it from me and went back inside.

My Uncle Sab was gone early every morning to his job as a draftsman at the Kauaʻi Pineapple Company in Lawaʻi. My Auntie Betty moved to Honolulu to be a school-teacher for several years before going to France and later Spain to teach for the military at the U.S. bases there. I continued to spend summers at Gramma's house. Sometimes, when she finished her housework for the day, she called me to go fishing with her at the landing.

The bay known as Kai Hoʻanuanu, where the camp at Pakala sat, had the best an-chorage for the early interisland steamers that connected Kauaʻi to Niʻihau. The Robinson family also owned the island of Niʻihau. Hawaiian people of mixed descent lived there. They spoke Hawaiian as their first language and lived more in the old way than anywhere else in the islands. The Robinsons were a very private and strongly Christian teetotaler family. They did not allow liquor or guns on Niʻihau. If anyone broke the rules, he was exiled and not allowed to return. I never understood it when I was a boy. Today I find the concept vaguely medieval, though I concede that the Robinsons' policies probably preserved elements of a fragile culture that might otherwise have disappeared.

The Robinsons had a surplus World War II landing craft that weekly plied the channel, carrying supplies and bringing the Niihauans to Kauaʻi. There was a landing just down the beach from Gramma's house. In the old days, before airplanes or freighters, the interisland steamers brought in stores at that landing. It was a sturdy structure, built of huge boulders from the shoreline. Farther out was a wooden pier extending beyond the surfline. I never saw any ships dock there. Another newer landing, inside the reef and farther up the beach at Mahinauli, provided a safer loading moorage for the Niʻihau barge. But the old landing was an excellent fishing platform until a tidal wave in 1960 washed it away.

When Gramma took me fishing, she would gather her fishing gear and her big hat, and we would cross the cattle guard into the pasture and walk to the landing. There were bulls in the pasture that always scared me a little, but the donkeys were worse. If I was with my grandmother, none of the livestock bothered us. If I was with other kids, the donkeys would charge and try to bite us. When I asked my grandmother about it, she just said, "Don't bother them and they won't bother you."

If we were going to the landing, or the river mouth beyond, it was easier to walk down the pasture road than to walk in the soft sand on the sloping beach. Without any adults, however, the beach was safer because even without any fence, the animals never went there. Sometimes, as I walked with Gramma, the big bulls would be standing right alongside the road. She walked calmly right by them, never even giving them a look while I fearfully watched them wide-eyed. Even when the donkeys stood in the road they moved when Gramma came along. They trotted out of her way almost as if they were afraid.

At the landing she would greet the other fishermen, and they would chat about the day's luck and what was biting. The prize catch was *papio*, but a fat mullet or *moi* was OK, too. Sometimes a *weke* would bite, but their mouths were soft and one had to be careful about setting the hook and hauling them up. I could always try for *aholehole* near the rocks, but the surge often washed my hook into the holes where it would snag. Then, shamefaced, I'd have to ask Gramma for another hook. Her fingers deftly tied the catgut fishing line around the tiny fishing hooks; for me, it was nearly impossible. Her patience with me, the fish, and everything else in her world had no boundaries.

When I was older I was allowed to swim unsupervised. I remember the water inside the reef was crystal clear. The steady flood of irrigation required for growing sugarcane stained the entire shoreline a dirty shade of red brown. In the early years, the ocean was clear enough for me to learn to spearfish. I spent hours diving all along the shore. My Uncle Sab was an expert spearfisherman. Occasionally, I would be allowed to go with Uncle Sab and his friends to other places on the island where the fishing was better. It was a wonderful time to be in a magical place with the imagination of youth.

One day two guys with surfboards tied to the roof of their car arrived and parked in front of Gramma's house. I had been vaguely aware of the waves breaking out on the reef, and sometimes I had joined the two older Pratt brothers, Lloyd and Terrill, bodysurfing or paipo-boarding in the little shorebreak on the far side of the landing. But the outside reef in front of the small fishing boat mooring might as well have been the other side of the moon.

The two surfers were excited that day. They looked at the waves while we gathered around looking at them, wondering at their excitement. Both were Kaua'i boys from Lihu'e side. One was named Carlos Andrade. In the following years, I would come to know him well.

Together they walked down the beach, sleek shiny surfboards under their arms and a flock of kids following behind. The surfers put their boards in and paddled out to the surf at the break in the reef where my uncle and the other fishermen drove their sampans through to get outside the waves. What happened next profoundly changed the direction my life would take from that day forward.

Both Carlos and his friend were expert surfers. The waves we never really had taken much notice of beforehand were, we saw for the first time, ideally shaped for long, graceful rides. Carlos and the other boy danced effortlessly to a tune we hadn't heard before that day. They were amazing, gliding and floating across the faces of those waves. Suddenly those waves, which I had looked at for the twelve long years of my short life, but had never before actually seen, took on a new light. I had surfed once several years before at Waikiki, but after the momentary thrill I had lost interest. My brother Victor had caught the surf bug the first time and had his own surfboard. I was not smitten until that day at Pakala.

The following year, in the summer of 1960, surfing exploded. Any place with a beach and waves became a surf spot. Everyone was learning how to surf, and I was part of the trend. Pakala quickly became one of the most popular surfing spots on Kaua'i. No one living in Pakala surfed, but boys from nearby Waimea, Kekaha, and Kalapaki flocked to the perfect wave. After long days of surfing, the big, heavy surfboards were left, leaned up against the spreading Milo tree in the pasture. The local surfers came and went, but the surfboards were safe and secure all summer long under the Milo tree. The surf spot had taken the name Infinity. It was given that name by Michael McPherson on a surf trip there from Kailua, O'ahu, with Roy Mesker, Chris Green, and Randy Weir in 1963. Randy was the grandson of Sinclair Robinson.

At lunchtime, the surfers who had the forethought to bring food with them ate fast before having to share with the others. I walked back to Gramma's house where she had lunch waiting for me. Although the concept didn't exist then, I guess I was one of the first Pakala locals. Localism, and being a jerk in the lineup, was still many years in the future. But at that time there was no hierarchy determining who got which wave, no jockeying for position, no such thing as dropping-in. Everyone took turns catching waves and always knew whose turn it was. Sometimes friends, or even strangers, caught the same wave and rode it together ... happily.

I spent the next couple of summers staying at Gramma's house and surfing every day at Infinity. Those days were, without a doubt, some of the best times of my life. Then several things happened to change those idyllic summers. My Uncle Sab built himself a new home in Kalaheo and moved Gramma there to live with him and his new wife, Auntie Hitoe. Gramma's house in Pakala was no more. I started surfing a place in Honolulu called Ala Moana and fell in with another crowd of surfers.

Things like that happen in surfing all the time. A surfer gets hurt and no one realizes he's even gone until he returns to the beach healed. A new surfboard comes along and the old one is forgotten. A surfer starts riding a new break and the old spot is barely a memory. Surfing happens best when it's in the present; the past is behind and the future not yet. The only thing of interest is what's here and now.

In June of 1966, I graduated from high school and made plans to attend college in Southern California. Surfing was not my first priority. But I discovered surfing again while in California and went on my first real surf safari in Baja, Mexico. I found a new commitment to surfing that surprised me. I thought I had liked to surf before; I now discovered that it was really all I wanted to do.

The summer of 1967 solidified my commitment; I became a surfer for life. The following winter, I began to surf the North Shore waves on a regular basis. Dick Brewer shaped me a surfboard that not only gave my own surfing a huge step-up but also turned the entire surfing world on its head. That surfboard was the opening shot of the shortboard revolution.

By the next summer, the growing surfboard industry was in turmoil. Surfboard design was evolving at a pace too rapid for the big factories to stay current. The backyard industry blossomed, and I became a part of it, finding myself swept up in a life lived from one surfboard to the next.

Other world events factored into the equation. The Tet Offensive in January of 1968 escalated the Vietnam Conflict into another dimension. In every place where young people gathered, old belief systems were cast aside and new ideas sprouted like mushrooms after a rain. We were all swept up in this time of exciting and rapid changes.

The youth movement rejected rigid establishment values with student demonstrations in Paris and throughout Europe, as well as on college campuses across the

United States. Violence hit the streets. Like many of my generation who grew up through the Kennedy and King assassinations to be confronted by the moral abyss of the Vietnam War, I found that the status quo of American values as espoused by leaders like Richard Nixon held little appeal. I found that surfing, to which Pakala with its special memories had opened a door, held out the promise of a better life. I dropped out of college and devoted my energies toward building a better surfboard.

A surfer I greatly admired named Herbie Torrens found a small house near the Menehune Ditch in Waimea. He called to tell me he was surfing a great break all by himself every day and wanted some company. I went to stay at my Uncle Sab's place in Kalaheo. Every morning I would borrow his 1956 Nash Rambler, drop my grandmother off in Waimea, and go on to Herbie's house. He was the only "mainland haole" in town and his place was called the "hippie house."

Together we would grab our surfboards, a little food, and begin the long walk along the beach from the Waimea River mouth to Pakala. A lot had changed since the early days when Gramma lived there and all the surfers left their boards under the Milo tree.

Sinclair had passed away, but not before he had closed the beach to surfers. Some visiting California surfers had abused the access privilege by chasing some of the Robinsons' mares ready to foal. The pregnant mares were always kept in that pasture between the main house and the surf break for close observation. It seemed that one of the mares had died; no more surfers were allowed across Robinson property. The only access was to walk from Waimea town on the beach below the high-tide line.

This was the reason the lineup was empty. The wave was still as good as ever and the walk always passed quickly. Herbie owned one of the new Brewer mini-guns just like the one Dick Brewer had shaped for me only six months earlier. I had an even shorter board that I had made myself. The surfboards probably didn't matter because we had our pick of any of the perfectly peeling Pakala waves.

George Weaver, another good surfer whom I had met in California, showed up one day and we became a threesome. A few days later another friend, Tom Gaglia, came over from Lahaina, Maui. Tom, George, and Herbie had all grown up together in Newport Beach. The four of us enjoyed day after day of perfect Pakala by ourselves. After surfing and the walk out, I drove over and picked up Gramma from my auntie's liquor store. Then we headed back to Kalaheo. Uncle Sab asked me what I did, and I told him we surfed all day. He didn't understand and just shook his head.

One particularly great day of surfing left us pretty tired. The four of us were dragging our feet on the walk out. Right at the very end, near the river mouth, in front of the Russian fort, there were a lot of rocks on the narrow, steeply sloping beach that made a tiresome climb. A row of ironwood trees above the high-tide line bordered a narrow dirt road alongside a cane field where the walking was easier. Normally we never used the road; we thought it was Robinson property. But, this day it was late, we were weary, and we weren't thinking. We stepped off the sand, up on the road, and had taken only a few steps when a jeep roared around the corner. Two guys dressed in khaki jumped out and yelled that we were under arrest.

Surprised, shocked, and a little scared, we jumped back on the beach and ran for it. When we got to the river, we hopped on our surfboards and paddled across. Looking up, I noticed a police car pulling down into the lot where fishermen parked. Tom and Herbie were already across and approaching the lot. I pointed out the police car to George and we both stopped in midstream.

"Who were those guys back there who were yelling at us?" George asked.

"That was the Robinsons, and I don't think it's over yet," I answered, watching the police car stop next to Herbie and Tom.

"Well, I don't think we did anything wrong," said George, "I'm going to see what's going on with those guys." He headed after Herbie and Tom.

I didn't know what to do. Sitting on my board I noticed a nice wave breaking off the river mouth. Remembering something I used to say to myself—"When in doubt, paddle out"—I paddled out to the break. I watched my three friends walk off with the police car following. A little while later, it came back. I saw the policeman get out, open the back door, and I watched my grandmother get out of the car. I paddled in immediately.

We were all arrested that afternoon for trespassing. We were told to appear in court in Lihuʻe the following week. My grandmother seemed more upset about riding in the police car in front of her friends than by my arrest. My uncle warned me that the Robinson family wanted to make an example of us and not to do anything foolish.

The four of us showed up at the courthouse in Lihuʻe for our appearance. A court official asked us if we had anything to say. He was looking directly at Herbie, whom he addressed as Mr. Porrens. George, Tom, and I looked at each other: "Porrens. What the heck?" Tom rolled his eyes.

"I think you might have made a mistake, my name is Torrens," Herbie stammered. Tom told us later that when the police were filling out the arrest report, they asked Herbie his name. In some far-flung hope to confuse them he had blurted out, "Porrens."

"That's what I thought," said the official. "You guys come on in now."

We looked like country bumpkins compared to the county prosecutor in his fancy suit and shiny shoes. We might as well have been in a foreign country when we walked into that courtroom. We were as out of place as anyone could be. We were directed to sit at one table, while the fancy "Portagee" (Portuguese) prosecutor took the other one and disdainfully ignored us.

We all rose when the judge entered and gave us the briefest look before sitting down. He said we were charged with criminal trespassing and asked us how we pleaded. We had agreed that we would plead no contest and throw ourselves on the mercy of the court. The look the judge gave us when we said that made us wonder whether we had made the right decision.

The prosecutor spoke first. He talked about surfers trespassing in the pastures, stampeding the cattle, chasing the horses, breaking the fences and on and on, until the Robinsons had no choice but to close down access through their property. He implied that we had done all those things, were criminals, and should be treated as such by the court. The judge listened and finally asked us if we had anything to say. Tom, Herbie, and I were shocked to silence, but not so George.

George politely asked the judge if he could use the blackboard to illustrate what had happened. With a piece of chalk, he drew the river mouth, the Russian fort, the beach, and the dirt road, explaining where we were and what we did every day when we walked from Waimea to surf in Pakala. Our intention was not to trespass. He showed where the Robinson boys had surprised and scared us in their jeep and where we ran into the water. The judge asked a few questions about exactly where we were and where the jeep was. Finally, George ran out of steam and sat down. The judge wrote something while everyone waited; then he looked at us and told us to stand up. We all thought he was going to lower the boom, but out of left field, he dismissed the charges against us.

The county prosecutor leaped out of his seat to protest, but the judge told him the Robinsons had overstepped their boundaries and no trespass had occurred. The prosecutor looked like his neck and face were going to explode: The prospect of the story of how he lost his case to a barefoot hippie with a piece of chalk circulating around the legal community of Kaua'i caused him dire distress.

The judge admonished me personally, telling me he was certain my grandmother had warned me about trespassing on Robinson property numerous times. He said he better not see me, or my friends, in his court again. I promised him that from then on we always would stay below the high-tide line. We walked out of that Lihu'e courthouse free men.

I learned a great lesson that day. Had Sinclair Robinson still been alive, I doubt whether any arrest would have happened. I met him once as a little boy with my grandfather; he bought me an ice cream while they chatted. He struck me as sincere, and as a visionary but down-to-earth person.

A man of vision embraces the future. Aware that all things change, he plots the best course through all the twists and turns of life. People who can't let go of the past try to build fences around the way things are. They hope to keep everything the same and refuse to accept change until it is forced upon them.

Sinclair's home in the sunny place overlooking the surf spot has become a vacation rental. People have come and gone, but the dry and sleepy southwest coast of Kaua'i has remained relatively unchanged when compared to other popular Hawai'i destinations. The summer wave off the little point of the bay at Pakala still spins perfectly around its arc of shallow reef, just as it did before my grandparents lived there, or later when a child looked up to notice its ample grace.

A First Time at the Pipeline

The first time I surfed at the Pipeline was in 1963 during my sophomore year in high school. My surfing partner, Tommy Chamberlain, and I were on the way to our class picnic at Pounders Beach in La'ie. The picnic was at the White Estate, a beautiful beach home owned by Pip White's family. Pip was one of our classmates at Punahou Academy.

Pip and his family moved in the upper circles of O'ahu society; Tommy and I were at the other end of the scale, which was why we had made plans to go surfing before the social event of our sophomore class. Surfing in the early 1960s was still considered to be on the low end of recreational activities. The surfing boom that was just hitting California's mainstream had not made it to Hawai'i yet. Surfers were still categorized in the same group as beach bums, con men, and gigolos. Parents frowned upon their children mingling with these social outcasts. My own parents reluctantly allowed it to continue in hopes that I would soon grow out of wasting time down at the beach and start thinking about important things like college.

Surfing was what Tommy and I lived for; we thought about it before anything else. La'ie was on the northeast side of O'ahu so going to the picnic by way of the North Shore with our surfboards was not out of our way. I was about fifteen years old, but Tommy was old enough to have a driver's license and he had a Mini Minor station wagon. It was a perfect surf vehicle; both boards would fit inside with me sitting in the backseat. Surf racks weren't invented just yet, but any seating arrangement that got us to the beach worked fine.

We both had Wardy surfboards from John Thurston's Wardy shop on Kalakaua Boulevard, just down the street from our high school. Mine was a green-tinted 9'8" with a three-inch redwood stringer down the center; it was heavy, but it looked good. Tommy had a beautiful 9'6" with redwood panel rails, a skinny redwood center stringer, and a lightweight glass job. Tommy's surfboard was half the weight of mine, but he was a much better surfer and could utilize the weight advantage. At my level of surfing, I would not notice the difference.

An early experience at the Pipeline before I knew
better about the break and the equipment needed
to have any success there. Photo: Art Brewer

It was Saturday morning as we drove by Hale'iwa, Laniakea, and Chun's Reef. But Tommy had the Pipeline in his mind so we kept heading north. We parked the Mini in the empty lot at 'Ehukai and walked out to look at the waves. It was one of those pristine clear days when we could see all the way to Kaua'i. It was still early in the morning with not another soul on the beach. Glistening, clean white sand spilled all the way to the water's edge.

A little way offshore, the waves were an ideal four feet. The wind was still and the waves were perfect: we ran back to get our surfboards.

The beach was empty as far as we could see in either direction. Tommy was an ebullient and expressive person, and he was whooping with delight as we jumped in the water. It was early fall, before any big swells had taken the sand away, and the waves were breaking very near the shoreline. That year was one of the flattest in North Shore history, but the size and conditions couldn't have been more perfect for our first time surfing the notorious Banzai Pipeline.

I paddled for my first wave, but it stood up so fast that I buried the nose of my board when I tried to stand up. Back then we called that a pearl dive. Tommy laughed but did the same thing on his first wave. Now we were both swimming in to get our boards. The waves were steeper and faster than any other waves in our experience. Tommy, the better surfer, figured we needed to catch the wave sooner and stand up more quickly. That sounded good in theory, but it didn't work. We both pearled on our next waves, and again we were swimming to the beach. This went on for half an hour and Tommy thought it was hilarious.

I was getting frustrated with one wipeout after another. I couldn't keep from pearl diving on the takeoff. Fortunately the beach was close and the swim a short one. We had more success bodysurfing than we were having with our surfboards. Finally, after eating it so many times, we left our boards on the beach and just bodysurfed.

After a while we were surprised to see someone paddling out wearing a coconut leaf hat. We saw that it was Jock Sutherland, one of the best young surfers in Hawai'i. We knew him by reputation but hadn't met him yet. After introductions all around, Jock proceeded to take the waves apart while we watched in stunned admiration. He had it wired; he never lost his surfboard or his coconut hat. We got so jazzed watching that we swam in and got our boards to try our luck again.

Jock told us to angle on the takeoff as we dropped in; don't go straight down. We tried it and started having immediate success. The longboard designs back then were primitive by today's standards. Our boards looked beautiful, but the shapes were not that different than an ironing board. Being straight and flat didn't help on the steep Pipeline waves. With the tip from Jock, we soon were having the time of our lives.

We lost all track of time until we remembered there was somewhere we needed to be. We asked Jock if he knew what time it was. No one wore watches in the surf back then. Jock looked up at the sun in the sky and said, "It's 11:46" How he knew it was 11:46 a.m without a watch we never knew, but the picnic was scheduled to begin at 11:00 a.m. and we were late. Thanking Jock for everything, we headed in. Three minutes later in the car, Tommy looked at his watch; it said 11:49 a.m.

We never figured out how Jock knew the time so exactly, but over the next few years, we figured out that he knew more than most people when it came to surfing. We became good friends and surfed together many times.

His style was unique, his surfing being both functional and progressive. No one came close to his surfing in the years when longboards reached their apex. Shortboards took over, and surfing went through the roof in terms of performance, speed, and covering more parts of the wave than ever before. Jock Sutherland led the charge in Hawai'i, inspiring every surfer of that new generation. His little tip about angling on the takeoff at the Pipeline would launch me into an intimate relationship with that spot that would last the next thirty years. It was a long and wonderful affair for me, some of the best times of my life. I will never forget how it all began on that one Saturday morning.

Above   Art Brewer, Gary Busey, Rory Russell, and me looking at Sunset Beach through Art's 1000 mm lens during the filming of the Hawai'i segment of *Big Wednesday*. Photos: Steve Wilkings

Right   Miki Dora possessed a surfing style that was entirely his own, with moves so highly advanced yet so subtle as to often go unnoticed. Photo: John Severson

a. GALLERY

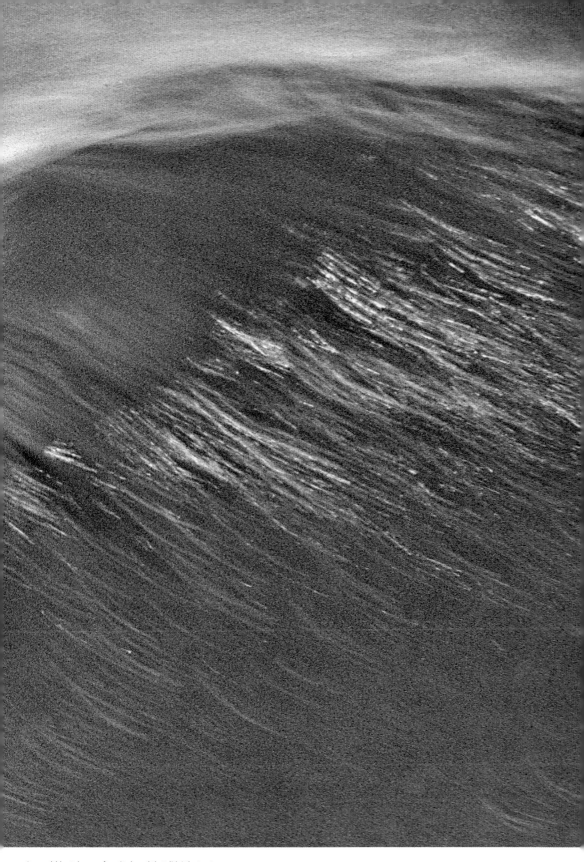

A speed-blur tube on a favorite board that didn't last out
the season and ended up where most Pipeline boards did:
on the broken-board pile. Photo: Jeff Divine

Above   Talking story on the beach at Sunset
with Herbie Fletcher and Barry Kanaiaupuni. BK
was the undisputed master of that break in the
1970s. Photo: Jeff Divine

Right   Classic Ala Moana (with Diamond Head in
the background), where I was during every summer
of my misspent youth. Photo: Steve Wilkings

Left   Don King, maybe the best water photographer of all time owing in great part to his superior swimming skills, lugs a heavy and ungainly 35 mm water housing up the beach for a film change. Photo: Jeff Divine

Above   A classic pose: Miki Dora perched on the tip at his favorite wave, Malibu. Photo: C. R. Stecyk

Previous spread　When a surfer did it right at the
Pipeline, it was a late drop to the bottom then a turn
straight into the tube. Photo: Dan Merkel

Above　An aerial shot of the Freight Trains break
adjacent to the Ma'alaea small boat harbor. McGregor
Point is in the background. Photo: Erik Aeder

Left   A wave during the 1979 Pipe Masters, just before
getting caught inside and experiencing a quite startling
out-of-body experience. Photo: Jeff Hornbaker

Above   Hanging out with J. Riddle and Billy Hamilton,
both surfing doubles for Jan-Michael Vincent, on
location in El Salvador during the second unit filming
for *Big Wednesday*. Photo: Dan Merkel

61

Walter Hoffman on his favorite Matchless, sliding
a turn on a dirt road of what is now Mission Viejo.
Photo: Hoffman collection

ii. THE BOYS

RB

DICK BREWER COMES TO HAWAI'I

Dick 'RB' Brewer came to Hawai'i from Whittier, California, in the underpopulated surf scene of the 1960s. He had a background in mechanical engineering and liked to build fast cars. These interests converged in this fertile surfing-ground; soon he was designing and building big-wave guns.

He opened Surfboards Hawai'i, building innovative surfboards for many top big-wave surfers of the day, including Buzzy Trent, Peter Cole, and even a very young Jeff Hakman. Brewer was a great designer and surfboard shaper, but he wasn't much of a businessman. After only a few years his shop was losing money.

On the strength of his reputation, Dick formed an association with Hobie Surfboards, the premier surfboard manufacturer of the period. After years of making surfboards out of balsawood, Hobie Alter pioneered the art of building boards with a polyurethane foam core. Hobie sold the business of making the foam cores to his partner Grubby Clark. He kept the surfboard factory business, which was home to many great surfers of the time: Phil Edwards, Mickey Munoz, and the great Waikiki surfers, the Patterson brothers. Dick shaped Hobie big-wave guns with offset colored foam T-bands that were popular during that time. After that, he spent a brief period working with Rich Harbour at Harbour Surfboards. Jackie Eberle and Jock Sutherland rode several of the Harbour/Brewer guns to fame at Waimea Bay. In 1965 Jackie rode a Brewer gun fading left backside at the Bay, a move that was talked about in the Country for a decade.

Next Dick hooked up with Bing Surfboards in California. In 1965, he began making the Bing Pipeliner series. The Pipeliner was the zenith of surfboard evolution at that time. The Pipeliner was the board to ride in Hawai'i then. They were thin, finely foiled, and had the most progressive rocker of any surfboards of the time. Brewer was shaping boards for David Nuuhiwa, Jock Sutherland, Jimmy Lucas, Jeff Hakman, and many of the young, hot, Hawaiian surfers of the period.

In 1967, RB had a falling-out with Bing. He sawed down all the wall racks in Bing's shop, claiming that the racks were twisting his shaped blanks. Soon after that he was back in Hawai'i.

I met RB when he arrived on the North Shore. Jock was unquestionably the Man then, with all respect due to Barry Kanaiaupuni for his unforgettable domination of Sunset Beach, a dangerous place then and now. Jock was kind enough to lend me his 9'4" Pipeliner. He did this on a regular basis and his 9'4" was the best surfboard I had ridden up to that point. RB saw me riding it one day at Velzyland, and while we were waiting for the next set, Dick offered to shape me a board of my own.

That pause in between sets at Velzyland was the beginning of our long and fruitful friendship. Soon after, RB moved over to Lahaina, Maui. Reno Abellira and I visited him there to get our boards shaped. RB told us to bring our own blanks.

We bought a couple of reject blanks full of holes from Fred Schwartz at Surf Line Hawai'i. Fred and his Surf Line shop carried boards from Yater, Hansen, Harbour, Dewey Weber, Gordon & Smith, Jacobs, and of course Bing. Surf Line Hawai'i was the main dealer for the Bing Pipeliner models, as their progressive shapes were best suited to the thick, fast waves of Hawai'i. Fred also carried a small supply of Clark Foam blanks. These were all rejects; they were cheaper and the only surplus foam Clark had for sale.

Reno and I flew into Kahului and hitchhiked to Lahaina with our precious blanks. RB had entered into an arrangement with 'Buddyboy' Kaohe, also known as 'Kolohe Joe,' a most notorious con man, but also one of the best surfers of his time. Kolohe Joe had a shaping room in the old Lahaina Cannery, where he put RB to work.

Buddyboy wasn't pleased when Reno and I showed up with our own blanks, expecting free shape jobs from Brewer; he had an eye for getting his part of any deal. We agreed to pay him a fee for use of the shaping room, and he graciously gave RB the green light to do our boards.

Reno got his board shaped first. His was a sleek Pipeliner gun shape scaled down to 9'6" to suit Reno's small stature. The next day it was my turn for a shape.

But things didn't turn out as I had expected. Up drove a car full of surfers, and out jumped Nat Young, Bob McTavish, George Greenough, Ted Spencer, Russell Hughes, and John and Paul Witzig. A big swell was forecast, and they had come over from the Country hoping to catch some good surf at Honolua Bay.

McTavish had shaped all of their boards. They were unlike anything any of us, including RB, had ever seen. These unusual boards were short and wide tailed with deep vee bottoms and long, finely foiled and raked fins. RB and McTavish bullshitted for hours before the others could pry the Aussie loose to look for waves.

McTavish would leave a lasting impression on Hawai'i surfers of the era with his performance on his Aussie shortboard in that year's Duke Kahanamoku contest at Sunset Beach. Sunset was for real that day. McTavish took off deep on the backside of the west peak, went straight down, carved a huge turn, and shot almost straight back up the pitching wall all the way to the top on a line no surfer before had ever taken while still standing on his surfboard. There he paused for a split second, with his wide vee-tail stuck into the face just under the lip, then proceeded unceremoniously to fall out of the sky. To his credit, he paddled back out. That one wave was the best he could do on his vee-bottom that day. But McTavish's advanced theories of board design would leave many unanswered questions among elite Hawai'i surfers about their own surfboard shapes. He also would remain etched into the lore for his sheer guts.

RB was lit up from talking to McTavish as we walked over to the shaping room, where my blank waited on the racks. I was about to witness one of RB's greatest assets. He possessed a quick and creative mind. He was able to grasp new or extreme concepts that passed over the heads of most of the other surfboard builders of the time. In addition, he had a spontaneous nature that sometimes got him into unfortunate situations. Still, he remained open and eager to try anything new and different.

RB grabbed his handsaw and, before I could say how long I wanted my surfboard, he sawed several feet off the blank. I had been hoping for a board similar to Reno's. I think I almost cried. But RB was on a roll and drew out a template radically different than any we had seen before. While Reno snickered over in the corner because he already had his board shaped, RB proceeded to put together a wide, hotdog nose with a drawn-out, full-gun tail blending the curves together into a smooth but very different outline. The length was 8'6".

He began planing away with his Skil 100, and before long a magically foiled board appeared. RB incorporated some of McTavish's bottom theories, putting in a slight vee-bottom. We knew the vee-bottom used to be a significant design feature on the old Hot Curl boards of the 1940s and 1950s, but that was prior to the advent of surfboard fins. When RB was done, we carried the shaped blank across the street to John Thurston's glass shop and put it on the rack.

John had come over from Laguna in the early 1960s to open a shop for Fred Wardy in Honolulu. Between 1963 and 1966, during my high school years, I had ridden Wardy surfboards that I bought from John. His shop was right down the street from our high school, so we had spent most of our after-school hours hanging out there.

I knew John quite well. John was involved with the Baha'i Faith and moved to Maui to start his own chapter. When Reno and I showed up with no place to stay, he kindly allowed us into his home in Honokowai where a whole bunch of O'ahu surfers, including Tom Stone, Gordie Benko, Pia Aluli, and Hoku Keawe, were crashing out.

I remember John looking at my shaped blank in his somewhat inscrutable manner behind his thick coke-bottle lens glasses. He commented simply, "Interesting."

John glassed it, Larry Strada sanded it, and in a few days my board, along with Reno's and Buddyboy's new boards, were ready to go.

The surf was big that morning as we drove out toward Honolua Bay. We parked down at the boat ramp and looked out to ten-foot waves pounding into the cave that fronted the takeoff spot. All of us paddled out on our new sticks. I didn't stay in contact with the others. I was looking out for my own interests. I was very tentative and wanted to be sure of my territory.

Honolua Bay is a board killer at any size; there are rock cliffs just inside the takeoff zone. Perfect as it may look, underestimating the power of the peak fronting the cave is a serious lapse of judgment. At that size, it was instant mayhem. This was years before the surf leash came into use, so once a board was out of a surfer's control he might as well just say aloha. Better that than to retrieve a board from the cave with its slippery seaweed-covered boulders and powerful waves funneling in the mouth and crashing up into the ceiling. By the time anyone could get to his board it would be splinters anyway.

Reno and I caught a few waves and played it safe out on the shoulder. But this was a north swell—it wasn't as cleanly lined up as a northwest swell would have been. Before long, I watched Reno wipeout and lose his board. There was no way I could go in

Top My first photograph at the Pipeline on the first mini-gun of the shortboard revolution. Photo: Tim McCullough

Bottom Shortboards were the beginning of successful tuberiding at the Pipeline and in Hawai'i: this 8'6" Brewer started the trend. Photo: Tim McCullough

and retrieve his board with the waves that big. I watched in horror as Reno's new board was smashed to bits.

Buddyboy was doing the Bay justice. He had every contour of it wired, even on this uneven swell. Folks used to call the place 'Buddy's Bay.' But in time he also got creamed, and his brand new board too was in pieces.

I guess my momma didn't raise a complete fool. Discretion took the better part of valor. After one wave all the way through the last inside bowl, I decided to paddle back to the boat ramp. My new surfboard was intact even if my dignity was not.

The Aussies had just arrived and paddled out on their strange-looking vee-bottoms. Nat's board tracked out on his first wave, much as McTavish would do later at Sunset in the contest, and being stringerless, it broke about two feet back from the nose. After a while everyone else went in except Russell Hughes. He had the whole bay to himself, and he surfed it well and with style. He was conservative, choosing his waves and his lineups carefully. Eventually the Kona winds came up and blew the surf out.

Meanwhile RB, Reno, and I went with Tom Stone. Tom said he knew another good spot on the other side of the island that was offshore when the Kona winds blew. We drove over to Kahului harbor and looked at some great lefts at Paukukalo. It had a bit of a rocky shore but was nowhere near as intimidating as Honolua. We all paddled out.

This was my first time there. Later, when I lived on Maui, this place would always be my first choice during any Kona wind conditions with a northerly swell. On that first day, my new board worked like a charm. My pals begged to try it, but I wasn't letting that board out of my grasp just yet.

Later on all the guys would ride it and realize, as I had, that RB had created a whole new generation of surfboards. We would call them mini-guns. Although we never knew it until years later, this was the precursor to what became known as the shortboard revolution.

Some weeks later, Nat came back to Maui. The surf was a more manageable size and groomed clean by the trades, and with his board repaired, Nat took the place apart. The smaller clean walls of Honolua were an ideal canvas for the lines that vee-bottom boards wanted to draw. Nat showed his surfing genius, and the vee-bottom became an integral part of surfboard design from then forward. We wouldn't, however, see anything resembling those radical prototype Australian boards again. Their weaknesses were harshly exposed during that first winter in Hawai'i. Those wide tails simply could not handle the thickness, speed, and power of Hawaiian waves at serious size.

Maybe McTavish and his crew had started their own revolution down under, but following that first 8'6" that RB carved out for me in a moment of visionary ecstasy, none of us ever looked back. Surfing and surfboards would never be the same again. A border had been crossed, and I was privileged and very lucky to be there when it happened.

MASTER SURFBOARD SHAPER

I became intimately involved with surfing and surfboards at that time and have been ever since. I give RB credit for almost single-handedly starting the shortboard revolution in

Hawai'i. As duly noted, McTavish and the Aussies had their own thing going. Also that chance meeting between RB and Bob McTavish certainly prompted part of the vision Brewer had as he shaped that first mini-gun. Maybe some guys in California were doing something with shorter surfboards as well, but in Hawai'i, it was all Brewer. He shaped that 8'6" in late 1967.

By 1968, the longboard was passé. The surfboard industry was no longer the get-rich-quick scheme it had tried to become in the heydays of surfing in the 1960s. Surfboard manufacturers built up an inventory of more or less mass-produced surfboards in winter to unload on kooks in the summer. The new surfboards were designed for surfers at the top of the pile who were innovative, progressive, and always in search of something that made them surf better.

It soon became difficult to get a board from RB because he was in such demand, so I started building my own boards. In the summer of 1968, RB asked me to come to Kaua'i, where he had moved, to ghost shape for him at Hanapepe Surfboards. It was an up close opportunity to see a surfboard genius at work. In all probability, this period on the Garden Island set the course my life would follow from that point forward. Dick Brewer will certainly go down in the history of surfing as the greatest surfboard designer to ever live.

During that time, we built Jock Sutherland his famous surfboard, Purple Haze. Jock stood the surfing world on its head riding that board at the Duke Kahanamoku contest that winter. Although he didn't win the meet, his surfing was far above the level of anyone else's. Next came Reno's Pocket Rocket that he wowed everyone with during the World Championships in Puerto Rico the following summer. Reno didn't win that event either, but his surfing was the most talked about. The surfing world got the message: The surfer has a lot to do with the ride, but the surfboard is the vehicle that will take the surfer to the next level.

It was a great time to be a surfer, and an even better time to be a surfboard builder working hand in hand with the most innovative designer of the period. I guess the best lesson I learned from RB was simple: As satisfying as it is to build a surfboard that works better than the ones before it, the joy is in realizing that it is just another step in an endless progression of design that is wholly fascinating and captivating.

Surfboards are in an infinite and endless evolution. Just when the shaper thinks he has built the perfect board, he thinks of something different to make it better. I'm still doing it. So is RB.

TWO BONEHEAD SURFERS

This next adventure occurred during my time in Hanapepe. RB and I had worked all day and then heard that the surf was up. We decided we would try for an afternoon session out on the west side of the island. We drove through the lush green sugarcane fields, passing by 'Ele'ele, Makaweli, Waimea, and Kekaha. We were headed out to the end of the road at Polihale, to a place called Queens Pond. It's a big, beautiful white sand beach with a clear view over to the island of Ni'ihau. It was a favorite spot of ours because there was always some kind of surf.

We pulled up, parked in the kiawe trees, and ran up the side of the sand dune to see what was in store for us. A broad, clean white sand beach sloped down from the dune a good quarter of a mile before disappearing into the water.

Our first sight was a lined-up set peeling from the left and right perfectly for a distance before they came together into a closeout. It looked like it was about five or six feet where it started and about half that where the left and the right finally met. From there the whitewater rolling in to shore looked only a couple of feet high. Small, but still, it all looked good.

We had surfed here fairly often, but usually it was a typical beachbreak, disorganized and all over the place. We had never seen it so lined-up and perfect-looking. Without a second glance we ran back to the truck, jumped into our shorts, grabbed our boards, ran back up the dune and full speed down toward the water's edge. We headed for the little channel where the left and right came together.

As we got closer, I began to see that maybe it was a little bigger than it looked at first. I slowed down a bit to check it better as we got closer. RB had worked hard all day, was hot and sweaty, and wanted to surf in the worst way. He kept running full speed, down to the water, threw his surfboard in, and started paddling out. The first thing I noticed was that the little whitewater that we thought looked about two feet from up on the dune was actually about six feet or more. Where the left and the right met, which we had thought was three to four, was at least ten feet.

It was breaking so hard that the whitewater and sand were exploding thirty feet up in the air behind the waves. The rip sucking out to the horrendous closeout was like a raging river, and it had RB in its grasp. I don't know what he was thinking, but it was obvious he wanted to get out there fast: He had his head down and was paddling hard. He hadn't looked to see the disaster to which he was inexorably being drawn.

Standing at the water's edge, I couldn't see how big the waves were outside as the whitewater in front completely masked the waves behind. But from the sound and the impact I could feel reverberating through the sand, I figured they had to be at least twenty feet. It was serious surf, and dangerous too. The riptide that I was standing in front of probably went all the way to Ni'ihau. The entire beach behind us was completely deserted. We were the only two people there. If we got in trouble, there were no lifeguards and no telephones to call anyone, even if there was someone to call. There was nothing, just us two fools.

One of us was a bigger fool because as I took this whole situation in, I knew I wasn't about to get into the water if I could help it. Just about then, RB got to the first big whitewater; it immediately ripped his surfboard out of his hands. He wasn't even near the closeout yet, which was fortunate because it didn't look like anyone was going to survive that meat grinder. His board washed in to where I was standing and I picked it up. Meanwhile RB put his head back down and swam as hard as he could back toward shore. He probably wanted to retrieve his board and try to get out again.

The rip, however, had other plans for him. Even though he was swimming in, the rip was pulling him straight out toward the washing machine closeout. Worse, there didn't seem to be any gaps in the waves. There were no lulls, just one wave after another. Back then we didn't have the luxury of wave forecasts to tell us if this was a growing swell or at what size it would reach its maximum. We hadn't even checked the tide chart to see if it was an incoming or outgoing tide. We were the real thing, genuine cretins challenging nature in the absence of a clue.

I could see RB wasn't going anywhere, at least not anywhere near shore. If he gave up swimming he would be sucked into the maelstrom of sand and foam. I had scant choice. As much as I didn't want to do it, I had to take a chance and paddle out to help him. I hoped we could both make it in before we got tired and were sucked out to sea.

I got out to him and he climbed on the surfboard with me; even with the board overloaded, it was better than swimming. Adrenaline charged our paddle strokes. Slowly we began to make headway. Finally, with some help from the incoming waves of white-water, we got to shore and safety.

The first thing RB did was turn around and gaze back out toward the waves. It actually seemed as though he wanted to try again.

He turned to me, "If Buzzy were here, he would have got us out there."

He was referring to Buzzy Trent, perhaps the greatest big-wave surfer of the early days, a man of steel and "huevos grandes." Buzzy wasn't afraid of any waves.

I just shook my head, "Well he ain't here, and I ain't going to try to go out there today, so let's go home."

With that, we walked back up the empty beach with our tails between our legs, got in the car, and went home. Score: waves 1, surfers 0.

A
Giant
Among
Men

In surfing, there are special people whose example can have as much impact on an in-dividual's journey of self-discovery as any epiphany, incident, or combination of events. They can be recognized not so much by their obvious skills, accumulated knowledge, or intrinsic wisdom but, more subtly and importantly, by the special relationship they have formed with the sea. They are masters of their element, completely at home in and around the ocean. This special bond puts them in touch with the currents of energy to such an extent that their actions sometimes seem to border on the miraculous. Just by being close to such individuals we gain some understanding of the flow and glide that is essential to the formation of our own ocean connection.

Around 1970 or so (dates become harder to remember as the years slide into decades), Smirnoff Vodka was sponsoring the first professional surfing contest in Hawai'i. Cash money would be paid out to the winners. This was a milestone event for the com-petitors. It was the first actual validation of the unthinkable notion that real surfers—not just journalists, photographers, garment moguls, and hucksters of every stripe, but actual blood-and-guts surfers—could reap some material benefits from their dedication and courage.

Of course, surfing pays dividends every time a good wave is caught. However, being available for every swell often equates to a negative cash flow. To surf and pay the rent each month was a major effort for many of us. The surfing industry was in an infant stage, and sponsorships as we know them today were nonexistent in the early 1970s. Simply put, no one was getting paid to go surfing, so a chance to surf for money was a big deal.

Golden Breed sportswear was also putting on an event called the Expression Session. Invited surfers would each be paid $200 to surf two times in a new, noncompeti-tive format at the Pipeline. Both events seemed to herald a time of change for the top surfers who dedicated their whole lives and entire beings to their sport. This was the first time they would be paid for doing what they had always done for free.

Unfortunately, fickle fate had its own ideas. The surf that winter seemed unwill-ing to cooperate. The first day of the Expression Session was slugged out in some weak

Rocky Point surf. The early rounds of the Smirnoff contest were held in small Laniakea. Then the waves came all the way up, closing out the Country as we knew and rode it then. The elements prevailed, and everyone decided to go west and check out Makaha.

The middle heats of the Smirnoff contest ran in pretty good conditions at Makaha. The field was narrowed to six finalists. The finals were slated for the following day. The Expression Session was moved to Maui. Apart from the Smirnoff finalists, the bulk of the top surfers invited to both events made plans to fly the following morning. The event organizers were hoping for some good Honolua Bay. As it turned out, they were forced to hold the Expression Session at Rainbows, a little-known and, in comparison to Honolua Bay, lackluster spot a few miles north of Lahaina. Notwithstanding the $200 show money paid to the surfers, the first Expression Session that promised such a bang ended instead with a fizzle.

Meanwhile back on the west side of O'ahu, Mother Nature had a better plan for the six Smirnoff contestants. The new sun rose to a stronger swell and solid, beautiful Point Surf Makaha in the fifteen- to eighteen-foot range. The towering waves were awe inspiring in the cool morning light. The winds were northerly, straight offshore on the west side.

A surfer couldn't ask for better Makaha. But it was big surf and very serious. Huge lines coming all the way from Ka'ena Point were peeling around Makaha Point as the contest got underway.

I recall those waves as if they loomed yesterday, but I have a hard time trying to remember who the finalists were. Likely this is an indicator of the magnitude of the

Buffalo Keaulana, the official (or unofficial, depending on who was asking) mayor of Makaha. Photo: Steve Wilkings

impression that those beautiful blue-green giants left inside me. I think the final heat included Nat Young and Peter Drouyn of Australia, Felipe Pomar of Peru, my good friend Jimmy Blears, either Mike or Jim Lolley (they were twin brothers whom I never could distinguish between because they looked and surfed exactly alike), and myself.

Jimmy's father, Lord 'Tally Ho' Blears, was the contest announcer. Lord Tally Ho was a huge man, a professional wrestler in Honolulu, with a deep booming voice that made him a standout at surfing events of the period. Lord Blears gave us our final instructions. He told us to watch out for ourselves and for each other, wished us luck, and sent us out.

Makaha has a deep and clearly defined channel that opens into a wide bay. The paddle out is easy, even when the waves are big. The challenge of paddling into big Makaha is in the mind. It is formidable. There wasn't much talking as we all stroked out, each of us deep in his own thoughts about what this day would bring.

It's a long paddle. We began to spread out. Everyone was on his biggest board. I had an 8'6" magenta pintail that I called the Purple People Eater, named after a corny song that played on the radio all the time when I was a little kid. I asked Jimmy where he was going to sit. He knew Makaha at this size a lot better than I did. The Blears family had moved out from town and lived right on the Point. Jimmy, his dad, his brother, and his two sisters all surfed there when it was good.

Jimmy and I had gone to high school together at Punahou Academy and had surfed together quite often; he was happy to share any tips he might have. Even though the best waves were from the Point, they were difficult to make all the way through the Bowl. Jimmy said he was going to play it safe and surf the Bowl. Most of the other guys kept paddling toward the Point, but Jimmy and I settled down in the Bowl and waited for our first waves.

We both managed to get a few nice rides from the Bowl. But it's only the big drop, then we were just cutting back in the whitewater as the wave mushed in along the edge of the channel. The real challenge at Point Surf Makaha is to ride from the Point and backdoor the Bowl section, which on occasion can get pretty hollow. Nat, Felipe, and Peter caught some waves from the Point but had to straighten out toward shore before the Bowl and prone out the rest of the way. The soup at big Makaha is harrowing. The surfer must hold on for survival. The careening bounce is like nowhere else.

There was one guy sitting farther up the point, beyond any of us. He had been out there alone when we paddled out. Jimmy and I could occasionally catch glimpses of him going over the swells on the distant Point.

Nat paddled back out and asked us if we were getting any good waves in the Bowl. We told him that we were making the waves, but it was mostly a mushy ride on the shoulder. I asked Nat who that was out there alone on the Point. He said it was George Downing.

To our generation of Hawaiian surfers from the early 1970s, George Downing was not merely a legend. He really was the father of modern surfing and big-wave riding as we knew it. Duke Kahanamoku was always the Man. But when we thought about what we wanted to do, our equipment or whatever, George was the guy to ask about it. He already had done it all, and like that day at Makaha, he was still doing it. He possessed a wealth of knowledge and experience, and in the true Hawaiian spirit, he was always more than happy to share it with us. We respected him above all others in the entire surf world. George was the real deal, not just some myth—a tangible hero whom we could talk to.

When Nat said that the surfer was George, an idea came into my mind. Just then we saw him take a wave and ride it all the way through the Bowl. As George paddled out near us, a set happened to be coming through, and I caught one of the waves. I rode the wave pretty far in before kicking out and starting the long paddle back out.

Felipe Pomar, the 'Bull of Punta Rocas,' had just chased his board into shore after a wipeout. I saw him behind me. Felipe was in his prime and at the peak of his surfing career. He came over from his home in Lima, Peru, to attend school at the Mormon College in La'ie. He spent most of his time surfing the big waves on the North Shore. He and Bobby Cloutier were on the Greg Noll Surf Team and were getting a lot of publicity for their surfing.

He was paddling hard to get back out to the lineup, but I wasn't going to let him pass me. We both churned the water in our little race there in the channel. Suddenly, I sensed Felipe cross over from my left. Looking back over my right shoulder, I saw him take a line right toward the Point, cutting the Bowl, a giant gamble on a day with waves this big.

I hesitated as I weighed the risk. I did not want Felipe to get a better position on me. I made my decision and cut to the right as well. I could see Jimmy sitting way outside at the Bowl. I knew he would be shaking his head when he saw what we were attempting to do.

No sooner than the dice were rolled and we were committed to our course, I saw Jimmy pointing outside. Going over a swell, my heart sank. I saw a huge set approaching. I turned my direction back out to sea. I was well out of the safety zone of the channel and directly inside from the Bowl.

As the first set wave approached, it looked like a four-story building. I remember hearing Lord Tally Ho on the PA system. His deep voice was carried out by the offshore winds. He was saying something about a giant set coming in. I was paddling for dear life up and up the face of only the first monstrous wave. It felt like I was paddling straight uphill for a long time, but I just kept stroking as hard as I could. I could hear Tally Ho shouting about two surfers paddling to escape this wave. I knew he was talking about Felipe and me.

Somehow we both managed to paddle over the first one. From that high vantage point before we crashed down on the other side, we both could see that the next wave was bigger. There also were plenty of waves behind that one. Heads down, we paddled as hard as we could, up and up again. Felipe was right next to me and must have thought he could escape by angling to the right because he started to veer away from me. I just kept paddling straight ahead. I never had been in quite that position before. Makaha is a very sloping wave, not steep like the waves of the Country. The uphill paddle seemed to last forever.

I was on my big board and had quite a head of steam going as I reached the top. I looked back to see where Felipe was and saw his board upside down with his fingers holding the nose as he attempted a roll-under. It was the wrong move. He had lost some

As his boat slid to a stop,
he casually stepped
out, lit another cigarette,
and walked away like
it was no big deal.
Soon after his departure
the two bedraggled
photographers crawled
out of the boat and
gratefully flopped down
onto the sand.

ground by veering to the right and was too late. I rocketed through the crest, holding on to both rails as I flew up in the air. Before I crashed down on the back of this wave, I saw the lip taking Felipe and his board back over with it. It was a horrifying sight. The thought of what he would be going through made me paddle even harder. I still could hear Lord Blears on the PA, saying something about only one surfer still scratching to escape the set.

Again I paddled furiously up and up, breaking through the crest. I could see Jimmy outside staring at me with a look of great concern on his face. He was safely outside and motioning to me, rather frantically, to keep paddling. I definitely was not going to stop after seeing Felipe get sucked back over like a rat in the lion's teeth. I kept at it for two more waves and somehow, by the grace of God, managed to make it over the whole set.

I paddled out to Jimmy and his first words were, "I thought you were finished."

I said, "I think Felipe is finished for the day; he got sucked over the falls on the second wave and there were three more behind that."

We both looked inside and shook our heads, thanking our lucky stars that it wasn't us. When I finally settled down enough, I told Jimmy I was going to try for one at the Point. He just said good luck; he was staying in the Bowl.

I paddled toward the Point from outside the Bowl, the safe way and the way that I should have done it in the first place. George was sitting deep. From that far out I could see all the way to Kaʻena Point. I had never sat that far outside at Makaha. The view was magnificent. The steep, green wall of the Waiʻanae Range rising almost straight up from the occasional thin finger of golden sand beachfront or the boiling white backs of huge waves, then the green mountains reaching into the clear blue sky. The sight took my breath away.

George was smiling when I paddled up and sat up next to him. I said, "Howzit, Uncle George," then asked him if he would pick me a good wave from the Point. He said sure. A set came that looked good, but George said no, not this one. Another set came and again George said it wasn't the right one. It looked good to me, but George was the master and I was out of my element. Finally, a wave came and I thought George said it looked good.

I paddled hard, felt the wave pick me up, and jumped to my feet. This wave however, in spite of George's benediction, had ideas of its own. When I looked down the line to my right, all I could see was an endless wall feathering the whole way to the Bowl. It was a complete closeout. All I could do was go straight down and straighten out. As I dropped down I thought about what a mess I was in again and what a beating I was going to take.

I sensed something to my left. Looking over, I saw Buffalo Keaulana in his boat, dropping-in next to me. He was standing tall in the stern, hand on the throttle of his outboard motor, with a pair of dark glasses on, smoking a cigarette, and looking over at me with a little smile on his face. Lying down in the boat, clutching the seat for all they were worth, were the two photographers from *Life* magazine invited by Smirnoff's PR department to photograph the event. Obviously they didn't know what they were in for when Buffalo offered to take them out in his boat to get some pictures.

Buffalo was quite a character, the unofficial mayor of Makaha Beach. He was another outstanding waterman whom everyone admired. Whenever we came to surf Makaha, the first thing we did was look for Buffalo to pay our respects before we went in the water.

A friend of Buffalo's who also came to surf Makaha during the surf season was Jim Arness, the well-known television star of *Gunsmoke*. Arness, in gratitude for Buffalo's generous Hawaiian aloha, went down to McWayne Marine Supply one day and bought a boat for Buffalo to use for fishing during the summer months when there was no surf. The new eighteen-foot Boston Whaler, deemed unsinkable by its manufacturers, would, with Buffalo at the helm, be put into situations undreamed of by anyone who had anything to do with the construction or sales of that boat. The Whaler soon became Buffalo's motorized surfboard, as he masterfully rode waves as big as they got at Makaha and Sunset Beach, and gave photographers a view of the surf and surfing never before seen. I'm sure, for his passengers, the thrill, or the scare, was an even bigger part of the experience.

I was about to get creamed by this giant closeout at Makaha and Buffalo comes right by and gives me a salute. I thought the situation was as bad as it could be, but Buffalo, cigarette in his mouth, dark glasses on, riding that boat like a surfboard, changed everything for me.

I had to laugh. Laughing relieved the tension that was in me, and that image of Buffalo probably saved my life because when that wave broke on me, the pounding I got was horrendous. Makaha is the type of wave in which the whitewater doesn't dissipate. It stays on the surface and keeps rolling without losing power. A steep, hollow wave may break harder, but the whitewater loses power almost immediately. I got tumbled and ripped for what seemed like a lifetime before finally coming to the surface. By the time I got to the beach, the contest was over and that was it.

Well, maybe not quite it. As we all were standing there waiting to hear the results and receive our prizes, I heard an outboard motor revving and looked toward the ocean. Makaha has a big sand beach with a high berm. The steep shoreline produces the famous Makaha backwash as the waves wash up the beach then roll back down and out to sea.

From where we were standing, we couldn't see the slope but we could hear the racing motor. Suddenly whitewater came washing over the top of the berm and right behind it came Buffalo's boat at full speed on the back of the wave. He rode his boat up the beach, over the berm, and high and dry far up onto the sand.

As his boat slid to a stop, he casually stepped out, lit another cigarette, and walked away like it was no big deal. Soon after his departure the two bedraggled photographers crawled out of the boat and gratefully flopped down onto the sand.

Again, I had to laugh. Buffalo had done what no other man could do. Not merely cruising out there surfing a small boat in huge Makaha Point Surf, but actually getting better rides than any of the contestants. I don't remember who received the trophies that day, but there was no doubt in my mind who stole the show.

No

Prisoners

After a long day of surfing great waves at Makaha, Wayne Santos and I were relaxing in the parking lot drinking a beer. A car pulled up next to us and out stepped Buzzy Trent. Buzzy was a hero to us, a "Man of Steel" when it came to surfing big waves. He, George Downing, Wally Froiseth, Woody Brown, Jim Fisher, and a few others pioneered big-wave riding—living and training for the giant winter surf, making it their lifestyle.

During the previous twenty years Buzzy seldom had missed a day of good big surf. On this day, although well into his forties, he was still built like a weight lifter, rippling with muscles that all had been earned from hard work and big water. Wayne and I were lounging on the fenders of our VW bug, but we stood to show our respect as Buzzy walked toward us.

"Hey guys, how're the waves today?" Buzzy asked us.

"Hi Buzzy, yeah, they were great. We thought it was supposed to come up bigger, but a couple of ten footers was about it. Now it seems like it's already backing off. Hey, can we offer you a beer?" I held out a bottle of Heineken.

"No thanks, it only takes one for me and I drop off the deep end, can't do it anymore," he declined. Then he added, "Used to do it all the time when I was your age, just make sure you don't let drinking get in the way of your surfing: Anybody says he can surf drunk is a liar."

"Yeah, back at Malibu we did a lot of drinking," he continued. "But the waves were small and didn't have the power like they do here. Try to surf Sunset when you've been drinking, and you're going to lose. The ocean takes no prisoners, she will let you play with her up to a certain point, then you find out who the master really is.

"Back in '51 we had a big day at Malibu, waves going all the way to the pier, pretty big surf for over there, but nothing compared to even today, right here. But that was a big thing back there, about as big as the place could hold. We lived for that stuff, loved it when it got big like that. There was this black boy named Nick used to come up

and surf with us. He would drive up from Santa Monica with all his friends from school; they were all black and he was the only one of them that liked to surf.

"He was in good shape, but he couldn't surf worth a shit. That was OK because the waves were usually pretty small. He would get a ride and all his friends would be hooting and hollering, the girls screaming, jumping up and down. 'There goes Nick, there goes Nick,' they would yell. He was a very nice guy and came up every chance he could.

"He got this new board from Simmons on the big day, he was pretty proud of it. I thought it looked like a barge, but it was the first new board he ever had, so he was happy about it. I had been out all morning, so I was sitting in the Pit watching when Nick walked through, showed us his new board and paddled out.

"The pier at Malibu now is a new one; the old one was further north, closer to the wave. The old pilings are still there in the sand. Back then it was a big deal to ride a wave all the way to the pier; that was a long ride. But you had to pull out real fast at the end or you would run right into the pier.

"So Nick gets on this wave, he's on the end, Bob Hogan is behind him, and I think Dick Jaeckle was behind Bob. It was a hell'uva wave and we're all standing up watching. Nick's friends were yelling, 'There goes Nick, there goes Nick!' They were pretty excited. The three of them rode the wave all the way across the Cove. Bob pulled out first, then Jaeckle got out but Nick kept going. His friends were still yelling, 'Look at Nick go!'

"I could see he was getting close to the pier, but he didn't pull off the wave, he just kept riding. I'll be damned, but he rode right into the goddamn pier. And that was it, no more Nick. His friends were all crying now, 'Nick's gone, Nick's gone.'

Photo: John Severson

"And he was gone, we ran over there as fast as we could but he had sunk like a stone. We found his body a week later. I think he was trying to save that new board. I mean he could have just jumped off the back anytime and nothing would have happened, maybe swept through the pier and cut up by the barnacles, but he wouldn't be dead. That just goes to show you, when it comes to the ocean, she's always the boss and she takes no prisoners."

With that admonition Buzzy bid us farewell, got in his car, and left. Wayne looked at me. "Jesus, that was some story."

"Poor Nick, what a way to go," I agreed.

Buzzy would remain a hero for all time. He would ride his last wave at Waimea a few years later, saying it was one of the best waves he ever got. There's a feeling at the end of a ride on a big, beautiful wave where the surfer does everything right. It feels like you've left this earth. Buzzy felt this many times in his life, earning for him an ocean-inspired humility.

As big, strong, and tough as he was, he always knew who the real master was. He believed the most important things to learn from big-wave riding were dignity and courage, values to carry beyond the surf.

Flippy,

Pipe Days

Flippy Hoffman with a pair of his outer-reef guns
long before outer-reef surfing was even a blip on
anyone else's radar. Photo: Jeff Divine

In the days before Internet surf forecasts, we just woke up in the morning and took a hopeful look out the nearest makai, or ocean-side, window. Those were the days when being a committed surfer provided benefits. A committed surfer was one who didn't have a steady job, relationship, or any other attachments that might impede his availability when good waves appeared on any given morning.

What I saw when I looked, sleepy-eyed, out the window that one morning in the early 1970s shocked me from slumber. I lived at the Pipeline and waking up to a solid west swell pumping into the lineup was not an everyday occurrence. Good Pipeline, when the swell is straight, the lines clean, and the direction correct, is something that happens only a few times during a season. It's much rarer when the swell is big enough to cap on the Second Reef peak and break nicely all the way through the inside.

Surfers in those days were considered moderately successful if they owned two pairs of shorts. The surf trunks were worn when surfing, and the walk shorts during dry time. Poor surfers only had the surf trunks, which they wore 24/7. I shaped surfboards and was more or less gainfully employed. I worked only when I needed a new board or there wasn't any surf to ride. I did, however, own two pairs of shorts.

I slipped out of my walk shorts and into my damp surf trunks, grabbed my 8'0" pintail, and headed for the beach. The paddle out at Pipeline when the swell is pumping is never an easy task. I paused at the high ground to give myself a better vantage point to choose the right moment, looking for a lull in the relentless surf. The waves were consistent, but I spotted a gap between two sets, ran like hell down the beach, and plunged into the water. The rip running along the beach was ferocious, but after paddling hard and rolling under the first two whitewater waves, I saw what I hoped I had seen from the beach. The third wave was small and not breaking.

This was my window of opportunity. By being able to climb over the top of the wave rather than roll under and through it, I gained enough ground to penetrate the pounding shorebreak and get outside before the next set arrived. The sweep had carried me quite a distance down the beach, but I was outside the breaking waves and only needed to paddle back to the lineup zone. The paddle provided a good view of the surf. The tubes were enormous, spray flying out of their gaping maws with a shattering crescendo of whitewater explosions.

The takeoff lineup on Second Reef is not as defined as the inside; the sets on the outside move around, covering a wide area. The best way to line a wave up is to see where one breaks, then go sit and wait there until another one comes. Otherwise it's a confusing chase from one peak to another, hoping for a lucky break. Actually, any wave at the Pipeline is a lucky thing. As a wave approaches, the kinetic energy seems to crackle, sparking off the face of the wave. If I decided I wanted it, and was in a good position, that energy would connect with me, surging into my body with a jolt.

That morning the sets were bristling with electricity. I remember dropping into my first wave; the further down the clean, ripple-free face I flew, the faster I continued to drop. My 8'0" pintail loved this kind of situation, but as I began to bank it over into a turn, the tail began to drift. A spinout in this position would not be good. I had to ease it back down and keep going straight. The face of the wave continued to fall away ahead of me in an endless drop. Further down the wave, I tried the turn again and once more I could feel the fin starting to break away. I backed it down onto a level plane again before it broke free. I began to wonder whether I was going to be able to make a turn at all. Finally, after one of the longest drops of my life, the slope near the base of the wave began to gradually flatten and I was able to gently bank a bottom turn. I pulled into the section as it started to run on the inside reef, a zone with which I felt intimately familiar. I shot through the spinning tunnel, out the end and exited over the shoulder.

For the next hour or more, I dodged rogue sets on the Second Reef and still managed to get a number of nice rides. No one else came out. I had no idea why. I looked toward shore just before kicking out of several waves and could see a few guys with surfboards standing on the beach, yet the lineup remained empty. After several hours alone, other surfers finally began to trickle out to join me. It was, after all, a rare and epic Pipeline day. They said they had a hard time getting through the shorebreak. They kept getting beaten back to the beach by the relentless sets.

Eventually I lost my board on a wave and swam to shore to retrieve it. The crowd that had congregated while I was surfing amazed me. The beach had been deserted when I first ran and jumped into the ocean. Now it was a large, festive gathering, mostly people just watching the big waves, but interspersed were surfers getting up their courage to give it a try. I saw Flippy Hoffman walking his huge board up the beach from the 'Ehukai Beach Park. The surfboard was big and Flippy just held the nose, dragging the tail behind him, leaving a deep furrow in the wet sand.

"Hey Gerry," he yelled, "I need to ask you a question."

I waited for him as he moved toward me in his characteristic rolling gait, that of an old sailor who spent more time aboard ships at sea than on dry land. Although he had spent many years of his life on boats, Flippy also was the president of Hoffman Fabrics, a wildly successful fabric conversion company. He and his brother Walter ran the company that their father Rube had founded, but they still managed to spend a lot of time surfing.

"What's the deal?" he asked. "I can't get through the shorebreak. What am I doing wrong?"

I glanced at his gigantic surfboard. It looked like it would be impossible to get that board under the whitewater, like trying to drag a small boat through the breaking surf. I scratched my head as I pondered a solution to his problem.

"I gotta get out there, I need to be where the action is, what do I do?" Flippy wanted to know.

He was no stranger to big waves; in fact he loved them more the bigger they got. On days when the lifeguards had closed the beach at Sunset because of high surf, he would sneak out with a pair of fins. Swimming to the outside lineup, Flippy would frolic in the punishing surf like an otter having fun, giving the guards on the beach fits when they noticed the lone swimmer. Finally, he would bodysurf one in and the frantic lifeguards would rush down to the water's edge, believing a rescue was imminent.

In response to their incredulous reaction when he strolled up the beach carrying his pair of beat-up, old swim fins, he would calmly say, "What's the big deal? I got fins, when I want to go down, I go down. When I want to go up, I go up."

The lifeguards would shake their heads in amazement that anyone would want to put himself in that situation.

Just then the younger brother of my good friend Wylie Artman walked up to say hello. He was carrying his swim fins, and an idea dawned in my mind.

"Flippy, this is Dennis," I said by way of introduction.

"Dennis, this is Flippy. We need you for a job," I continued.

Dennis was on vacation, staying with his brother. For Dennis, anything legal that would pay him to be able to stay longer in Hawai'i rather than having to go back home to California was worth talking about.

"OK Flippy, all you have to do is pay Dennis here ten bucks to paddle your board out. You take his fins and swim out. When you get outside, you can swap. How's that sound?" I announced, thinking I had come up with an easily workable solution.

Dennis was all for it, but Flippy muttered and scowled. His eyes darted between Dennis and me in that perpetual squint from looking into the sun for too many years without sunglasses. Finally, after much deliberation—testimony as to why his fabric business was such a financial success—he looked at Dennis and asked, "Will you do it for five?"

Top I lost my board on the wave after this one and swam in, only to find Flippy on the beach frustrated from a number of unsuccessful attempts to paddle out. Photo: Art Brewer

Bottom Both the waves and the strong rip current, a result of the relentless swell, conspired against all those attempting to breach the shorebreak to gain the outside lineup. Photo: Jeff Divine

Jan's Board

My *Big Wednesday* costume and prop: trunks
and surfboard were all that was needed for this
Hollywood surf movie. Photo: Art Brewer

I was at home that day; the surf hadn't been exciting enough to make the long, narrow, winding drive down the hill for a closer look. From my front window I could see the sweep of the north shore of Maui, and at a glance the paucity of whitewater lines told the story. The waves were flat. It was a day to curl up with a book on the couch and rest. The surf, on its own schedule, would come the following day or some day thereafter.

As it happened, I was stretched out on the couch when the phone rang, startling me with its shrill ring in the silence of upcountry Olinda, high up on the slope of the Haleakala volcano. My golden retriever, Blue, raised an eyebrow at the sound, glanced toward the couch to determine whether action on my part was forthcoming, shifted positions, sighed loudly, and slipped back into that wonderful instant slumber only dogs of his ilk can achieve.

Normally I could rest, not in the least disturbed by the ringing phone. I might vaguely count the number of rings until it stopped, feeling no guilt whatsoever for not summoning the energy to connect with the person making the effort to call. It was a bad habit, but I enjoyed the solitude of my home high in the hills. I justified my unwillingness to be imposed on by thinking that he or she would call back if it was important. For some unclear reason this time I rolled up off the couch, took the required three steps, grabbed the phone off its hook, and returned to my supine position on the couch before answering.

"Hello," I said into the receiver.

Afterward, I would wonder whether maybe subconsciously I had some inkling that this phone call would be different because making that connection would, quite literally, turn my quiet life upside down in the months to come.

"Hello," a strange woman's voice said. "Is this Gerry Lopez?"

"Yes it is," I replied, thinking who in the heck could this be now.

"Will you please hold for John Milius?" I heard the click of the call being transferred, and before I could wonder who John Milius was, although the name did sound vaguely familiar, a strong voice came on the line.

"Gerry? Hi, this is John Milius, how are you?"

"Well, I'm fine ... John, do we know each other?" I had to ask because I was at a loss to place the name.

"Not yet, not yet," he quickly answered. "But we will. Let me explain."

He went on to tell me how Warner Bros. Studios was producing a movie about surfing. He and a guy named Denny Aaberg had written the script. It would be called *Big Wednesday*. There was a cameo part in it that he wanted me to play. My old friend surf-filmmaker Greg MacGillivray would be directing a second unit to film the surfing sequences.

I listened and wondered what the heck a cameo appearance or a second unit might be, but I marginally understood the importance of our conversation. This was Hollywood calling. This was the call that everyone dreams about. I checked whether I was still breathing. Even Blue was awake now, watching me closely, sensing something in the air.

A few days later I was driving on Ventura Highway and following the directions John's secretary had given me. I came around a curve and over a slight rise, and there sprawled before me was the small city that is Warner Bros. Studios. A big sign told me I was at my destination. A huge fence ran, I imagined, around the entire complex. The fence ran as far as I could see to either side of the gate I was approaching, at least a mile in both directions.

A guard gave me directions to the *Big Wednesday* office. I drove down row after row of huge metal buildings that were all separate sound stages. Everywhere there were extras in costume: cowboys, Romans, 1920s zoot-suiters, showgirls … the works.

I drove past a completely deserted suburban neighborhood with 1950s-style houses lining the street. The next street was a typical turn-of-the-century city, with old buildings and businesses bunched together. As I passed I saw that these were only false fronts. There was another row of false fronts backed against them. I passed a dirt street of a Western cowboy town complete with saloons, horse troughs, and hitching rails. I was in Hollywood, Tinsel Town. Only a few days before, I had been sprawled on my couch in a different life.

I gave my name to the series of secretaries and moved deeper into the inner sanctum of the temporary *Big Wednesday* production office. John's personal assistant greeted me.

Then John, a bear of a man, rushed forward, shook my hand, and ushered me into his small office saying, "Glad you could make it, this is great, we're going to make a terrific film."

He went on to fill me in on many details of the upcoming production. I was in a Hollywood daze, barely hearing what he said as a host of different crew members trooped through John's office to ask some question or another and briefly say hello to me. The producer, Buzz Feitshans, joined us and informed me of "my deal," membership in the Screen Actors Guild, and other pertinent information regarding my new employment.

"Sure, it all sounds good" was all the answer I could muster.

My new Hollywood experience peaked when the star of the show, Jan-Michael Vincent, walked in with his rugged good looks. Only a short time before I had watched him on the big screen in "The Mechanic" with Charles Bronson; now I was meeting him in person.

The general atmosphere of informality surprised me. Hollywood always had seemed to me distant and larger than life. I was stunned to recognize that, when it came right down to it, these people were just regular folks like me.

Jan-Michael and I became fast friends. His successful acting career didn't prevent Jan from being an avid surfer, and we had a lot in common. I was a regular guest at his Encinal Canyon home during the L.A. shooting portion of the movie. I had only light surfboard-shaping responsibilities for my business, Lightning Bolt Surf Company, and even lighter duties to the Bolt Corporation, our licensing company. I was free to play my new Hollywood role.

And quite a role it was. Besides reveling in the glamour of the movie-making process, I also enjoyed a spectacular social life hanging with the stars. Gary Busey, the other main actor, was married and had a young son but spent most nights out on the town with us. Mostly those evenings were spent watching Jan operate. He was the

consummate ladies' man; the women loved him, and he was seldom without their company. He was separated from his wife, a situation common to the tabloid lifestyle of Hollywood.

During the next several months of partying with him, I understood why Jan's movie-star nightlife couldn't support a marriage. Near the end of the shooting I reached my limit. I awoke one afternoon and knew I was done. We stayed up far too late to enjoy any sunrises or mornings, unless we stayed up the entire night. High on the hillside, Jan's home had a view of Point Zero and Zuma Beach. I could see a swell running but the wind had already blown out the waves. Jan was still asleep, and it was too late to catch any good waves. I was disgusted with myself. From that moment forward, I vowed never to drink or party like that again. That was thirty years ago, and I haven't had another drink since.

The moviemaking was fun. Most of the filming was done on the Warner Bros. lot where sets already were in place. A few scenes were shot on location. The draft board scene was filmed in the actual building where the draft board conducted the physical exams prior to sending those selected away to Vietnam. Another scene required a pier where the 'Bear' had his bait and surf shop. That location was the Gaviota Pier north of Santa Barbara.

Big Wednesday is a movie about three friends who grow up surfing Malibu in the early 1960s and spans the carefree years of youth when the movie characters, Matt, Jack, and Leroy, live to surf and little else matters. Come the early 1970s, the friends get jobs, have families, move away, and leave their youth behind. *Big Wednesday* is a day when the surf gets bigger than ever before, reuniting them one final time. It's a movie about youth and friendship. The details are exacting. John Milius and Denny Aaberg had spent a portion of their own youth surfing the 'Point' and hanging out in the 'Pit.' They set out to re-create authentically what for them had been the sweetest of times.

By far the best location work was where they set up the Pit area. The Pit was painstakingly re-created in amazing detail at Cojo Point on the Bixby Ranch, just north

Top   I'm pointing out some nuances of the break to
John Milius, the director, and Jan-Michael Vincent,
the leading actor, before we all paddled out for their
first attempt at surfing some big waves at Sunset
Beach. Photo: Dan Merkel

Bottom   One of the sets at Cojo on the
Bixby Ranch built to look like the Pit at
Malibu of the early 1960s. Photo: Dan Merkel

of the famous Hollister Ranch. Cojo is a perfect right point, highly coveted during the south swell season but entirely off-limits because of the privately owned ranchland. Cojo's splendid waves break mostly unridden, except by adventurous boat-in surfers.

For three wonderful weeks Hollywood moved in and took over, renting the area from the Bixby Ranch. The cast and crew were housed in nearby Lompoc, but Jan and I were exempted. His personal motor home, a classic Airstream, was leased by the production company for his own use during the entire shoot and parked on location. It was quite a deal. The movie paid him to use his own motor home.

It was my first experience with a motor home. I marveled at this complete home on wheels. For the entire three weeks, Jan and I spent our nights on the set. We would awaken on many occasions to the quiet solitude of Cojo Point with perfectly peeling waves. There was a night watchman, but we never saw nor heard him. The catering manager would make sure he left a large tray of food and drink for our dinners each evening. Every day, two busloads of beautiful Santa Barbara girls were hired as extras and bussed to the location. Jan would work his charm and magic to entice some of them to camp out for the night.

Despite the excesses of his nightlife, Jan was a professional when it came time to do the job. When the director said, "Action," Jan delivered his lines perfectly. That he had been up the entire night before drinking didn't matter. It helped that the character he played was supposed to be drunk most of the time, but still it was amazing to see him perform.

Acting isn't easy. To do it well takes a lot of—well, I'm not sure what. Believable acting takes talent, but also lots of concentration, dedication, and focus. Many actors are professionally trained, spending years at acting schools or with private acting coaches. Some use what is known in the film industry as "method acting," where they substitute a previous personal experience to set the mood for the particular emotion required by the scene. Jan was a completely natural actor, able to get into his role with little preparation or research.

I had done some very lightweight acting in a few surfing movies. In the surf movie scene for *Big Wednesday*, I was only required to play myself, walk through the crowd, and make brief eye contact with Matt. The location was an old theater that actually had been used to show surf movies during the 1960s. John and Denny wanted every detail of the movie to be authentic in order to preserve on film the nuances of their former lives.

I had no lines to speak and only a moment on film, but I was nervous to a point near catatonia. Jan noticed my discomfort on the first rehearsal and gave me some pointers. He simply told me to remember being at a real surf movie and to re-create that memory here. It was my first lesson in method acting.

There was a scene on the Cojo set that required a little more from me. In the scene I would drive to the beach during the big swell, get out of the car, and pull my surfboard out of the back. When the time came to shoot the scene a small problem became apparent. I didn't have a surfboard to take out of the car.

Luckily, I had made a surfboard for Jan. It was an 8'0" Lightning Bolt with an orange bottom, red deck, and black and white bolts. It was inside his motor home. One of the assistant directors rushed to fetch the board and we shot the scene. Later when we filmed the surfing sequences in Hawai'i, I built myself a matching board. At that point the producers decided that only the big winter surf at Sunset Beach could make the necessary impression. So the new plan was that we would finish the movie on North Shore, O'ahu.

The water unit, main stars, and quite a few of the crew enjoyed a nice month at the Kuilima Hotel while shooting film all over the North Shore for that final day of the story. I made a new board to ride big Sunset, glassed exactly the same as Jan's board. George Greenough and Dan Merkel took some heavy wipeouts filming from the water at inside Sunset with bulky and unwieldy 35mm cameras in water housings. Greg MacGillivray masterfully directed all of the shooting from shore. His brilliant editing of the footage created an exciting and totally believable final surfing scene.

The *Big Wednesday* of surf did indeed come across as a day like no other. The main character's (Matt Johnson) surfing, cleverly doubled by Billy Hamilton and J Riddle, was spectacular. Jan did some of his own surfing at Sunset. Although a bit outgunned by the premier North Shore surf spot, he definitely set a high bar for actors and was dubbed "the best surfer in Hollywood." His real-life surfing allowed the editing team to cut to close-ups in the surf sequences, which helped to sell the scene.

In the movie, the three friends come back to their favorite break, and although now considerably older and perhaps slightly over-the-hill, they rip it up one last time. Matt takes a vicious wipeout on his last wave, ending his surfing career. He passes his special big-wave board, built by the Bear, on to one of the younger surfers when he gets back to the beach. For the wipeout the stunt coordinator, Terry Leonard, hired Bruce Raymond, now a chief executive at Quiksilver International, but then a starving young surfer. For $100, Bruce paddled himself over the falls on wave after wave until Terry, the second unit director called, "Cut!"

After reviewing the daily film, both MacGillivray and Milius decided that Sunset Beach just didn't look terrible enough. They came up with an idea to get a goofy-foot surfer to take some gas at the Pipeline; they would flop the negative to make the left become a right. For another $100, Jackie Dunn agreed to be the human dummy. Why anyone would deliberately launch himself into space again and again at the Pipe was beyond me.

Flipping the negative cut perfectly into the film sequence. Jackie Dunn actually looked much more like Jan than did either of the other stunt doubles. Apart from breaking several of the prop boards, shaped by Tom Parrish and airbrushed to look like balsawood—and probably almost breaking his neck—Jackie was little worse for wear after the stunt. The final sequence of the movie was a complete success.

Big Wednesday, authentic in every detail, well-acted, well-directed, and a cinematographic tribute to the sport of surfing, was doomed to a life of mediocrity. Rejected by the suits at Warner Bros. Studios, the film was sold in a package deal to an independent distributor rather than marketed by the formidable studio distribution system. This decision precluded allocation of any large marketing dollars to help sell the film to the public. Even the surf media reviews of the movie were lackluster to outright negative. *Big Wednesday* wasn't going anywhere in the U.S. Nobody wanted to know about longboard surfing in 1978.

Ironically, the film enjoyed great success in both Italy and Japan, quickly becoming a cult classic and enjoyed for years. However, *Big Wednesday* had a snowball effect on the surf world in several ways. Not only did it become a standard by which the era depicted would forever be measured, but it also single-handedly launched a resurgence of longboard surfing that took the surf world by storm a few short years later.

Big Wednesday rose to its well-deserved prominence eventually, but only by coming in through the back door. Real surfers found this to be appropriate. Just like its subject matter, acceptance was based on the unspoken and unacknowledged nature of the sport.

Despite the negative public opinion that pervaded mainstream culture during surfing's first ascension to notoriety in the 1960s, our way of life continued to grow. Surfing is, for surfers, the only life, and will always be the only life. Today the surf industry is mainstream, but like the rip currents that are common to many of the best surfing areas, the sport and the lifestyle it spawned had to battle against the current to gain acceptance from nonsurfers.

Ironically, the only surfboards from the early shortboard period that remain in my possession are the *Big Wednesday* boards. Somehow the one I rode at Sunset during the filming, and Jan's board, escaped the rubbish heap. Hi-Tech Maui, the premier surf and water sports store on Maui, used them for display boards. This further helped them to avoid being sold or thrown away. Randy Rarick recently sold Jan's board at his world famous surf auction. It was a beat-up old board that had definitely seen better days, but it had a superb pedigree. It sold for more than $12,000.

The Track

of the Cat

Shoe stores in Hawai'i must not have done much business with children's shoes during the 1950s. No kid I knew wore shoes when we were growing up. The first time I owned a pair of shoes was when I was entering seventh grade. Until then everyone went barefoot.

The best thing about not wearing shoes was that the soles of our feet got so tough that they were impervious to kiawe thorns or hot pavement. With the bottoms of our feet like leather, it was as though we had a pair of built-on shoes. My grandmother would throw us out of her house in the morning. Because we had dirty feet, we couldn't come back inside until we took a bath that evening and washed our feet before dinner.

The surf lifestyle was not particularly big on shoes either. Who needs them at the beach? After an early, and brief, surf fashion statement with Sperry Top-Siders and huarache sandals, most Hawai'i surfers just wore rubber slippers if they didn't go barefoot. For us, dressing for comfort and not for speed was more in line with being a surfer.

Growing up in Hawai'i was the perfect place to dial in the minimalist surf dress code. A pair of shorts, a tee shirt, and a surfboard were all a surfer needed. But a cool pair of trunks wasn't easy to find in the early days. There weren't any Quiksilver or Billabong surf companies making functional and stylish surf trunks. Surfers in the know would go to a custom sewing shop like Take's, M. Nii's, or H. Miura's, be fitted for shorts, pick the fabric, and practically live in that pair of shorts once delivered. A couple of tee shirts rounded out the uniform.

On early trips to Bali, Indonesia, we reverted back to those carefree days of youth. We packed a couple of pairs of shorts, a small stack of tee shirts, two or three surfboards, and a sturdy pair of Rainbow Sandals. But the beaches were clean, so once we arrived we ditched the slippers and toughened up our feet that had grown soft from too many years of wearing shoes.

One of the big training programs that became part of our Bali lifestyle was the run-swim-run. We would start from Mike Boyum's house near Kuta Beach and run down the dirt road barefoot and along the shore in our Speedos, swim goggles on our heads. It was easier to run on the packed wet sand near the water's edge, but it was a better workout to run in the soft sand further up the bank. The dry sand, however, was hot. There was a risk of burning our feet if we hadn't broken them in properly.

This breaking in was a careful process of feeling the soles of our feet getting hot, then dashing down to the wet sand to cool them off before resuming the run in the hot soft sand. After several miles of running, we would jump in the water and swim back about halfway, then run the rest of the way home. It was a great workout, and we did it religiously whenever the surf was small. If the surf was up, of course we just went surfing all day.

One day when the waves were small we did an early yoga session and decided we would extend the run and swim distances. We wanted to come back and reward ourselves with a big lunch without feeling guilty about eating too much when there was no surf. So we headed out in the midmorning. The sky was clear, the trade winds had kicked in combing the small wave faces into perfection, and it was a joy to run along the seashore watching the surf. Occasionally a wave would peel and we would mind surf it. We imagined turns, cutbacks, off-the-lips, and tuberides. In that way we received all that those waves offered.

Several miles down the beach was another little village called Legian where there was a hotel, more losmen, and some small shops. I guess Kuta and Legian had been there a long time, because both had very old temples and huge trees. The big trees were a sure sign that people had been living in an area, as they provided a priceless service: shade.

The sunshine of Bali is deceptively inviting. Overexposure can be serious. Light-skinned tourists not acclimated to the intensity of the sun near the equator pay dearly. For very obvious reasons, local people value shade, and cutting down a shade tree is a high crime. If the numerous large shade trees were any indication, Legian was probably a more popular area than Kuta at one time.

Kuta grew quickly with the recent influx of Australian and American tourists looking for less spendy digs. But Legian has something the beachbreaks of Kuta will never have, which may have a big effect on future growth, at least for surfers. There is a more pronounced bend in the curve of the beach at Legian, which affects the riptides. Sometimes as a result of these rips a sandbar will form creating beachbreak waves of world-class shape. I had heard about this break, but until this day I had not seen it.

Mike and I were running up the beach and could see surfers in the water, but we were still too far away to make out any detail. As we got closer we saw the surfers getting long rides, unusual in shorebreaks unless they are really good. In Hawai'i there are not many beachbreaks well suited to surfing—bodysurfing yes, but not boardsurfing. To a surfer raised on reefbreaks, and with the excellent reefbreaks of Uluwatu and Kuta Reef, the beachbreaks of Bali didn't hold much appeal for me.

But, we could see as we came closer, this Legian break was as near perfection as a beachbreak can be. Maybe the surf was coming up, because the waves looked really good. The surfers were all sitting in one spot where a nice peak consistently broke. Sometimes it would break better left, other times to the right, but most often it went both ways equally clean. It appeared that the right was giving longer rides, all the way into the knee-deep water inside. Hot and sweaty from our long run, we stood there in shock, watching wave after wave peel off.

Back then there were not a lot of surfers on Bali. The more skilled ones naturally gravitated to the better reefbreaks, while those of lesser skills enjoyed the more gentle waves on the beaches. The level of surfing was not quite up to the quality of the waves on that day with one exception. We had seen one guy styling across a wave when we were still a distance away, too far to tell much except that he got a long ride.

As we stood nearer the break he caught another wave, but as he made his first turn some beginner took off in front of him going straight off and he was forced to kick out. There was something very familiar about his surfing style. A few minutes later, he caught a wave that somehow reminded me of First Point Malibu as it peels into the Cove.

Watching this guy climb and drop, smoothly cutting under the whitewater when the wave sectioned ahead before sweeping back up onto the green, I realized why the wave looked like Malibu. It was because this guy surfed just like Miki Dora, the King of Malibu. He rode the wave to its end, kicked out, and paddled back to the peak.

We sat and watched more rides, waiting for the good surfer to get another one. When he did, again he rode just like Dora: the characteristic slouch, knees forward, upper body leaning back, the hands held stylishly. Either this had to be the real thing or the best imposter I had ever seen.

"Mike, let's swim out there and see who that is, I think it's Miki Dora," I said.

Mike knew the history of Dora and was as keen as I was to see if this was really him. So we put on our goggles and swam out to the lineup.

"Hey Miki," I yelled when we got close, but he glanced sideways at us, turned the other way and paddled for a wave.

We waited until he paddled back out, but could tell he was trying to avoid us. I'm sure we looked like two geeks in our swim goggles and Speedos swimming after him in the lineup. Every time we tried to get close, he would just move away. He had much more mobility on his surfboard than we did swimming.

We weren't getting anywhere this way, so I suggested to Mike that we run back and get our surfboards. So we ran back to the house as fast as we could, grabbed our boards and a motorbike and blasted back. I drove while Mike sat behind holding both surfboards. Back then nobody cared if we drove on the beach because there were so few people. We knew all the lifeguards anyway.

We got back to Legian, parked the bike, and paddled out. He was still there, sitting farthest outside alone. Mike and I paddled up and introduced ourselves.

Miki Dora styling through another section
at Malibu. Photo: Leroy Grannis

"Hi Miki, I'm Gerry and this is Mike," I said.

"I think you've got me mixed up with someone else," was all he said, but the furtive head gestures and shifty eyes gave him away.

"You're Miki Dora and you're our hero; what are you doing here?" I blurted out.

"Are you guys FBI?" was the only answer.

"FBI? If you mean feeble-brained idiots, yeah I guess so. What the hell kind of question is that?" I was puzzled.

"Well, you don't look like federal agents, but if I ask and you are, you have to say so," he answered.

"So you're Miki Dora and you're here in Bali. What's going on?" Mike and I wanted to know.

"I might be who you say, but don't say it out loud any more. I don't know who the rest of these guys are," he gestured toward the other surfers around us who sat there totally oblivious to our conversation or our identities, their only interest being the next set of waves.

"You guys live here? You know where the good surf is?" he asked.

"Yeah, you want to go out and surf some bigger waves at Ulu? Where are you staying, we can send a *bemo* around to pick you up and head out there right now, if you want. It kinda looks like the surf came up a little so it should be pretty good out there," I replied.

Being in the presence of the Great Miki Dora had us nervously motor-mouthing. But after all we had, more or less, the undivided attention of one of the biggest legends in modern surfing.

He looked at us a little suspiciously, but it seemed like it was his first trip to Bali and we sensed a kindred spirit of adventure in him. He agreed, told us where to find him, and that was how we first met Miki 'da Cat' Dora.

We picked him up at his losmen in our bemo-for-the-day. A bemo is a small Datsun pickup with a covered bed and bench seats along each side. They serve as the main means of transport for the local people. A bemo was the best way to get ourselves and our surfboards out to Ulu. The exhaust fumes flowing into the open back mingle with the rest of the too-numerous-to-list odors that permeate the Balinese atmosphere. We were well used to it, but Miki's discomfort was evident.

"I'm used to a little higher standard of transportation; is this all that's available?" he asked as we bounced along the road to Uluwatu.

In contrast to our dirty surf trunks, grubby tee shirts, and dusty running shoes, Miki was dressed immaculately in a stylish tennis outfit with sparkling white tennis shoes.

Forty-five minutes later, after a bumpy ride over a twisted narrow road, our bemo pulled off under some trees. As always a group of young kids waited for our arrival. They greeted us with big smiles and shouts of "me carry, me carry," as they jostled each other hoping to get picked to carry one of our surfboards down the trail to the waves.

Miki was pretty game after we informed him of the three-kilometer hike to get to the surf. I think it was the young board carriers that made the difference. If he had to carry his own surfboard up and down the rugged path in the boiling midday sun, he

"I think you've got me mixed up with someone else," was all he said, but the furtive head gestures and shifty eyes gave him away.

might not have been so willing. Mike and I took off running as was our usual practice, a warm-up before the waves. Miki took one incredulous look at us and said he would stay with the surfboards and their carriers.

When we got to where we could see the surf, one glance showed us that the swell had come up. After a few days of no surf, Mike and I were raring to go. We climbed down the rickety tied-together sticks into the sea cave that was the easiest access to the shoreline along the steep, rugged limestone cliffs at Uluwatu. Eventually, the boys brought our boards down the makeshift ladder in their bare feet, as surefooted as monkeys.

Dora, perched above, called down to us, "I'm supposed to climb down this?"

I guess at first sight the final part of the trail didn't look very secure, and it would have been a long, ugly fall. Actually, it was an ingeniously designed, although very primitive, ladder system that worked perfectly well, until it fell apart and had to be rebuilt. Miki came down the ladder very tentatively.

"So how's the surf look?" Miki asked. The board carriers, interested in neither the waves nor in Miki following, had come straight to the cave without bothering to take a look.

"It's good, it came up," I answered, as Mike and I waxed up, eager to get into the water.

"Well, where do you paddle out?" Miki asked as he got his own equipment ready.

"No sweat, just follow us right out of this cave and you'll see the lineup," I told him. He looked at us a little dubiously as we strapped on our leashes and pointed the way.

The paddle out from the cave at Uluwatu is normally a stunning experience. Paddling out of the darkness into the sunlight to be greeted by a panorama of beautiful surf after the long, hot hike feels like finding the pot of gold at the end of the rainbow. This time was an altogether different reward. Apparently I hadn't done my surf check diligently enough. When I burst out into the sun, instead of a sigh of joy, I uttered a serious, "Oh Shit!"

The swell was a lot bigger and more powerful than I had expected: eight- to ten-foot waves crashed down in relentless fury. The tide, at its peak, coupled with the strong surf, produced a rip of prodigious strength. I was immediately swept sideways, backed up against the rugged cliffs, fighting desperately to keep from being washed into the rocks. Normally it's a two-minute paddle out. I struggled for a difficult fifteen to twenty minutes before finally breaching the surfline, at which point I saw that the sweep had carried me over a half-mile down the shoreline.

Once through the waves, I started the long paddle back up to the lineup in front of the cave. Mike joined me a short time later, having been right behind me as we went out of the cave. In the riptide and breaking waves, we separated, and it was every man for himself with no stopping along the way.

Over an hour later, Miki came paddling out. "Is that how the paddle out is every time?" he deadpanned.

Not knowing what to expect, he had followed us out from the cave and was caught in the rip. There was no turning back nor any relaxing. He had to battle to keep from being pushed up into the rocks at the base of the cliff. Finally, much further down than Mike and I had been swept, he managed to break through the surf and get outside.

"So is getting back in as exciting as trying to get out?" he wanted to know.

I knew that we had to wait until the tide went out and were kind of stuck out there. It was possible to go in to the small beach just upstream from the cave, but at high tide there was no escape. The tunnel back into the cave would be underwater and practically impassable. If a surfer was lucky he might ride a wave right into the cave entrance, but if he missed, it would be a repeat of the paddle out. Mike and I informed Miki of all this. He calmly took it all in, but I'm sure he thought we were a couple of lame turkeys.

Trying to make up for the surf thrashing, we took Miki to dinner at the Sunset Beach Hotel. The owner there, Francois Faust, was from the Grand Duchy of Luxembourg, he had moved to Bali, married a Javanese gal, and had two little boys. He not only ran a great hotel where I usually stayed but also put on a great meal each night.

Miki questioned Francois about whether he had been a Hitler Youth who had fled Europe after World War II. Francois ignored Miki while I tried, to no avail, to let Miki know that Francois and I were about the same age, both born well after the war.

Francois' friend, Hans Snell, a Dutch artist and also married to an Indonesian and living up in Ubud where he sold his beautiful paintings, had brought his family down to have dinner at the hotel. Miki insisted that Hans looked like an ex-SS man and both Francois and Hans belonged to an Indonesian cell of ex-Nazis hiding out in Bali.

This was more than a little embarrassing for Mike and me. It appeared that Miki had some obsession with Nazi Germany; I'm sure the wine with dinner didn't help.

Apparently Miki's ranting didn't make any impression on our host or his friend, and as most nights in Surf City Bali, ours thankfully ended early. We left it with Miki that we would meet him early the following morning to see whether we were surfing or doing something else.

The next day, our ill-fated surf adventure behind us, the surf had dropped dramatically. An unusual storm swell, intense but short-lived, was probably the reason for our rough handling at Uluwatu the day before. Overall, that day of surfing had not been Miki's best, nor ours.

With the surf gone and the day still young, we thought a run-swim-run would be a good thing. Miki somewhat reluctantly agreed to accompany us. He declined a pair of Speedos but accepted the swim goggles as we stripped down to our essential equipment. We always started out running near the water's edge but as we left the lifeguard station behind, the beach quickly became devoid of people. We moved up into the soft sand and Miki followed us as we concentrated on our breathing and pace. The sun was up, the day warm, the air clean and fresh, and the sea sparkling off to our left.

Suddenly Miki veered down toward the water, ran right in, and sat down. Mike and I stopped, looked at each other, and went down to see what was going on. Miki was sitting in the shallow water looking at the soles of his feet.

"Are you guys some kind of masochists or what?" he said.

"What's the matter?" I asked.

"That hot sand just burned the shit out of my feet, didn't you guys feel that? Are you torturing me just for fun, or did someone put you up to this? Yeah, you can go ahead, I think I'll just stay right here." Miki was done for the day.

He waved us on, cooling his hot feet in the water. I guess those California guys didn't go barefoot enough because the sand wasn't that hot yet, and we were less than ten minutes into the run. Mike and I kept going, feeling bad about trying to show Miki Dora a good time in Bali and doing a terrible job of it. We didn't get to surf with Miki any more over the next ten days we spent with him, but he schooled us in a fierce way at tennis, which he played expertly.

A year or so later, I found out that Miki was on the run from the FBI for some crime he allegedly had been involved in. Apparently they caught up with him. I think the story goes that the FBI always gets their man.

Many years later, I ran into Miki in Biarritz, France, at a dinner party in another friend's home. I asked him if he remembered the brief time we had spent together in Bali. He answered with a trademark Miki Dora hand gesture and a twinkle in his eye: "You must have me confused with someone else."

Momentary

The surf at G-Land had always produced for us. Year after year, trip after trip, the waves pumped. We came to expect it, thinking this was just the way it always would be. But the reality of surf is that it is almost never consistently reliable. That is one of its greatest lessons: To lessen disappointment, one must first lessen expectation.

The surfing experience teaches this lesson over and over again on a regular basis. How many times does a surf report instill high hopes that are only dashed, when after much effort the surfer finally arrives at the seashore to find no waves at all?

The good thing about G-Land was the lay of the land and its orientation to the predominant incoming swell. The southeastern tip of Java sticks out like a hook, trapping the southerly Indian Ocean swells and funneling them into the surf spot. It also has an offshore submarine trench, which helps enhance the consistency of the surf. The waves in front of the surf camp are at least twice the size of Uluwatu on the nearby island of Bali, even though both coastlines face in exactly the same direction.

So it was a big shock to arrive and find minimal surf trickling into our most reliable surf location. My brother Victor and I knew it had to be flat sometime; surf everywhere else on the planet is like that. But when the days passing stretched into a whole week without waves, we began to worry. The arrival of a surf charter sailboat broke up the monotony of laying around in the tree houses carefully watching the horizon in hopes of another arrival: the forerunner sets of a new swell. These were the early days

Photo: Jeff Divine

Entertain-
ment

before surf forecasting became the enterprising science it is today. Other than taking a look out to sea, there was no way of knowing whether any surf was coming. Several Brazilian surfers had arranged for the boat charter and having a few extra berths, they allowed two Hawaiians to fill the empty space.

One was Don King. In between his junior and senior years on a water polo scholarship at Stanford University, Don came out to shoot photos in Bali and joined us for a ton-day run at G-Land. The surf, as usual, was magnificent and the place had the same effect on Don that it had on us: love at first sight. Several years later, living in Hawai'i and with his fame in water photography gaining momentum, Don was on assignment full-time as a staff photographer for *Surfing* magazine. Indonesia was the hot spot for surf during the months of April through October, and Don was there to film the action.

For this trip he had enlisted Mike Stewart. Mike's career as one of the world's leading boogie boarders was just around the corner ahead, but his water skills were already well developed. Both friends were like fish in the ocean. Even without fins they moved through the water with ease. Don regaled Mike with stories of great waves at the remote G-Land surf camp, and they had taken the extra berths on the chartered boat.

They heard we were on the beach and came ashore on the inflatable dinghy to say hello. The captain of the sailboat was a dour, stern taskmaster who took his work and his equipment very seriously. He drove the inflatable over the reef and stayed with it on the beach while Don and Mike tracked us down in our little tree house. None of us knew of any imminent surf, but we traded tales of great waves we had ridden here on past trips. Finally, one of the camp boys came to tell us the boat captain was getting impatient and wanted to leave before the tide got any lower. He need not have worried as we were in a full moon cycle of tides, the highest water of the entire month. Our friends informed us that the Brazilians had been giving the captain fits the entire voyage with their wild behavior. Don and Mike wanted to stay on his good side, so we all said goodbye for the moment.

The next day was no different: The surf remained flat. The offshore winds that normally would have combed the long walls into perfection howled through the trees and over the wave-barren reef. We lay in our tree house, reading and bored out of our minds, but without surf, there was little else to do. Victor has never been a patient man, and the long week of inactivity was wearing thin on him. To put it mildly, he was one grumpy person ready to snap at the slightest provocation.

Meanwhile back on the sailboat, the captain must have found some qualities he liked in Don and Mike because, contrary to his nature, he agreed that they could take his precious inflatable for a cruise. Equally bored out of their minds, the boys eagerly jumped into the little dinghy and fired up the outboard engine.

Up in the tree house, I happened to hear the faint whine of a two-stroke motor and glanced up from my book. When the tide is full on the big tide cycle, there is plenty of water over the reef. The small surf size meant the waves were insufficient to even break over the normal or most inside lineup. But over the shallow inner reef, the tiny swells were pushed upward and little waves were formed for a short distance before they again sank down into the deeper water closer to shore. Don and Mike were using the inflatable like a motorized surfboard and riding these miniscule waves. Back and forth they wove, trying to milk the longest ride possible out of the short-duration waves. When the wave they were on petered out, they would wheel the little boat around and race back to catch another one. It was the only surfing anyone had done for over a week, and they were having a blast.

The noise from the outboard was slightly irritating in the serene jungle setting, but they were having fun and it was harmless ... or so it seemed. I just happened to look up as Don was driving back outside when another wave popped up right in front of them. Apparently he failed to warn Mike who was sitting up front on the opposite side. When Don suddenly turned to catch the wave Mike must not have been holding on and flew right off the boat. The loss of Mike as ballast greatly upset the delicate balance on the tiny inflatable and the result was the boat tipping the other way. This threw Don off the other side. I put my book down and sat up so I could see better.

The driverless boat completed the turn into the wave and toward shore. Without any weight in the boat, the brisk offshore winds lifted the bow until it was at an impossible angle and on the verge of going over backward. It was also racing at full throttle straight toward the beach. I sat up a little straighter to see where it would crash into the shoreline.

But, as the little boat came into the wind shadow near shore, caused by the thick jungle, the nose came back down into the water. There must have been a very slight tilt in the angle of the outboard's tiller because the boat made a sweeping turn and was now headed straight back out to sea. Just when it looked like it would run into the little waves, the driverless boat made another big turn and was again racing back toward the beach. The wind got under the nose and put the little dinghy into the wheelie position it had assumed on the first lap. Inside the wind shadow of the trees, the bow dropped, and like before, the boat swept around and blazed back the other way.

"You need to see this," I said to Victor who had his nose buried in his book.

Removing his reading glasses to look where I was pointing, he muttered, "What the heck?"

Meanwhile in a desperate effort to retake control of the lost boat running at full throttle before the captain on the sailboat realized what was going on, Don and Mike swam to intercept it. With the binoculars, Victor watched the action up close and gave me a blow-by-blow description.

"These idiots are going to kill themselves," he exclaimed.

This did seem likely: There was that spinning prop on the outboard that would have shredded flesh and bone. The boys tried to grab at the speeding boat, but at the last moment had to hurl themselves out of the way of the slicing propeller. As the boat made another lap, Don and Mike tried again, but it was an impossibly dangerous feat.

Victor was enjoying himself for the first time in several days and kept the running commentary going for my benefit. We lost count of the laps and speculated that the engine would run out of gas. Meanwhile, the boat raced around its big oval course.

Finally, in an act of complete desperation, Don put himself directly in the boat's path and made a flying leap as it came at him. Somehow he got a hold of the side. Through the binoculars, Victor's glee at their predicament turned to horror as he could see Don was slowly sliding down the side, closer and closer to the spinning propeller. When it looked like the worst was about to happen, and Don clutching the side was about to slip under the stern where the racing outboard waited, it was suddenly over. By hanging on, Don had slowed the boat enough that Mike was able to chase it down. He managed to climb on, and just before it appeared Don was about to be filleted, Mike killed the motor.

We watched the boys pull themselves back aboard, restart the engine and very slowly motor back toward the mother ship, tails between their legs. The episode had energized Victor and brought him out of his funky mood. We laughed and laughed about it. The next day the surf finally came, and we were back in the money. We surfed our days away as usual, spending most of the daylight hours on our surfboards and limping back in at sunset to eat and fall into a deep sleep, and then do it all over again the following day.

On a recent trip with Don, I reminded him of the incident, and he just laughed and shook his head. Surfing is and always will be a series of close calls and near misses; danger always lurking, but the attraction never fades.

For any surfer, there is always one place that will challenge his skills and experience more than any other. For me, that place is G-Land. Photo: Art Brewer

b. GALLERY

Top and Bottom The Ala Moana Bowl was where the most progressive summertime surfing in Hawai'i went down. The surf leash indicates this was the later 1970s, before that there were many long swims to retrieve lost boards. Photos: Steve Wilkings

Left Photo: Steve Wilkings

115

The photographer, Denjiro Sato, and I call this photo the
banzai picture because of the arms raised in the traditional
Japanese celebration of life. Photo: Denjiro Sato

Above   Flippy Hoffman grills me on the technique
to paddle out during a large, consistent swell at the
Pipeline. Photo: Art Brewer

Right   The price of not catching the wave at the
Pipeline was costly, not something any surfer liked
to pay more than once. Photo: Jeff Divine

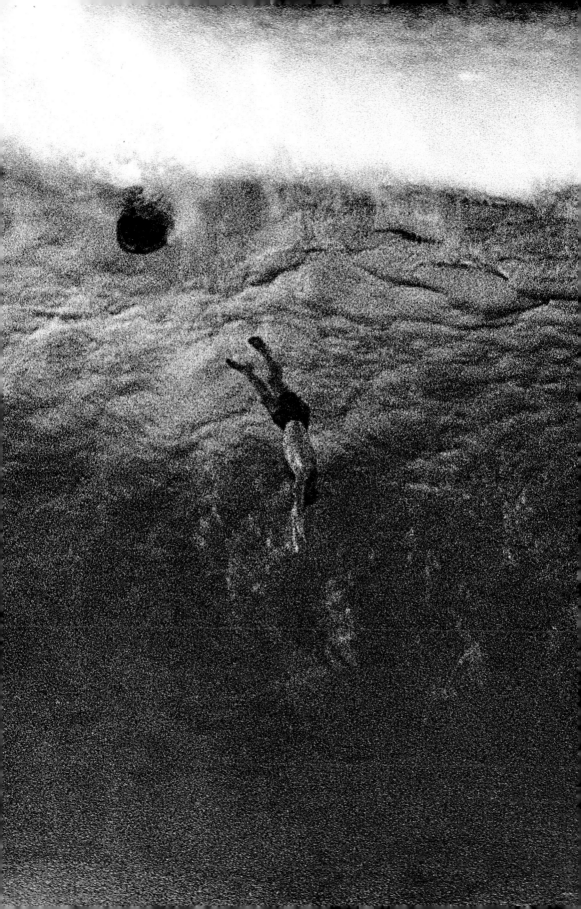

Herbie

Herbie and his Kawasaki in the front yard
of the Pipe house, looking for some help to
launch his ski. Photo: Denjiro Sato

Herbie Fletcher is one of the surfing world's most colorful characters. If a single word could most completely describe his life, that word would be passion. Herbie always has something going on, something that momentarily consumes him with passion. This trait is infectious. It permeates his whole family.

There were plenty of good times over the last forty years, but a lot of them centered on the time we owned the Pipe house together. His boys were growing up fast. Christian was just beginning to polish up his high-flying act. Nathan was still a youngster but had a memory like a steel trap. He could tell me what everyone was wearing as many days or weeks back as I wanted to go: shirt, pants, shoes, right down to the color and style of the socks and how high or low they were.

Dibi, Herbie's wife, was in a class all her own, an avid and intense pursuer of most anything life threw at her. She went after, in turn, athletics, business, art, music, and dance. She embraced each with that characteristic Fletcher passion. She mastered it, wrung from it all she could get or want, then moved on to something new and completely different with undiminished zeal.

Dibi's enthusiasm is illustrated in the example of her receiving a call from the high school administration to report that Christian was being disruptive in class, and to inquire whether she would care to accompany him for a day to see for herself what the problem was. Certainly, she agreed, saying she would be there for his first class of the day the following morning.

The bell rang to start school. The class members seated themselves, and the teacher settled in to begin the day's lessons. Suddenly the door swung open with a loud bang and in walked Dibi. She was dressed in a very short leather mini skirt, a skin-tight net top, high-heeled boots up to her knees, and sporting her hair ratted out in a Tina Turner-style hairdo.

Dibi is a very well-built woman and dressed in such fashion was a sight to turn heads at the Academy Awards ceremony, let alone in a ninth-grade class. She stood in the doorway demurely looking in on the shocked students, who, along with the teacher, gaped with their jaws hanging open. The room emanated a silence as if to invite heavenly sounds, perhaps the wings of angels softly stirring.

What came instead was one of Christian's friends whispering, "Christian, it's your Mom."

Dibi announced to the teacher and the class that she was there to spend the day with her son, who didn't seem to understand the importance of school—and furthermore, that the lessons to be learned there might grow in importance as life unfolded.

The class was utterly disrupted, albeit duly impressed. The unfortunate teacher was in shambles. Nothing in her career had prepared her for the radiant apparition of Dibi the Disco Goddess at 8:00 a.m. None of the students could take their eyes off Dibi, who sat there like a queen, aloof and undisturbed by the hubbub around her. Christian, of course, was trying without success to melt into his seat and disappear. When class ended, everyone bolted, running to tell the rest of the school about Christian's mom.

Christian tried to steer his mother around the back way to his next class. Dibi would have none of it. She flatly informed her errant young son, "No way buster, we're going right down the middle, where everyone can see us, and if this doesn't teach you a lesson about how to behave here at school, wait till you see the outfit I have picked out for next time."

Life in the Fletcher family could make Technicolor blush. This episode, centered on the head of the family, Herbie, began early one morning at the Pipeline house I shared with them. We all woke up to a giant swell hitting the Country. Huge waves were breaking out on the third reef in front of the house, way out of control and unrideable.

"Come on Herb, let's go check Waimea," I suggested to Herbie, as we absorbed our morning herb tea while watching mountains of whitewater churn the Pipeline into chaos and confusion.

Eventually we stumbled out to Herbie's station wagon and drove out Ke Nui Road. The sun had not yet come up over the hills that shadow the beachfront of the North Shore. Going by Three Tables we got a quick glimpse of the surf and it had Waimea Bay written all over it. Turning the corner by the Waimea Tower, I looked back and saw a set pouring into the Bay. It was definitely Waimea size. As we pulled into the parking lot the set was still going. The waves looked good in the twenty-foot range with clean, morning offshore winds careening the spray back off the crests as they climbed into the sky.

"Herbie, don't even stop, let's go get your ski, you're all over this," I said to him.

We circled the parking lot, but Herbie, ever the careful surfer, said "Hey, we gotta check this out a little better."

So we turned right and drove up to park alongside the road up above the Bay where we had a nice vantage point to look down on the lineup. There were a few guys sitting outside and the lighting was still dim where they were waiting. The sun had yet to emerge from the hills shadowing the lineup, but way out to sea, light was shining on the next set marching toward shore.

Those waves looked majestic in the morning light. The lines were tall and thick; they looked solid. We watched as the surfers in the lineup spotted the set coming and paddled to get into position. One of them spun around and paddled for one of the bigger waves. It jacked up like only Waimea can, hanging the hapless surfer in the lip until he freefell into oblivion.

No one else tried for any of the other waves. The wiped-out surfer finally surfaced after long, scary seconds. He was swept in toward where his surfboard already had washed ashore.

"Come on, Herbie," I taunted. "This is what you want, this is you, there's hardly anyone out, it's perfect for your ski. This is what you've been waiting for."

"OK, let's go get it," he agreed, and he turned the car around and headed back to the house.

Herbie's Kawasaki Jet Ski was a product of years of trial and error. He was one of the few guys to really push riding the machine in big surf. His experiences at Outside Pipeline were heroic, downright death defying. Randy Laine was another surfer who was jet skiing in the surf, although not very much in the big waves that Herbie liked.

Herbie paid particular attention to the engine on his ski. That motor had more time, work, and money invested in making it run better than the cost of a whole new ski. It was tuned as finely as was possible for this machine. Herbie had big Pipeline and Waimea in mind as he was paying to have the motor prepared for him.

That morning at Waimea was everything he had been hoping for during all the preparation and months of waiting. I kept reminding him of that. If it had been me about to do this, go out in giant Waimea, I would have said, "Shut the hell up so I can think and mentally prepare myself for what is ahead." But Herbie is a mellow guy, and all my bantering and telling him to hurry up had little or no effect on his state of mind.

Maybe he needed someone to push him a little bit. Those were some pretty huge waves he was about to challenge. While he had been in a lot of big surf in front of the house at the Pipeline, he had never ridden his ski at Waimea. The specter of Waimea Bay and all the scary stories that surround it are pretty heavy stuff.

Back at the house we got the ski loaded up, collected Herbie's sleepy son Nathan, who had just woken, and headed back to the Bay. As we pulled into the parking lot a set rolled through that broke across the entire front of the Bay, closing it out completely. It was a chilling sight. Herbie started to slow down a little as the whitewater closed down the channel. Still, I kept pushing him.

"Come on, there should be a nice lull after this set and you can get out easy," I said as we pulled the ski out of the back of the car.

Herbie had this clever little sand trolley with fat tires so that he could roll the ski down to water. We got him going, pushing his ski down the beach right in the middle of the Bay. There was a long lull, so the shorebreak was pretty tame for the moment as Herbie got the ski down close to the water. I grabbed the trolley while he waited for a surge to push the ski into the water.

Nathan and I dragged the trolley up past the high water mark and went over to the empty lifeguard tower where we could watch the action. A little wave washed up the beach. Herbie pushed his ski into the water, fired it up, and zoomed out toward the lineup.

Watching a guy who knows what he's doing in big surf, especially on a souped-up jet ski, is very exciting. Herbie was probably the world's leading expert for this specialized exercise, and he had it completely dialed in. He blasted out to the lineup at high speed just as the next set was arriving. On the first big one, he did what we call the "berm shot."

Riding up on the swell, he banked it back around, carved a perfect track 180 degrees, and dropped into a beautiful, big wave. Stalling a little at the bottom, Herbie let the wave stand up taller before making his turn toward the shoulder. Just like any surfer would want to do if his surfboard had a throttle, Herb turned, cutback, and weaved all over that wave, riding it all the way into the Bay. The two waves behind were bigger and were breaking across the whole channel again as he pulled out of his wave. It was another closeout, but Herbie was an expert at this. He stalled around, waiting for the whitewater to dissipate a little before punching over it just at the moment it was backing off before it lurched up again and dumped in the shorebreak.

Stalling again for the next tumultuous wall of whitewater, he played it perfectly once more. He barely got splashed as he waited for exactly the right moment to go over the closeout. In the lifeguard tower, Nathan and I were fighting each other over the single pair of binoculars so we could see the action up close.

Herb motored back out toward the lineup. Through the binoculars I could see a lone surfer sitting over in the middle of the channel away from the lineup, probably resting after that last closeout set. From the vantage on top of the lifeguard tower and through the magnified binocular lens, I suddenly spied what seemed to be perhaps the biggest set of the day so far.

Herbie was in position and this time decided he was going to go for the biggest wave since it appeared that none of the surfers in the lineup were interested in those waves. He went over the tops of several twenty-foot-plus waves, dropping out of sight into the trough for a moment before reappearing in front of the biggest, meanest-looking wave I had seen all winter. Banking around in his patented "berm shot," he dropped over the edge and down the face of the enormous wave.

This, however, was one of those killer waves, thick and extremely powerful. It kept jacking up, ledging like only Waimea outside the boil will do. I had Herbie centered in the binoculars and could feel the incredible power of this wave as he gassed it down the face. That wave was feathering across the entire bay and was still outside the boil that is the normal takeoff at Waimea.

It was a wave of gargantuan proportions, probably a death wave on a surfboard, but I felt Herbie had the perfect tool in his souped-up Kawasaki Jet Ski. As he got near the bottom of the wave, I figured he would just throttle up and drive away from the wave face, staying safely out in front of the maelstrom. Squeezing hard on the binos, as if that would make me see better, I could see he was not leaving the wave behind, but in fact was staying dangerously close to the face.

Is his super-duper, blueprinted, and ported engine crapping out on him? I asked myself. That would be very bad. Or maybe he was just stalling to play it tight. This was potentially the wave of a lifetime, and Herbie seemed to be aware of that as he weighed his options.

I watched the wave grow more in height as the thick lip, arrayed across the width of the Bay, pitched up and out. It landed with an earth-shattering crash right behind him; the explosion seemed to blast him and his ski up in the air. Herbie's body was fluttering like a flag, his hands on the handlebars his only attachment to the ski as the rest of his body flapped like a towel on a clothesline in brisk wind and his mechanical savior bounced like a ping-pong ball in the whitewater.

"Gas it, Herbie, run away from there, what the hell are you doing," I muttered.

But he couldn't seem to get away from the wave. The whitewater boiling behind threatened to eat him alive at any moment. The ski bounced so high in the air that I thought it would come down nose first and endo before our eyes. But somehow Herbie maintained a death grip and hung on through it all. Later he would say that he had the throttle wide open but to no avail. The wave was too big and strong; he simply couldn't run away from it.

He hung on, heading to shore and finally running right up the beach as far as he could, high and dry and, more importantly, safe and sound.

I remembered the guy sitting in the channel. I swung the binoculars back toward the channel, searching in front of the whitewater of the next wave, which also had closed

out across the bay. Suddenly I caught a glimpse of a surfboard's nose but no person as the next wave came relentlessly forward. Almost the instant before the whitewater washed over it, I saw a head surface and then get buried again by the mountainous foam.

"Nathan, I just saw someone caught inside of that wave," I said to him sitting right beside me on the lifeguard's seat.

"I don't see anyone," he answered. He was uninterested because there was nothing to see except boiling whitewater.

I kept looking through the binos, watching as the next wave approached, another closeout. The surf had definitely come up since this morning and it wasn't even 8 a.m. yet. Again as the whitewater rolled in, I saw the board come up and like the last time, only a moment before the wave hit, I saw the head again.

"There he is again," I told Nathan. He looked and saw only whitewater; there was nothing else to see.

"I think you're seeing things," he said, "There's no one there."

But I had seen someone, and I knew he wasn't getting much air as the sets churned over him. He must be on the verge of drowning. The shorebreak was tremendous in a set like this. The explosions were sending water thirty to forty feet in the air and shaking the sand under the tower. We could feel it where we sat.

The next closeout came on, and once again I caught a quick glimpse of the board and head of the surfer before it hit. This time Nathan was looking at the right time.

"I saw him. Oh man, I sure wouldn't want to be where he is," he said.

We kept watching as the next two waves came on, seeing the guy for just an instant before the wave rolled over him. He probably only had time for a little gulp of air before he went under again. The power of those big closed out waves was staggering. I could only imagine what kind of thrashing this guy was going through underwater. Finally the outside sets stopped, but still he had not come to the surface.

Herbie does his patented berm-shot takeoff: going
full speed toward the incoming wave, then power
turning on the face, and banking it back around a full
180 degrees. Photo: Jeff Hornbaker

At last he popped up as though the ocean was done chewing on him and spit him out. He was directly in front of the lifeguard tower. Nathan and I sat there, rendered speechless by what we had just witnessed.

Somehow the guy flopped on top of his surfboard. He was only about twenty feet from shore. Without a backward glance he paddled straight in.

Normally there in the middle of the beach at Waimea on a swell like this, the shorebreak would be backbreaking and deadly. But it was as if the Bay had had its way with this poor surfer and was giving him a momentary reprieve. Not another ripple came as he paddled, pretty fast considering what he had just been through, to the safety of the dry sand. Likely, seeing the beach so close galvanized him with one last rush of adrenaline after the horrible pounding he had just received. He made the shore, staggered up, and just keeled over face first in the sand.

Kenny Bradshaw was just walking down to the corner to paddle out. He put his board down and walked down to the collapsed surfer. Kenny is a strong man. He picked up the guy by his shoulders, stood him on his feet, wiped the sand off his face, and appeared to ask if he was OK.

Nathan had the binoculars and exclaimed, "It's Scott Farnsworth."

Once Kenny stopped holding him up and let him go, Scott immediately collapsed again. Ken picked him up and literally carried him further up the beach. Kenny dropped Scott in the sand, grabbed his own surfboard, and headed out.

Herbie, walking up to retrieve the trolley to go get his ski, looked over at Farnsworth lying in the sand and asked, "What happened to him?"

I just shook my head. Nathan went off with his dad to bring the ski back to the car, and I could see the hand gestures and body language as he told the story as only a thirteen-year-old could.

Herbie had had his fill of Waimea for the moment. He would return later that afternoon and completely rip the place apart on his jet ski. No one would ever ride a ski like that, at least not that I've seen in my life thus far.

Herbie was riding one of the early standup-model jet skis, a notoriously unstable machine, in enormous waves, bigger than anyone else had ridden at the time. What he did will be remembered. Herbie was the Man when it came to jet skiing the big surf.

A few days later when the surf had dropped and the Pipe got good, Scott Farnsworth was out surfing, took a late drop, got slammed into the reef and washed, momentarily paralyzed, up on the beach. Herbie, Fast Eddie, a few other guys standing in the yard, and I went down and carried him up the beach on his surfboard. As if we were carrying a fallen warrior on his shield we brought him into the yard, hosed the sand off him, and waited for the lifeguards to run down from 'Ehukai.

I said to him, "Scott, this hasn't been a few good days for you. I watched what you went through the other day at Waimea and now this."

He was in pain. He told me his parents were coming in that day from California to watch him surf. At that moment he didn't feel like ever surfing again. But he was a very good surfer, young at the time with a pro career ahead of him. I knew that how he felt then would change. The ambulance came and took him away. Sure enough, he returned with his father a few days later to thank us for helping him and pick up his surfboard left in the yard.

I had been right, too. Although a little stiff and sore, Scott was most anxious to get back in the water.

Herbie and I would go on to have a lot more adventures together in different parts of the world. Nathan would grow up to become not only an outstanding world-class surfer, but also a top-notch skateboarder, high-flying motorcyclist, daredevil snowboarder, as well as a rock star in his own band.

The Fletcher family still goes through life at their own pace, in their own way, setting standards everywhere and in everything they do. I feel fortunate to have them all as friends.

The Fastest Wave

in the World

The State of Hawai'i small boat harbor at Ma'alaea is just that: small. It's too small to handle all the boats that would like to use it. For over thirty years, there have been plans for expansion, but they have not been without controversy.

One of the sticky points is that the harbor lies next to one of Hawai'i's premier summertime surf spots. Ma'alaea is nestled in the corner on the right flank of the south-facing bay, like a catcher's mitt for the summer swells. The left curve of the bay sweeps toward Kihei. Heading right out from the harbor, the bay ends at McGregor Point. From there, the coast continues swinging west around the Pali toward Olowalu and eventually Lahaina.

Actually, there are several breaks directly in front of the harbor break wall, but the spot that would be most affected by the proposed expansion is called Freight Trains. This break has the reputation among the top surfers as being the fastest wave in the world. It works best only on rare direct south or south-easterly direction swells and can go years without breaking big, but when it works Ma'alaea Freight Trains is the crown jewel of Hawai'i's summer breaks. None is more challenging, nor more spectacular.

The U.S. Army Corps of Engineers has been at the forefront on this and all other coastline projects in the state. The Corps' past track record has been, in a generous view, somewhat spotty. Surfers were not happy when Magic 'Tragic' Island was constructed in the mid-1960s directly over an excellent and very consistent surf spot called Garbage Hole, along with several other popular breaks in the immediate area. Not long after, the Corps took out another great wave at the famous Maile Cloudbreak by building a drainage canal.

In the 1980s, the Ma'alaea Harbor expansion project was granted federal funding and the State of Hawai'i pushed to initiate construction in a required time period so

Left The proposed expansion to the small boat harbor at Ma'alaea would put the break wall right into the lineup of the wave that you see in this photo. Photo: Jeff Hornbaker

Above My brother Victor locked into a speed trim at Freight Trains, hoping his board will be fast enough to make it out the other end. Photo: Jeff Hornbaker

as not to risk losing the government grant money. The State Department of Land and Natural Resources (DLNR), Harbors Division, along with representatives from the Army Corps of Engineers, set up a public meeting at Kihei School.

This is standard procedure to allow parties affected by any public project to ask questions and air grievances. Those in favor of the expansion were, of course, the boat owners who were crammed into the small harbor. Many operated boats for tourist fishing, diving, or sightseeing charters. These businesses were becoming very popular in the 1980s, with the rapid growth the Valley Isle of Maui was experiencing.

The most vocal, however, were the local fishermen for whom the harbor had originally been built. They were getting elbowed out of their harbor slips as the bigger- and better-financed tourist operations were granted slips. Opposing the expansion were the surfers and concerned property owners from the various condos and homes on the beach near the harbor.

The protocol is for anyone who wishes to speak to sign up on a roster and wait to be called. The DLNR and Army Corps representatives spoke first. They told of the rising need for more harbor space and showed some preliminary plans for how they proposed to address those needs. Their plans were to extend the existing front break wall toward Kihei, right over the entire Freight Trains surf spot.

Finished with their presentation, the government representatives explained how the rest of the meeting would work and began calling for those who had signed up. Several boat owners spoke about the lack of space and the long waiting list for those wanting a boat slip. Some condo owners asked the Harbors Division representative how the new harbor would affect their property; according to the proposed plan, boat slips would replace the beachfront. A surfer got up to state that the break wall would permanently erase one of the best surf spots on the island, but before he could finish, catcalls and loud heckling came from the back of the room.

A number of the local fisherman and boat people had been getting well-oiled before the meeting, drinking all afternoon and evening before the 8 p.m. meeting. They were very vocal about any opposition to what they wanted. I felt sad knowing they would be the last to benefit from a bigger harbor. The big-money tourist operations, without a doubt, would have first pick.

John Kelly from Save Our Surf had flown over that afternoon to attend the meeting. I had arrived just after the meeting began and had no time beforehand to so- cialize or see who was there. I was surprised, but elated, that the great champion of the surfers' cause for the past twenty-five years was about to speak. He had been involved in the Ma'alaea project from its inception.

I knew John well from surfing, had gone to high school with his daughters, and had supported all his efforts toward the preservation of surfing areas around the state. As he took the podium, I was certain he would present a reasonable, historical perspec- tive that would lay bare the foolishness of this latest harbor plan.

John began by saying that he had come over from O'ahu to be here, but sens- ing that he was opposed to the new harbor, the hecklers began shouting for him to go back. John looked to the DLNR and Corps people supposedly conducting the meeting to take charge and allow him to speak. But I could see from their smug attitude that this was just what they wanted. They didn't want any opposition to their agenda. The noise level became so loud and angry that it seemed the situation was on the verge of erupting into something violent and physical. John Kelly had no choice but to sit back down. It was a sad moment.

Next to speak was probably the oldest person there that night. It was Woody Brown, an old friend of John Kelly. I knew Woody lived in Kahului and was sure they had come to the meeting together. Both Woody and John, along with George Downing, Wally Froiseth, Fran Heath, and others had been the pioneers who paved the way for riding big surf. Theirs was a colorful and wonderful history in the beginning of the modern era of surfing in Hawai'i.

Woody was well into his eightieth year and his seemingly frail appearance belied a quick wit and sharp mind. As he shuffled to the podium, the entire gathering quieted down in deference to his age. None of the boat owners, especially the drunk ones, knew who he was or which side he represented.

Woody took the stand and looked out over the crowd, the twinkle in his eyes obvious to all. As he began to speak in his soft voice and easy manner, the audience hushed further to hear what he was saying. He spoke of a time long before the present harbor, of spending time on the sandy beach with his Hawaiian wife, of fishing, of surfing the waves, and of enjoying the beautiful and idyllic spot. He spoke of other Hawaiian and local families who had also enjoyed it and the times they shared there together.

The attention in the room was rapt as Woody took all of us to a place and time of a natural Ma'alaea that none of us knew had existed. He paused and let the moment to which he had transported everyone sink into our hearts and minds.

Then he added, "I remember the first time the government came to Ma'alaea. I was there."

Woody paused again and glanced toward the seated officials with a look I interpreted as, not so much disdain, but one of pity. The two government men seemed to wither under his calm and steady gaze, checking their shoelaces and fingernails.

Looking back over the silent group, he finished by saying, "The first thing they did was build a shithouse right over the freshwater spring."

As he sat down, silence still pervaded throughout the crowd as the government men squirmed in their seats and even the loudmouths looked sheepishly at each other, their beers forgotten.

It's now almost twenty years after that meeting. The Surfrider Foundation has become involved and is currently monitoring the State of Hawai'i's ongoing plans for the harbor expansion. I'm happy to report that, as yet, the government has not built anything over the surf spot. The Ma'alaea Freight Trains has enjoyed several epic sessions in the past few seasons. The fastest wave in the world, for now at least, still lives.

Whitey and the Duke

One day over on the Big Island of Hawai'i, Grubby Clark and I were driving around looking for a place to surf. Our first stop was at Kawaihae Harbor break wall, which catches the swell pretty good but is kind of a mushy wave. As we pulled up to the edge of the break wall and looked out at the waves we saw two surfers out and a set coming in. Jumping out of the car, we watched as one surfer paddled for the biggest wave of the set. His positioning was perfect and he caught the wave easily. As he stood up, we both recognized the familiar style; it was Lorrin 'Whitey' Harrison. He was probably in his early eighties, but his surfing was skillful and sure as he made his turn and trimmed across the long wall.

Seeing us on the break wall as he got to the end of the wave, he turned toward shore and rode the wave all the way in. Climbing out of the water, we exchanged greetings. He was wearing the coconut leaf hat that was his trademark. He wove them himself and wore them out surfing until they fell apart, then just made himself another one.

For one with so many years behind him, most of them spent surfing, he didn't look like most eighty-year-olds, and in fact he fairly bubbled with health. There was a spring in his step as he climbed up the rocks to where we stood in the parking lot. The familiar twinkle in his blue eyes was more pronounced after his surf session, and he still had the broad shoulders and good muscle tone of an active surfer in spite of his advanced years.

"Lorrin, you're surfing with your daughter again," Grubby said, stating the obvious as all three of us turned to watch Lorrin's daughter, Marion, catch a wave of her own and get a nice ride.

"Yes, she drives me down here because I always lose the car keys when I drive myself," Lorrin answered.

Whitey Harrison at home in San Juan Capistrano
with the first Hawaiian outrigger canoe used to surf
in California. Photo: C. R. Stecyk

"Gerry, I saw you in here and had a story I wanted to tell you," he said turning to me. "I haven't seen you in a long time and I've been wanting to tell you about this one time back in the '40s on the North Shore; you know every time I see a picture of you surfing out there, I think about this story and was hoping I was going to run into you so I could tell you about it.

"It was a long time ago when not many guys were surfing out there. You know, you would have to get a bunch of the fellows in Waikiki together to make a surfing trip, and sometimes it was hard just to find everyone. Then maybe they had something else to do, so it was hard to get a group all together to go surfing out there, and you didn't want to go surfing by yourself especially when the waves were big. Well, I heard about the surf being up, but no one wanted to go so I just thought I would head out there with my wife ... that was my first wife you know. I thought we would just take a drive out there and have a look at the big surf.

"So we got the car and drove out from Waikiki; it was a long drive back then—you had to go through Pearl City and take the back roads—they didn't have any freeways then. But when we were driving down the hill from Wahiawa, through the pineapple fields, you could see all the whitewater down by Hale'iwa, and it looked so good.

"We got down by Jerry's Sweet Shop across from the park where we could look out the channel: It was a big swell, and it was breaking best way out at Avalanche. There was so much 'ehukai, or surf spray, in the air that it was hard to see, so I say to my wife, why don't we paddle out tandem on my surfboard and we can sit in the channel and watch the waves from up close. Well she was a real go-getter so she said OK. I got the board out of the car—you know there wasn't a soul around, it was just the two of us. So we got on that board together and paddled out the channel.

"We got out by the side of the Hale'iwa break when this big old set comes in and closes out the whole channel. Of course, it took the board away from us and we were left in the water. The rip running out the channel was real strong, and even being good swimmers we had no chance to swim against it. Swimming as hard as we could, we were still being slowly dragged out the channel.

"Pretty soon we're way out by the channel buoy so I tell her to swim over and hold on to that. The current is so strong that the buoy is leaned way over sideways, but at least we can hold on to it. I can see the shore and there are people in there now looking out at us but none of them are surfers, so no one can come help us. Boy, I'm really in a fix because we can't get in. My wife thinks it's fun, which is a good thing, and she is just expecting me to figure out what we are going to do next.

"Well, I'm really starting to get worried when I happen to catch a glimpse of my surfboard way over on the other side of the channel; it's caught in the rip too and heading out to sea. I tell my wife that I have to take a chance and swim for the surfboard because it's our only chance. I say to her that I may not get it and then I will be swept out to sea for a while, so she should just keep hanging on to the buoy and someone will eventually come for her.

"So she says OK, and I kiss her goodbye and dive into the current to go find my surfboard. I swim and I swim, and it's real choppy in that channel and hard to see, but after a long time I finally see my board. By now I'm way outside past Pua'ena Point, but I have my board so I'm not worried. I fight the rip in and get back to the buoy where my wife is waiting.

"She just says 'I knew you would be back,' and jumps on the board. We paddle back to the beach where all these local people are gathered because they saw what was happening, but no one could do anything. They didn't have a fire department back in those days to call to go rescue people, so they were all worried because they thought we were going to be killed by the waves. But they are all relieved and even have some food so we all sit down and have a picnic right there on the beach.

"The next day when we were back in Waikiki, the Duke comes down and finds me at the beach and gives me a good scolding. He said I never should have taken my wife out there with me, and it was a good thing I made it back safely. He scolds me a little more, then gives me a hug and a big smile, and says he's glad we are both OK.

"So that's my story of the North Shore. I thought you might want to hear it," says Lorrin as he grabs his surfboard and starts to head back out to the waves, where his daughter is still surfing.

"I'll see you guys later, I have to get a few more waves before Marion wants to go home." With that he paddles back out to the surf.

Grubby and I look at each other, kind of in shock. "He was scolded by the DUKE," we both say at the same time, "Can you believe that?"

Dr. Surf

Doc and his paddleboard, a classic 1930s Tom Blake
hollow-construction design. Photo: Jeff Divine

Dr. Dorian Paskowitz will always be a great man to me. He has devoted his life to surfing as a means to help people understand the true value of health. No one I know has given more of himself in this way than Dorian.

My parents met him in Waikiki back in the mid-1950s when I was a small child. Our family frequented the Queens Surf part of the beach every summer day for years on end. Dorian had a small clinic and ding repair business and was consumed with surfing. I was too young when we met to remember him from those days, but he always remembered me. This was a trait of his character that I grew to find fascinating. He seldom forgot a child he met and with whom he interacted.

Dorian went on to father a large tribe of his own, nine to be exact. They all grew into great, very enthusiastic surfers. The kids, with his help and guidance of course, would go on to open the most successful surf school for youngsters in the history of surfing.

On a trip to Tel Aviv he brought his surfboard and astounded the beach kids with his demonstrations of wave riding. When he left, the surfboard stayed and started their surfing craze. He later helped form the first surfing club in Israel. Today there are many surfers from Israel with world-class skills ripping waves all over the planet.

Dorian often said that Eleanor Roosevelt's quote, "Health is more than the mere absence of disease," would propel him into discovering what health really is. By seeking to understand the meaning of health, he would come to realize the most advanced yet simple medical principle to be found in his fifty years of practicing medicine. Health, Dorian learned, is the presence of a superior state of well-being, a vigor and vitality that must be worked for and earned each and every day.

To achieve this required maintaining a lifestyle based on a correct diet, sufficient exercise, proper rest, recreation, and the right attitudes of mind. This was how he lived his life. Dorian's long-sought-after understanding of health is the foundation of my own lifestyle.

My wife Toni, son Alex, and I were in San Jose del Cabo one spring break to get a little warmth and sunshine after a long, cold winter in Central Oregon. I was out surfing while Alex frolicked in the shorebreak and Toni soaked up the sun on the beach. When I came in, she said an old guy with a surfboard had passed by and that he looked like someone I would know. She couldn't tell me any more than that except that she had noticed quite a twinkle in his blue eyes when he had said hello on his way by. We lay on the sand together watching our little boy have a grand time, getting smashed in the shore pound and washed squealing up the beach.

Finally, covered in wet sand, Alex came up to dry off and warm up. We were all sitting happily when Toni said, "Hey, here comes the guy I was telling you about."

Even with my poor eyesight, in a glance I took in the old beachboy style of carrying his surfboard up on one of his broad shoulders, the generally fit shape, the even tan and lean waist. Memories from as far back as those my son was now forming crystallized in a delighted certainty of recognition.

Sure enough, when he got closer, I could see it was Dorian. Then well into his eighties, he was as fit as I ever remembered him. We greeted each other warmly, as it had been several years since we had last seen each other. He joined us on the sand, and

"No one's ever too old if he wants to surf, and he's living proof of it."

I introduced Dorian to my wife and son. He immediately told Alex that he had met me when I was about the same age as he and doing the same thing, rolling around in the Waikiki shorebreak and loving it.

He told us he had driven down on his own from California to go surfing; his wife didn't like the rats at the campground so she had stayed home this trip. I asked him where he was camping, and he said that he usually just stayed in the arroyo, but had made some new friends who were letting him stay in their empty lot next to the arroyo. The lot was safer and more secure.

He then lowered his voice as he said, "These guys are the Mexican Mafia, and they own that new restaurant over there where my camper is."

We started to turn that way to look when he quickly warned us, "Don't look over there, they're watching us, they're always watching."

We all dropped our eyes, trying not to look obvious. But now we looked at Dorian with rapt attention. He certainly had piqued our interest. We wanted the whole feast and dessert of this story, as Dorian was a master at storytelling.

"I was eating some lunch in the restaurant when I noticed these guys looking at me; I didn't know who they were but I could tell they were hombres malos. They were

Doc, well into his eighties, comfortably surfing one of his favorite breaks at Waikiki Beach. Photo: Art Brewer

sitting by themselves over in one corner of the place and no one was going near them. Then the waiter came over to me and said that these guys wanted me to join them.

"So I walked over and said, 'Hola, buenas dias, senors!'

"They asked me to have a seat and if I wanted something to drink.

"I could tell right away which one was El Jefe, their chief. This guy didn't say a word; one of the other guys did all the talking. The Jefe and some others sat there with dark sunglasses on and just looked at me. The one guy doing all the talking asked me what I did. I told him I had been a doctor for fifty years, but had done a lot of other things too.

"They talked about that in Spanish among themselves, nodding their heads, and then they just sat and looked at me some more. It wasn't uncomfortable even though they were a scary-looking bunch. I had a feeling these guys were Mexican Mafia. They didn't seem threatening toward me, they just seemed curious.

"Finally El Jefe took off his dark glasses and looked me right in the eye: 'Eh gringo, you are el doctor, but I think you have done other things, yes?' he said to me in his heavily accented English.

" 'I have … lots of other things,' I answered him. He nodded and said something in Spanish to the others who all seemed to agree with him.

"A period of silence passed as they all looked at me until he spoke again: 'Eh gringo, I look at you and I think maybe you and I are alike. Maybe we have done some of the same things.'

"Well I didn't know what he meant exactly, but I nodded in agreement with him. There was a little more murmuring among themselves, then more of the piercing looks.

" 'Gringo, I think maybe you have killed men, yes?'

"He asked me this with a penetrating look deep into my eyes. If there had been silence before this, now you could hear a pin drop as the others all sat forward in their chairs awaiting my response. I returned the Jefe's look unwaveringly as I thought about all the patients over the years that I had misdiagnosed and had probably died because of my failings.

" 'Yes … yes, I have,' I answered quite truthfully.

" 'I knew this, I knew it,' he almost shouted, slapping the table with his big hand.

" 'I could tell from the first moment I saw you. Eh, amigo, we are the same, you and me.' He was smiling broadly as were all his men, clapping each other and me on the back, offering me drinks, everyone happy.

" 'You are mi amigo, we are brothers, I own this place, these are my people, anything you need here is yours, mi casa, su casa,' he proclaimed to me and all the others."

With that, Dorian hoisted himself to his feet, still spry in spite of his advanced age, the twinkle in his eyes more pronounced than ever. He shouldered his longboard, bid us adios with a wink, and headed back to the restaurant where his newfound friends waited for him.

"Isn't that man too old to surf?" my young son asked as we all watched Dorian head off down the beach with, I might add, a definite spring in his step.

"No he's not," I answered, still smiling. "No one's ever too old if he wants to surf, and he's living proof of it."

Comin'
Down

Rory Russell and I were best of friends, especially during the period when we both made surfing the Pipeline our life's mission. I was older, and Rory was always trying to one-up me whenever he got a chance. It wasn't out of any malice or jealousy; it was just the nature of our relationship.

We would see pictures or movies of ourselves surfing those great waves, and Rory would shake his head and ask, "Do you pose in front of a mirror to practice those moves before you do them on your board?"

"What moves?" I would answer, playing dumb but knowing what he wanted to figure out. Back then in the early 1970s, we tried to make our surfing look effortless when, obviously at a place like the Pipeline, it wasn't.

The Pipeline had a reputation as a wave that could kill a surfer and a record to prove it. Photographers liked the spot because it broke close to shore, making the photography easier than trying to shoot photos at an outside break like Sunset Beach. But they liked it even more because it just looked spectacular in pictures. On those rare days when the swells rolled in cleanly from the west or northwest and the trade winds blew straight offshore, every surf photographer worth his salt was on the beach hoping for a cover shot or a center spread. This made for a competitive and crowded playing field in the lineup.

One of my favorite surfers from the generation before us who also made it look easy was Walter Hoffman. 'Big Wally' was a legend among his peers, being one of the early California surfers to go to Hawai'i and seamlessly fit in with the local crowd there. His surfing skills were elevated enough that he was instantly accepted by the top surfers and beach boys at Waikiki as one of their own. 'Waltah' often regaled me with wonderful stories of those heydays of the 1950s and early '60s. Generally this took place in between sets at places like Cottons Point or the Garden right in front of his Southern California home at Poche Beach. To be honest, I lived for those moments, for Walter had been in the front ranks of a special time in a special place.

One time, during a beautiful swell at Cottons, I watched him as he exercised his *droit du seigneur*, as King Cotton. Because he knew the lineup better than anyone else out there, he chose the perfect position for the next good set. When it came, he lined up the best wave, as usual, and, as was also his way, whenever he tied into a good one, yelled out in a booming voice, "Comin' down!"

And, as if by magic, the path before him through the other surfers clustered in the lineup miraculously cleared. In reality, it was probably the loud bellow and the specter of the big guy on the big board, double-arm paddling into the biggest wave of the set that caused the other surfers to scatter like a school of minnows before a charging, hungry barracuda. After he rode his wave almost to shore, he paddled back through the crowd, only now like a Southern politician: campaigning, glad-handing, accepting the congratulations and acknowledgements of the last wave as his due. He sat down just outside of me so as to be in position for the best wave of the next set, pulled a small comb from the pocket of his surf trunks and slicked his hair back. As he slipped the comb back in his side pocket, another set loomed and he was off again. I had to smile at his entire act; it was an Academy Award performance, honed to perfection long before I had ever been on a surfboard. I especially liked the combing his hair in between sets and filed that away for some future use of my own.

The day was one of those classic Pipeline days, and Rory, as usual, showed up at the crack of noon to take his place in the lineup. With long arms, huge hands, and a loud mouth, he was a pig when it came to getting waves in a full lineup. This entitlement attitude was actually well deserved. Rory had put in his time and paid his dues long before many of the other surfers who were there. There were a few who had been there on a regular basis before him, but Rory was always acutely aware, if not perfectly polite, to those few when they were out, and always knew exactly where they were.

On many occasion, I had witnessed him in that sudden, explosive, totally focused paddling effort necessary to catch a set wave at the Pipe, twist his long neck, look over, and ask in all innocence, to the surfer right next to him, trying to paddle into the same wave, "Are you going on this one?"

Since it was often me he was asking, and I was trying my damnedest to catch the wave he was paddling into in front of me, I seldom had time to respond. Afterward I would wonder what in the world had he thought I was trying to do? Of course I was going on that wave, or at least attempting to. There were times when, beforehand, we would purposely plan to take the wave together to see if both of us could fit into the big Pipeline tube.

Today, however, was one of those days where every person out wanted to get a wave all their own. Besides, I was also trying to set Rory up for something that I knew would shatter his beady little mind.

The waves that day were of a quality that a good ten- to twelve-foot one would be a lifetime memory for any surfer. The Pipeline had the ability to sear an indelible impression into a person's soul, an impression that would stand out over a thousand other waves. Sometimes it would come not even from a wave ridden, but from one watched from the vantage point of paddling back out.

Rory was in his usual white-hot surf frenzy. I had already been out all morning and that had been his first question to me when he joined the lineup. I told him I came out early, so he knew I was already four to five hours ahead of him in my wave count. But he was trying hard to catch up. I sat patiently and waited for that right moment. I wanted him to be paddling out when I rode my wave.

Finally, the perfect opportunity presented itself. Rory took a wave that I was certain he would make. Several waves after, the one I was waiting for came my way. I paddled out to meet it, turned around, and paddled hard. I felt the swell lift my board and propel me forward. I jumped to my feet as the board fell away beneath me. Lightly setting my edge, I dropped down the steep wall and kept my eyes open for Rory paddling out. Sure enough, there he was, in perfect position to see my wave. I ran my drop out into the flat in front of the wave, putting my eight-foot gun up on its rail and carving it around in a long bottom turn that would set me up for the bowling section ahead. Coming out of my turn, I stalled on the tail to slow down and position myself for the barrel. Rory was on the other end of that tube section.

As the thick lip curled over my head, I stood tall and reached into my wax pocket. I pulled out a comb, and with my eyes locked on Rory, I began to comb my hair in the tube. I almost lost it when I saw his jaw drop open and his eyes bug out. I combed my hair all the way through that tube. As I came out, I slid the comb back into my pocket and glided straight at him, carving a small arc in front of him and splashing some water into his wide-open mouth.

Without even a glance his way, I slowly began to paddle back out. I could hear some strangled, incoherent mutterings from behind that I casually ignored. With his long arms and my slow pace, he finally caught up to me, but poor Rory was still in shock. I had to bite my lip to keep a straight face as he tried to form one question after another and had no success with any.

Some months later on, in between sets during another California session with Walter, we were "talking story." I told him about the trick I had played on Rory and Walter laughed heartily. Then a set came and as we scrambled for it, I found myself perfectly outpositioned by a master. All I heard was a deep bellow, "Comin' down!"

Big Wally

Many surfers agree that the second best thing about surfing is talking about it afterward. As we tell and retell surf stories, waves grow ever more enormous and frightening, wipeouts ache immeasurably more each terrible time, and our heroes dwarf human scale. Often our stories so delight tellers and listeners alike that these epic tales become legends, and even approach the status of mythology.

Just as in tales of the Norse, the Greek, the Samurai, and in many more of the world's cultures, at the center of each surfing fable stands the hero or heroine. This individual is extraordinarily brave, skillful, or funny. The surfing world is blessed with many characters to serve as models for these modern myths. A select few heroes gain the special status of icon. Attaining this exalted perch, surveying all of surfdom, arises from signature moves that render the particular hero unique amid the masses of the paddling humanity. Devotees to such a wily Odysseus will recite all of his legends from the epic to the mundane. Sycophants literally quiver in awe when granted an audience before the hero.

Those few individuals who attain such a following often have a follower or two who may feel an imperative to keep the legends alive. A teller of the tales rises to the call of duty by reciting the mythical deeds whenever possible. In my own small way, I feel an obligation to record at least some of the stories I have lived and heard. Let not my generation of surfers vanish quietly like spindrift on a clear offshore day. Better to raise our voices in unison, as Dylan Thomas urged, and to rage against the dying of the light.

The many thick layers of tales form like enamel around legendary pioneer Walter Hoffman. Hoffman's broad influence during the early years of California surfing secures for him a knight's nobility in the hierarchy of surf prestige. He was a stylish surfer who developed grace and skill in the all-but-empty breaks of post-World War II Southern California. Pursuing his dream in 1948, he advanced to Hawai'i, origin of the sport of chiefs.

The beach boys of Waikiki, masters of Hawaiian surfing and ambassadors of aloha, recognized Hoffman's abilities and welcomed him to join among them. Hawaiian

Above   Walter, at the Waikiki Surf Club, with a balsa board he made out of wood salvaged from a surplus World War II life raft. The life rafts for ships used heavy wood, but the aircraft life rafts were made out of the lightest balsa and were ideal for surfboards ... if one knew where to find them, and Walter, of course, had it figured out. Photo: Hoffman collection

Left   At the 1954 Makaha contest, Duke Kahanamoku and the 'Queen of Makaha' flank Walter Hoffman and his tandem partner, Gwynn Davis. Photo: Hoffman collection

tradition dictates that a great surfer is always accepted with open arms into the ranks of local surfers. A Waikiki beachboy, even a haole from the coast, must have a nickname. Walter became 'Wally,' and graciously slid into "livin-on-a-easy." When the waves were up, he surfed all day. When rich visitors brought food to the beach, he ate like a prince. Wally learned to play the 'ukulele and to dance the hula. He sang golden summer notes in the beachboy chorus.

Wally surfed tandem so well that beach beauties competed to be his partner. An excellent canoe surfer, he was one of the first to return to California beaches with a Hawaiian outrigger. Only Lorrin 'Whitey' Harrison had a bigger canoe than Wally. He was one of first to pursue free-dive blue-water spearfishing, going after big tuna long before this became an international sport. He survived several close calls when a speared fish swam loops around him, wrapping Wally in the spear's line to take him to the bottom in the fish's dying spasms. He was first in at many of the premier diving locations in Baja in his legendary pursuit of the great Guadalupe grouper and the coveted giant jewfish. He bore early witness to California's undersea gardens where, in his own words, "the bottom was red with lobsters."

Walter's innate business acumen also served him well. After investing fully the years of his youth in surfing and diving, he and his brother Philip settled in to work for their father Rube's company, Hoffman Fabrics. Philip focused on selling to fabric retailers. Walter quickly recognized the market potential in the fledgling surf apparel industry. He supplied printed fabric designs and set cloth standards for most of the trunks, aloha shirts, and other woven garments of the American surfwear industry. Walter was also a financial flat-tracker. He reaped a vast personal fortune in investments by his uncannily shrewd ability to anticipate profit or loss.

Walter always loved dirt bikes. A racer at heart, he was at his best on the starting line of a desert race. He loved lining up handlebar to handlebar with racing legends like Dick Vick, Malcolm Smith, J. N. Roberts, and Dick Mann, as well as alongside friends and fellow surfer/racers Grubby Clark, Dave Rochlen, Rennie Yater, Phil Stubbs, Hobie Alter, Bruce Brown, and Jim Jenks.

Through the years Wally's motorcycles were gleaming examples of brush-tuning and high standards of maintenance. His bikes were custom built to his own specifications for his daring riding style. He immersed himself in every aspect of dirt bike racing. He studied every move and all of the statistics. He became personally acquainted with many of the top racers, who often were equally honored to meet Walter.

He was a regular at the Friday night flat track races at Ascot Park in Gardena and a personal friend of J. C. Agajanian, promoter of the events and track owner. Walter would gather his friends every Friday afternoon at his home in Capo Beach, and then they made the trek to the speedway, where this particular Big Wally myth begins.

This would not be just any Friday night race. This was the once-in-a-season American Motorcycle Association half-mile Grand National. All the national number riders were there, racing for points and glory. The purse was less than an afterthought that Friday night. The favored nationally ranked racers breezed through their heat races on toward the main event, easily leaving behind the local fill-in riders.

Walter and his Dana Point cronies were all there, hollering the dead to dance. Surprisingly, the son of an old friend of Walter's, who was attending UCLA, managed to locate Wally and the Dana Point crew. This was quite a feat in itself as the race was sold out and the stands were choked with howlers. The schoolboy's father had long ago moved the family from California to Hawai'i to pursue a career in construction and a pastime in surfing ... or maybe it was the other way around. The son had grown up on the North Shore of O'ahu, a local island boy; the youngster didn't know many people on the mainland.

His father had suggested calling Walter, who was known for his Hawaiian-style hospitality. Walter immediately invited the lad to the races. Walter said that a ticket would be waiting at will call and described how the student could find the group. They always sat in the same place near the first turn after the start line.

Seated at last next to a red-faced, heavy-breathing Walter, the kid was a little uneasy. The area near the raceway he'd driven through to find parking was sketchy at best. Most of the race enthusiasts present, excluding Walter's crew, were either motorcycle gang members, assorted motorheads, or otherwise didn't fit any familiar profile in the experience of the kid from Hawai'i. Being a freshman college boy, he was the one who drew hard looks as he jostled his way through this foreign territory.

Notwithstanding the noisy, chaotic atmosphere, Walter observed the kid's frayed nerves. In a gesture consistent with Big Wally's simpatico nature, he draped a heavy sweaty arm over the youngster's shoulder and yelled in his ear. "You got here just in time, they're getting ready to start the main event. Let me tell you, this is the finest racing known to man."

"You see those riders on the line out there?" Walter continued. "If they screw up, they go over the falls with a Harley. Guys get killed hitting the wall in this turn all the time. That's why we always sit here. These are MEN."

Walter had to shout to be heard as the noise level grew.

"You see that little guy, number 7, that's Sammy Tanner. They call him the 'Flying Flea.' He weighs 125 pounds soaking wet, but his balls must weigh twenty-five pounds each. Jeez, is he something—these guys put it all on the line."

The din rose as the racers found their places on the starting line. At the core of the sound were the revving engines, deep throbbing bass notes of 750cc Harley Davidson motors. Individual rhythms were set by each rider's hand on his throttle. This cacophony of sounds crackled like electricity in the air around the track, stimulating the crowd to its feet as the noise level steadily intensified.

The crowd's roar seemed to issue forth from the depths of a single living creature, born of age-old excitement, anticipating the coming spectacle. This was a modern chariot race. The feelings of these spectators were every bit as primal as the Romans felt at Circus Maximus.

Everyone in the stands was up and screaming as Walter yelled into the boy's ear. "You've never seen anything like this. This is the finest. You know what it's like? This is like ... PIPELINE!"

The moment of urgency drew near as the flagman moved off to the side of the track. He still held the flag motionless to indicate the last seconds before he would drop

"You've never seen anything like this. This is the finest. You know what it's like? This is like ... PIPELINE!"

it. The riders were absolutely focused on that flag, their engines at full roar, bursting to engage. Completely focused in turn on the riders, the crowd was on fire. The noise was near wholly full. Walter himself was in frenzy, short of breath and red of face. He yelled again, spittle flying.

"This is like ... BIG PIPELINE."

Walter appeared crazed in this moment. The flagman held the flag up, ready to sweep it down. The riders were poised, intent. The bikes looked and sounded deadly.

"BIG ... OUTSIDE ... PIPELINE!" bellowed Wally.

The flag dropped, the bikes roared off the line quickly accelerating, thirty, forty, fifty, sixty, seventy, up to eighty miles per hour, handlebar to handlebar, flying into the first turn where Wally and the boys stood on their seats elbowing each other to get the best view.

Out on the track, the riders pitched their bikes sideways entering the turn, inside leg locked open at the knee, steel sole strapped to their left boots, foot down sliding, throttles pegged wide open. The pack was still tight, jockeying for the inside, or for any advantage to get ahead.

A daring rider hung it out, dove in front of the whole field, passing four or five bikes in one move, the finest moment. Walter was at the absolute zenith of moto ecstasy. His mind still frantically searched for that elusive last surf analogy to hold out the moment in perspective, so the college boy could fully grasp it.

The dirt rooster tails filled the air in the first turn. The view abruptly changed from head-on to going-away as the leaders made the turn. The bikes were all still sideways and bucking violently over the ruts in the track. The riders slid delicately on their steel shoes. It would be bad to catch a foot, to slide-out, or worse, to high-side in front of the pack. The oncoming bikes would chop the fallen rider into hamburger. In those last, most frenzied moments after the start, before the riders began to string out for the long twenty-four laps ahead, where the passes would still be exciting but more calculated, singular and never as tense as in the beginning of the race, it finally came to Wally. A maniacal gleam formed in his eyes, panting heavily, giggling out of control, his voice a strangled, barely intelligible shriek:

"BIG, OUTSIDE PIPELINE ... WITH SHARKS!"

iii. ALL SHOOK UP

The steep drop at the Pipeline sets up the bottom
turn that, if it is performed well, allows the surfer to
exit the turn with more speed then he had going in.
Photo: Jeff Divine

Everything Bad Goes Down in Parking Lots

In the 1970s and 1980s, I traveled with a terrific surfer named Roy Mesker. He had the smoothest style of anyone I've seen before or since. 'Big Roy' riding a wave, any wave—big, small, perfectly peeling, or blown-out slop—looked as natural as a palm tree swaying in the wind, or water running down a stream.

We surfed both south and north shores of all the Hawaiian islands; took surf trips to California, Australia, the South Pacific, and Indonesia. Still the wave dearest to our hearts was always Ala Moana. Any hint of south swell would find us perched in the parking lot of the Ala Wai Yacht Harbor. At the right moment of tide, wind, and swell, we would paddle out and turn the dial up loud.

Roy had an uncle we both admired. Not only was he a great guy, he was a veteran FBI Special Agent with lots of good stories to tell. Uncle Chuck ended every tale with the admonition, "Stay away from parking lots. Everything bad goes down in parking lots."

We didn't have the heart to tell him that most of our adult lives up to that point were spent in parking lots. By the sum of our cumulative experience to that time, Roy and I both knew that the only place to be during the summertime south swell season was the parking lot at Ala Moana.

That parking lot was, in my opinion, the staging area for some of the most pro-gressive surfing on the planet during the early days of the shortboard revolution. This is not to suggest that the surfing of the 1960s longboard era was less than progressive. It was spectacularly so. Ala Moana drew the best of Hawaiʻi's small-wave surfers and made them better.

The 1970s, however, formed into a special and unique period of surfing history. Our hot, flat, little concrete and asphalt spike into the Ala Wai Yacht Harbor was the epicenter of a swiftly developing lifestyle and culture that was attractive for its uniquely

Following my friend George Sakamoto as we thread
the bowl section at Ala Moana. Photo: Steve Wilkings

Uncle Chuck ended every tale with the admonition, "Stay away from parking lots. Everything bad goes down in parking lots." We didn't have the heart to tell him that most of our adult lives up to that point were spent in parking lots.

individualistic values. That lifestyle would play a key role in what would eventually become a multi-billion-dollar industry.

The lure of the great surfing conditions at Ala Moana produced a generation who understood that being there to ride those gracious waves required its own set of rules. They understood this not so much by conscious thought than by internalizing the experience of the vagaries of wind, tide, and swell. A regular life of employment and relationships was a difficult fit with the fickle surf schedule. We put off growing up as long as possible. Life is what happened in the process.

If a surfer didn't work because he was always down at the beach waiting for the surf to come up, people who didn't understand called him a beach bum. That was fine as long as Mom and Dad fed and housed the bum. When, inevitably, the bum burned that bridge by not showing up for a family gathering because a set was picking up momentum down the line at Kaisers, getting creative quickly was mandatory. At some point an actual adult emerged, maintaining some position as a functioning member of society, while simultaneously maintaining flexibility to pursue the surf on a full-time schedule.

This phenomenon would ultimately change the way the rest of society regarded people who at first were seen as merely selfish and irresponsible. Kerouac and Dylan's "straight" world, the man in the grey suit, came at last to see surfers as dedicated athletes with superb physical conditioning and a clearly defined goal in life. When an individual tries to change commonly held opinions and perceptions on his own, he is labeled a freak. But when everyone's children are doing the same thing at the same time, parents find this activity more difficult to condemn. At some point parents stopped asking the "What are you going to do when you grow up?" question. They realized that their sons had grown up and were already doing it. Parents heaved a great collective shrug and accepted it.

The 1960s and 1970s were times of great change across all barriers of Western society. In a significant way, Ala Moana parking lot consciousness embodied changes that were taking hold everywhere in the West. No one among us had any idea that we might be any kind of avant-garde for changing mores in the larger society. We were just there for the waves. But somehow, in the ignorance of youth and in the bliss of those moments of magical ocean energy, our behavior must have managed to transmit some kind of folk wisdom we had acquired, because life around us seemed to alter ever so slightly for the better.

The first time I surfed at Ala Moana, I was still a kook. The first thing I learned was that until I learned to surf a lot better, I had no business being out there. The caliber of surfing was at an expert level.

Located in front of the Ala Wai Yacht Harbor, Ala Moana is a great wave from two to ten feet. There are several different breaks within Ala Moana. Paddling out from the break wall beyond the cars, a surfer passes through the first spot, the inside break.

This break within the break was made popular by a great surfer back in the 1960s named Benjamin 'Buzzy' Kneubuhl, a smooth goofy-foot who was the consummate "soul surfer" before the phrase was even coined.

Paddling past the inside break, straight ahead there is a pole that marks the east side of the harbor channel. The pole there today is a new one. It replaced the original pole put in when the channel was dredged back in the early 1950s.

The original pole was washed away by a big swell sometime in the 1980s. The new one was relocated further outside to prevent the waves from taking it away again. When the surf was at least six feet, the sets would come in right at the old pole and we would use it for our lineup. Those were the fabled "Pole Sets" at Ala Moana.

Further over toward Diamond Head is Middles, which is the main break at Ala Mo. From two to six feet this is the premier left slide on the entire south shore of O'ahu.

The case can even be made that it is the best summer left on any of the Hawaiian Islands, although Pakala on Kaua'i and Mala Wharf on Maui must be considered. Apart from the waves themselves, Ala Moana Middles has been home to the majority of the best of Hawai'i's summer surfers.

The Middles wave is a long, fast-peeling left that when ridden properly can be connected through the entire inside break for a long ride. To do that requires negotiating the inside bowl section directly inside from the pole. A shallow reef there causes this section to peak and break ahead of the curl from Middles. To make it through requires speed and swooping down around the soup, or climbing up on the whitewater and floating over the section without losing momentum. Either way, it was a troublesome section to get beyond, so there was always a group of surfers sitting there to take any unmade waves.

On the far side of Middles is Ala Moana Rights. There was another whole group of guys who came out just to surf this unpredictable and seldom productive wave.

There remain a variety of other breaks at Ala Moana proper. Further down from Ala Moana Rights is Rockpiles Lefts, and then Rockpiles Rights. Beyond those is Kaisers Bowl, which has a decent left and a short right. The right at Kaisers breaks into a channel and is a mini version of Ala Moana Bowl, a hollow, hooking wave that can completely bury a rider, then spit him out again.

Ala Moana is a man-made surf spot created by the Army Corps of Engineers. This fact compels interest because of the remarkable quality of the wave, which no one even considered at the time the project was begun. The channel at Ala Moana was made for boats. There is no evidence that surfers participated in planning the project. One wonders what might be possible if the Corps, or some similar entity, actually set out to create a wave in Hawai'i.

The Corps dredged out the mouth of the Ala Wai Canal in the early 1950s. The Ala Wai Canal was built in 1928 to drain the swamp and floodwaters behind Waikiki. The Canal's dual purpose was to make more room for development, as well as to alleviate the chronic problems caused by standing water. To make a safer passage through the natural break in the reef, and to create more space for boats, the Corps dredged the harbor inside the reef and the channel out through it. This wide channel generated the left at Ala Moana. It also made a great little right peak on the other side that eventually was named Garbage Hole because all the crap from the canal and the small boat harbor collected there. The Army Corps of Engineers made friends by creating Ala Moana. Unfortunately, they would lose those friends in later years by destroying Garbage Hole when they built Magic 'Tragic' Island and by destroying the famous Maile Cloudbreak surf spot on the West Side by building a questionable drainage canal.

They are still not making any friends among surfers with their latest endeavor to expand the harbor at Ma'alaea on Maui. Any plans that will ruin the famous Freight Trains break there can, and should, be averted.

The cast of characters who have frequented Ala Moana rivals the great waves in colorful splendor. As far back as I can remember, it was always the gathering place for the best surfers on the island—a group populated by folks who were a show even on land. From the early days, guys like Donald Takayama, Paul Strauch, Fred Hemmings, Peter Cole, Fred Van Dyke, and Joey Cabell were regular faces in the lineup.

The real masters, however, were not quite as well known outside of Hawai'i. Conrad Cunha and Sammy Lee were two of the best surfers in the water on any given day. Both were experts at shooting the tube, as tuberiding was called back then. From my earliest memories of surfing come images of one or the other of these great riders. They would stall themselves back into the curl, disappear from sight into the inner bowels of the wave, then fly back out into the light in a burst of spray.

Other great Ala Moana regulars of the time included Shoyu, Toku, Tony 'Grapevine' Irvine, Robbie Rath, Roy Mesker, Freddy Fong, Ivan Vanatta, Ivan Harada, Franny Lum-King, Michael McPherson, Dynamite, and Jack 'Ganzi' Gonzales. Joseph 'Joe Kolohe' Kaohe, also known as 'Buddyboy,' was on a planet all by himself, the essence of Ala Moana smooth.

Those were the days when all the surfboards were long and heavy, a far cry from the sleek, lightweight longboards of today. To be an adept surfer back then took a lot of skill, strength, and practice. The Ala Moana surfers of the early 1960s also had an innate understanding of, and close relationship with, the ocean. Surfers then were more complete watermen. Most of them spent time paddling outrigger canoes or paddleboards and fishing in all its forms.

An ordinary sight back then was one of these guys spearfishing outside the lineup on a small day to fill the grill. There was always a hibachi going in the parking lot for the after-surf feed. As much time as was spent out in the surf, perhaps even more was spent in the parking lot talking about it or waiting for it to happen. A lot of beer drinking and other activities went on at all times whether there was surf or not. Any news of interest, as well as a lot of gossip, was passed around and the parking lot became a clearinghouse of information on any and all subjects.

I was only a little kid hanging around on the edges of this great happening, but the tradition continued as I got older and eventually took a place in the lineup. Unless there was something else to do, everyone in the group always had it in mind to end up at the parking lot at some point in his day, if not for most of it.

Later on when I had passed through my Ala Moana phase and had the opportunity to look back on that period, I was amazed at how all-consuming the whole surf experience was at that point in time. As the Ala Moana consciousness got left behind, it seemed that the surfing part happened more in the water and less while out of it.

During the Ala Mo period, that place was a full-time passion. Even if I was doing something else entirely—school, work, family, girlfriends, whatever—Ala Moana was always an open window in my mind that never went away. If there were any hints of surf, or especially word on the grapevine about "Pole Sets," I could forget about getting anything constructive done until after a trip down to the parking lot for a mingle with the crew and a surf session.

Even then, the "talking about it with all the boys afterward" part was sometimes harder to break away from than the waves, regardless of how important any other thing was supposed to be. It was quite a crew too: my brother Victor, Reno 'Hamajanga' Abellira, Wayne 'Ultralizard' Santos, Lionel 'Pudgy' Judd, Roy 'Mr. Hollywood' Mesker, Ben Aipa, Rick and Keone Hoopii, the Mahelona brothers, Alden Kaikaka, the Dumphy brothers, Hoku Keawe, Les Wong, Calvin 'Naka' Takara, Roger Hayashi, 'Turtle,' the Ham-Young brothers, Davey Smith, Mike Smith, Rusty Starr, Tommy Winkler, the Bradley brothers, the Titcomb brothers, the Ho brothers—the list went on endlessly.

In 1970, Jack Shipley (also an Ala Mo regular) and I started our own surf shop. Before that, we had both worked for Fred Schwartz at Surf Line Hawai'i, the premier surf shop on the island. We named our new shop Lightning Bolt. This was a problem at first when people phoned then hung up before they heard the "surfboards" part of the name. But both shops were in close proximity to Ala Moana and our connection there was unbreakable. Anytime there was any hint of surf, we were on it. The short surfboard designs had begun to stabilize at that point in time and, more than at any previous time in surfing's history, surfboard designs began to get specialized for each wave type.

The designs for Ala Moana and other south shore breaks were the focus of most of our efforts. With a huge surf team and extensive rider feedback, the shapes improved rapidly, and with it, so did the level of performance. I traveled internationally a bit at the time. I remember thinking every time I surfed another spot that the overall level of surfing at Ala Moana was dramatically higher than anywhere else. That was a function of both the advanced surfboard designs and the competitive nature of guys who surfed there. Being part of Ala Moana drove everyone to want to improve his surfing. To hold a place in that lineup required effort.

Ironically, the Ala Moana style of surfing always was very smooth relative to the rip and tear styles of today. Even when Larry Bertlemann on his Aipa Stingers started his run, his style, though quite a bit more energetic than the others, was still smooth and flowing. The original Ala Moana style, maybe most clearly personified in Buddyboy Kaohe, was a postwar adaptation of the Beamer Brothers' "real old" Waikiki style, its roots nourished all the way back to Duke himself.

That contrasted with the cruise-oriented California styles of surfing; at Ala Moana no one was willing to let his level of surfing cruise along. Overall, everyone was elevating his own surfing performance in order to stay in the lineup. Generally speaking, a surfer can reach a certain level of surfing relative to the board he rides. To progress beyond that requires a better surfboard. If the number of surfboards we built at Lightning Bolt was any indication, the level of surfing was elevating at a very rapid pace.

It was a grand time and I wouldn't have traded it for anything, nor changed any of it for something else. The people were terrific, the times were great and the surf was outstanding. Every man was a King.

Top and Bottom   **Ala Moana was all about small-wave, high-performance surfing, and it drove surfboard design to new heights every day of the summer. Photos: Steve Wilkings**

Cannons

There was a lull after
that wave, and I
paddled farther outside
to be ready for the
next set. Looking back
at the boys, I could
see Carlos standing
still and silent,
while Howard and my
brother were rolling
on the ground laughing.
My big idea about
showing off for
my friends had ended
with a huge
lesson in humility.

This surfboard was state of the art in 1968–69, but
in short order its limitations were revealed. The
shapes and designs evolved dramatically from one
board to the next. Photo: Art Brewer

One morning Carlos Andrade, the best surfer on Kaua'i, came by to take my brother Victor, Howard Fukushima, and me to a surf spot in Ha'ena. When I asked him about it, he just told me that it would be a spot I'd like. The year was 1968 and I was living in Hanapepe town working as a shaper for Dick Brewer at Hanapepe Surfboards.

All of my mother's family were from Kaua'i, so Victor and I had spent a lot of time all over the island beginning when we were kids. We were very familiar with the area near the dry cave in Ha'ena, having camped there with our Uncle Sab many times over the years. The diving was exceptional during the summer months when the surf was small.

The reef Carlos had in mind—as well as Tunnels on the opposite point of the bay that over the next few years would become a frequently ridden spot—were my uncle's lobster grounds. I had spent many days being bag boy while Uncle Sab and his friends pulled lobsters out of the holes in the reef and filled the bucket in the center of a float tube I held for them. Any thoughts of waves or surfing in the area were absent from my young mind then.

On that morning when Carlos offered to show us a new break, I was eager to jump in the car with him. After the long drive from Hanapepe, through Hanalei to Ha'ena, we finally reached our destination. As Carlos pulled his car over to the side of the road, he pointed out a perfect-looking left that peeled along the edge of the reef. We were just a little way past Ha'ena Beach Park and the dry cave where Uncle Sab used to bring us. Here the road starts to go back uphill, winding along the Na Pali cliffs for a few more miles before it comes to where the End of the Road meets the beginning of the hiking trail into Kalalau Valley.

"What is this spot?" we asked Carlos, watching a nice set roll in.

"I call it Cannons," he answered with a smile, pointing toward a handsome wave that broke with a loud boom spitting a spray of mist out the mouth of the tube. It did seem like a cannon firing.

"What's it like? Do guys surf here a lot?" I asked. I was very much intrigued by this new surf spot.

"Nobody comes out here," Carlos said, but I noticed a small twinkle in his eye and knew that he had probably surfed it.

"How big is it?" I wanted to know. My first impression was that I liked this wave, a clean, hollow left. But from our lookout point up on the road above, it was hard to tell the size. "It looks like it's about four feet, huh?" I continued.

"Paddle out there and find out; I think you'll like it," answered Carlos, but the bigger smile and mischievous twinkle failed to register with me.

I needed no other prompting as I grabbed my board and ran down the little hill toward the beach. The sand was white and sparkling out to the dry reef. The air was still and the sky, blue and clear. On my head was a coconut leaf hat I had made. The waves didn't appear to be too big, and back then in the days before sunscreen, the hat was some protection from the hot sun.

I picked my way across the rugged coral to the edge where it dropped off into the blue-green water. After waiting for the next surge, I jumped in and rode the surge back out as the wave receded. I was safely off the jagged reef and into the deep water.

I paddled out during a long lull and reached a point where I thought the waves were breaking. I glanced back at the car and waved with my coconut hat to the guys. They waved back and pointed toward the outside.

As the next set approached, I jammed my hat down firmly on my head and began to paddle out. I paddled over the first couple of waves, keeping a sharp eye out for any big waves. Although brimming with the confidence of surfing in front of my friends, I kept in mind that this was a new and unfamiliar lineup. As I paddled over the second wave, it seemed as though the water level behind it had sunk. Instead of facing another four-foot wave like the ones before, I was suddenly looking at a ten-foot monster that was going to break on my head.

I paddled furiously, knowing already that I was caught. As the wave threw out, I turned turtle and hung on tight. The wave exploded on me, tossing me around like a wet leaf. My surfboard was ripped away instantly. When I surfaced, the next wave was bearing down. My surfboard was to one side of me, and my coconut hat floating on the other. I had a moment to decide which to grab. I chose the surfboard and somehow managed to hang onto it through the next wave. But my coconut hat was gone.

There was a lull after that wave, and I paddled farther outside to be ready for the next set. Looking back at the boys, I could see Carlos standing still and silent, while Howard and my brother were rolling on the ground laughing. My big idea about showing off for my friends had ended with a huge lesson in humility. I stayed out for about an hour and managed to catch some waves. Those guys never came out; they just watched and waited until I finally lost my board and came in.

I loved that wave. During the rest of that winter season I went there at every opportunity. Cannons became the wave that showed us how poorly our surfboards worked in the tube.

In 1968–69, all surfboards had a round belly in the nose. We thought it made them looser and easier to turn. Soon we would try a flat-bottom nose, but we still had round, turned up rails in front. This design tended to push water, and once pitted in the deep barrels of Cannons, the board would slow or stop dead, causing us to wipeout.

It was a frustrating period in the evolution of wave riding and surfboard development. We had the uncrowded, pristine tubes of Cannons to ride, but we were getting our butts kicked. Finally, Mike Hynson let us try his boards that had hard-edged, turned-down rails from tail to nose. Although his designs used a round-bottom belly in the nose to compensate for the sharp, low rails, this was the breakthrough we had been seeking. We incorporated the turned-down rails with flat bottoms and that was the ticket. The tuberides of our dreams finally became a reality.

Carlos showing us Cannons was the key to a particularly difficult period in surfboard evolution. Carlos Andrade went on to become a noted professor of Hawaiian history. He still surfs with the same style and grace. And he still has the same big smile and wonderful twinkle in his eye.

The

Big

Swim

Curt Mastalka's first movie, *Sea Dreams*, enjoyed some financial success. He plunged right into his second one, titled *Red Hot Blue*. He was a one-man show, doing the entire process on his own. Scripting, filming, editing, producing, marketing ... Curt did the whole ball of wax. He also was an amateur pilot, and he asked Barry Kanaiaupuni, Rory Russell, and me if we would fly over to the island of Kaua'i to film a sequence for his new film. Curt had some information about a pending new swell, which would hit Kaua'i first. It seemed like a good idea at the time, but in hindsight I can't believe any of us ever let ourselves be talked into it.

We arrived at the far end of Honolulu airport where the private planes were kept. Curt rented a Cessna 172, a single-engine plane with slightly more room than a VW Bug, but also slightly more flimsy construction. Somehow we stuffed three surfboards, Curt's camera gear, and incidentals into the small cabin and crammed ourselves in after it. Curt was flying, BK sat in the co-pilot seat, and Rory and I were stuffed in the back with the rest of our junk.

A strong Kona storm had begun to move into the island chain, but we foolishly paid it no heed as we taxied down the runway while Curt called for clearance to take off. There weren't any other single-engine planes flying in the bad weather that day, so we were quickly cleared to go. We lumbered up into the air, and I had my first inkling that this trip might be a mistake.

The labored roar of our one engine straining to keep the overloaded little plane aloft made conversation nearly impossible. To communicate at all required shouting. Curt was a decent pilot but without much experience. The weather didn't help the situation. We flew into the strong southwesterly headwind, and the Cessna was buffeted horribly, bouncing up, down, and sideways.

I'm not much for flying and immediately began to feel nauseous. It's roughly a hundred miles to Kaua'i, but it seemed to take forever. With the cloudy, stormy weather, there was a point midway where we lost sight of both O'ahu and Kaua'i. I hoped the gauges were all working properly, especially the compass and gas gauge. The relief was palpable when we finally saw the coast of Kaua'i. I believe there was a point when even Curt began to have reservations.

Landing in Lihu'e was a relief for everyone; it was great to get out of the crammed cabin and put our feet back on the ground. I was still woozy from the bumpy flight, so I delegated Rory to unload the equipment while Curt and Barry went to get a rental car.

We headed out of Lihu'e toward Hanalei, where we had planned to surf, but that prospect was looking unlikely due to the Kona wind conditions. We talked it over as we drove through Kapa'a and decided our only bet was Cannons in Ha'ena. Hanalei Bay, when we got there, was a mess from the onshore wind, so we just kept going, hoping for the best.

Passing the dry cave of Ha'ena, we could see the surface conditions were not ideal, but it looked like Cannons might be surfable. Finally, parked on the road overlooking the surf spot, we saw the waves were far from perfect. The north shore of Kaua'i receives northwest swells before O'ahu does. That extra hundred miles of ocean seems to do a lot of combing. The waves are smoother and cleaner by the time they reach

Sunset Beach, Hale'iwa, and the Pipeline. The waves we were looking at were a little ragged, and it was apparent that this was not a very clean swell. The interval was close and the faces were bumpy.

But we came to surf, so Rory and I told Curt we would paddle out if he wanted to film. Barry just shook his head; he had no interest in the rough-looking lefts. He had come on the trip with hopes of riding some of the long, clean walls at Hanalei, and the waves here at Cannons were a far cry from that.

While Curt set up his camera, Rory and I headed down to the beach. Since we were the only people around, I told Rory we needed to keep an eye on each other. The surf was in the ten- to twelve-foot range, not dangerous, but sizeable enough that there was a need to be careful. The tide was low, and the inside reef at Cannons was very shallow, the edge of it like a small wall. Jumping in was no problem, but I could see that getting back ashore would require some good timing, a little luck, and maybe a short climb.

The waves weren't that bad. With no one else in the water, we could take our pick of the best ones, so we got some fun rides. Cannons starts at a definite peak so lining up was easy. I had surfed Cannons quite a bit in the late 1960s, but had not been back in the past few years. After a couple of waves, I started to feel comfortable again.

This was Rory's first time here, but he followed my lead and matched me wave for wave. I got a little too ambitious and took one too late. It dumped me, and my board was gone. Rory caught the next one and made it. As he paddled back out, I yelled to him if he could see whether my board had gone in over the reef or out in the rip. He sat up, looked in, and told me my board was up on the reef. The choppy water made it hard to see for myself, so I took his word for it and swam in.

I got in to the reef's edge without incident, but it was tricky trying to get up on top. Eventually I timed a surge just right and let it carry me up over the wall on to the dry reef. I looked for my surfboard where Rory said it would be, but it wasn't there. I looked all over but no luck, my board was gone. I whistled up to Curt and BK and saw Barry point out toward the channel. Looking out to sea, I caught a quick glimpse of my surfboard floating far out in the channel. I was used to long swims from far offshore breaks like Sunset Beach, so without a second thought, I dove back off the reef and began swimming to get my board.

Rory Russell and me laughing about one thing or another; with Rory there was always something funny going on. Photo: Jeff Divine

As I swam further out the water began to change color. Near the reef it was green, but as I got into deeper water, it started to turn blue. About 200 yards offshore, I stopped to try to spot my board again. I saw it rise up on a swell, but it was still a good distance away. Again, without thinking, I put my head down and swam hard. I reached where I thought it might be and I stopped once more. My board was a little closer than the last time, but I still had a way to go.

The water had turned dark blue, and as I turned back toward shore, I was shocked by how far out I was. There was a rip running out to sea, and both my board and I were in it. I had to get my board or the next stop, if I was lucky, might be the French Frigate Shoals. I put my head down and swam hard. The water was so deep it had turned to black, and I began to have weird shark vibes.

I've always felt I had good karma with sharks, but I never took any dumb chances, giving them respect and a healthy distance in any encounters. This time I was putting myself right into their territory and there wasn't anything I could do about it. To take my mind off the sharks, I started getting mad at Rory. It was his dumb ass that had gotten me into this situation. If he had just looked a little better and had actually seen my board before assuming it had just washed in, I wouldn't be in this predicament. Cursing him, I swam like I was in a race.

The water was black and ominous. I was a mile out to sea when I finally saw my surfboard just ahead. A wave of relief washed over me as I grabbed it and climbed aboard. A surfboard is probably the best life-saving device for any open-water situation. A boat with an operational means of propulsion is better, but if that boat is broken down, even with a paddle, the occupants are at the mercy of the currents. If the paddler has experience, a surfboard can be paddled at a decent rate of speed, usually fast enough to overcome most rip currents.

I was so pissed off at Rory that I could have paddled against any rip just to get my hands on his throat. As I got closer to where he was sitting in the lineup, I started yelling at the top of my lungs. Later Rory told me he thought I just went in after my board and never came back out. Then he heard me screaming at him from out in the channel, figured out that he had screwed up and what had happened. Being Rory, he panicked when he realized how mad I would be. He caught a wave and went straight in before I got to him.

By the time I got back to the beach, my anger had cooled. Back on the beach, I found Curt and Barry both laughing, having witnessed the whole episode. I didn't see Rory, so I asked them where he was. Curt told me Rory was so scared that he had quickly changed his clothes and hitchhiked back to the airport hoping I would cool down by the time we got there. We had a good laugh about what had happened while we packed up our stuff and headed back to Lihu'e.

We didn't get the waves we hoped for that day, but we did have some good laughs. I kept Rory thinking I was pissed off at him, and he acted like my slave, doing anything I asked him to, giving me any wave I wanted. But it wasn't long before the fear wore off, and Rory was his old selfish self, hogging all the waves and taking off in front of everyone.

Caught

Inside

Again

In the winter of 1980, I felt like I was sitting on top of the world. I had spent a long spring and summer embroiled in an exhausting legal battle over the Lightning Bolt Company. My part in it was finally settled. I put it as far behind me as I could.

I was the marketing director of a new company called Pipeline and loved the responsibilities that entailed. My friend John Porter and I had just finished our new beach house at Pipeline and were enjoying the thrills of being ringside at this great surf spot.

Lastly, I was to leave that night for Spain where I would be joining John Milius and Arnold Schwarzenegger to play the co-lead in *Conan the Barbarian*. I felt like everything was going my way. But life has a way of surprising a person when he least expects it.

The Pipe Masters was being held that day, and even though I was leaving that night, I planned to surf my heat and enjoy myself. There was a rising swell out of the west with light offshore winds, a perfect Pipe swell. In my mind, it couldn't have been a more fitting send-off to my six-month acting job in Spain: some perfect Pipeline before I left.

There were only six guys in the sixth and last heat of the first round. It was an ideal amount of surfers for the Pipeline lineup. Hans Hedemann, Mark Warren, and Steve Massfeller were riding backside and not regular faces at the Pipe. Eddie Rothman and Brian Bulkley were there every time the place broke. Brian was our neighbor and one of the top underground surfers at the Pipe. This contest was a big deal for him. For me it was a lark. I only had this one session, and then I would be high and dry for the next half a year on a movie set. I wasn't serious about the competition, but I am always serious about surfing the Pipe, especially when the waves are in the eight- to ten-foot range and tubing out of the west.

It was a beautiful swell. Standing on the beach before we paddled out, I remarked to Brian that we were both sure to get some great waves. These were the best conditions one could hope for at the Pipe Masters. I wished him the best of luck in the heat and the continuing contest after I was gone. We got out to the lineup and waited for the horn to begin the heat. The surf appeared to be on the rise, but the sets were clean and beautiful, and all of us were anxious to start surfing.

The heat started. Brian and I, both very comfortable with the ideal conditions at our home break, immediately got a couple of good waves each. I was leading the heat with Brian in second when a good set started to show on the horizon. It was my turn, and I had my eye on a good wave approaching. Brian, sitting next to me, surprised me by asking if he could have this wave. We could both tell it was a beauty. He said he needed a good ride to elevate his surf career and, since I was already famous, could I please give him this wave.

I couldn't refuse a plea like that. I pulled back, signaling him to take it. It really was a great wave and I sat for a moment watching it. I heard the crowd roar and knew he had done exactly what I would have done: pulled in, got tubed, and spat out the end. It was the best ride of the heat and pushed Brian into the lead.

As I turned to see what was next, I caught a glimpse of some much bigger waves outside. Thinking I could get a bigger and maybe a better wave, I paddled hard out to sea to get into position. The other competitors must have all been inside because I was alone on the outer lineup. As I crested the next wave, I could see that the waves

Walking up the beach after a near-death experience, still a little spaced out, and probably trying to forget how close I had come to the 'Big One.' Photo: Denjiro Sato

175

behind were quite a bit bigger than anything that had come in so far. I paddled harder, but it was obvious that I was too far inside and was not going to be in any position to catch this next wave.

As I paddled, the wave continued to grow bigger and bigger. I knew I was in a race just to get out of its way. The biggest sets up till then had been ten feet; my first impression was that this was about a twelve-foot wave. I quickly realized, however, that it was already in the fifteen-foot range and still rising. I was now paddling as hard as I could. As I started up the face of this monster, it was still growing. It must have been twenty feet when it began to throw out at the top, and I was still only halfway up the face.

I attempted to duck-dive my board through the wave, but it was just too big and too powerful. I couldn't penetrate the wave at all. Instead it felt like I was in an elevator on the way up. I just kept going upward, still in the face of the wave, not able to go any deeper. I rose farther up, then I felt the rise slowing and for a long moment I was floating. Then I started to drop; down and down I plunged.

I had paddled out almost to the second reef to get this wave and now it had me. The water is much deeper out there and down I went into it. The deeper I went, the darker it got. So far everything had been smooth without any rough stuff. I could tell by the pressure on my ears that I was at least twenty feet deep. I had a brief thought that maybe I was deep enough to escape a pounding. But no sooner had that thought crossed my mind than I found myself in the most violent wipeout of my life. It spun me around like a rag doll, over and over again. I struggled to maintain my sense of direction.

In a bad wipeout it is very important to remember which way is up. If I lost my direction, it was possible that I could swim the wrong way and find myself going deeper instead of up, a bad position if I was low on air.

The thrashing was not letting up. To this day, I still wonder how that wave could have been that intense so deep below the surface where the wave's energy seldom reached. It was like being in the jaws of a huge dog and being violently shaken. Every time I tried to get away and swim up, the turbulence grabbed me once more, pulled me back down and thrashed me all over again.

I was becoming desperate for air. My struggles were to no avail. I couldn't get free. I kept getting pulled down into the turmoil. I somehow knew which way the surface was but I couldn't do anything about it. I must have been near the end of my will to resist. I still had my mouth shut against the water, but I could feel everything becoming sort of dreamy.

I happened to look down, or I thought I did, and there below was my own body tumbling around in the whitewater. Somehow I knew in an instant that I was having an out-of-body experience. Through my interest in yoga I had read many books on this subject. I had marveled at yogis who described astral traveling.

I had also read about ordinary people talking about out-of-body experiences. I knew that these occurred in near-death situations. The ones who had lived to talk about it said they found themselves floating above their physical bodies and experienced re-entering their bodies before coming back to consciousness. I knew I had to do that.

The thought of what I needed to do helped me somehow, and I managed to dive back into my body. I don't really know how to explain that moment except to say that I was filled with energy and revitalized. I felt strong again and easily swam away from the powerful pull of the wave. I ascended to the ocean's surface and got my head above the water just as the next, even bigger wave broke right on top of me.

I didn't get much of a breath, and this time the thrashing was even more violent than the first. For some reason though, I was at ease, in control, and feeling powerful. I relaxed and had no trouble riding out the pounding this wave gave me.

When I resurfaced inside, I looked back out and saw Brian Keaulana, the water patrol, frantically searching the whitewater outside. He had seen me get caught by the first wave, but did not see me surface. He watched uneasily as the second wave rolled over my position. He had been over one hundred yards inside of me on the first wave, and now I was at least fifty yards inside from him: I had been dragged about 150 yards underwater by the two waves.

Brian couldn't believe his ears when I yelled to him from the inside that I was all right. I swam in, retrieved my board, and paddled back out to catch another wave before the heat ended. I placed third behind Bulkley, who took first, with Rothman in second, but the contest was over for the day. The wind had turned onshore, ending the perfect surf conditions.

I wish I had spent more time examining what had happened to me out there. I filed the incident away as just another wipeout, one of many more to come. I was young and foolish at the time. Sadly, I let some of the vividness and the color of this experience fade, even though the significance had left an indelible impression on me. I'll never forget that sensation of being filled with a strength and power that came when I needed it.

Getting caught inside is such an everyday occurrence in surfing that it becomes a metaphor for dealing with adversity of any kind. Obviously any lessons learned in the water can have a significant application back on the beach. We live today in a civilized world where life-or-death situations are rare in our everyday lives.

Sometimes, however, those critical moments when a person's whole life flashes before him is an opportunity to see into the inner self. The inner self is a part of each of us and holds answers to complete happiness and a life free from pain and suffering.

This inner place of harmonious bliss is layered over with ego, individual belief systems, and mundane concerns. We live in the past where nostalgia makes us sad or in the future where our worries cause us anxiety. We fail to grasp that this moment we are in is all there ever was or ever will be. Life is, was, and ever will be, simply now.

Moments of surf realization are here to remind us of our true potential. If that is why we surf, that's good because surfing reconnects us to who we really are. This is all the more reason to keep surfing. Life is good. Surfing reminds us of how good life is.

c. GALLERY

Left   Carefully threading the deep line on a Pipe beauty—
total concentration, nothing else going on except my board,
the wave, and me. Photo: Steve Wilkings

Above   With Rory Russell, my team rider, and
Jack Shipley, my partner in Lightning Bolt Surfboards,
and a yard full of boards. Photo: Steve Wilkings

Next spread   Photo: Jeff Divine

Rory confidently deep in a beautiful
tube at the Pipe, a position he was very
familiar with. Photo: Jeff Divine

Above   A view from Pupukea of the corduroy lines of big waves marching in. Photo: Jeff Divine

Next spread   This shot gives an interesting perspective of a tuberide at the Pipeline. The wave will break in front of the surfer, but it is the Pipe so he will be able to ride through the tunnel ... or so he hopes. Photo: Jeff Divine

Photo: Denjiro Sato

Above **My last wave at the Pipe before six months in Spain filming** *Conan the Barbarian* **with Arnold Schwarzenegger. Photo: Cordinha.**

Next spread **Before the duck dive was possible, a good, hard, and well-timed shove was a surfer's only hope of getting his board through a wave when he was too late to paddle over or around it. Photo: Jeff Divine.**

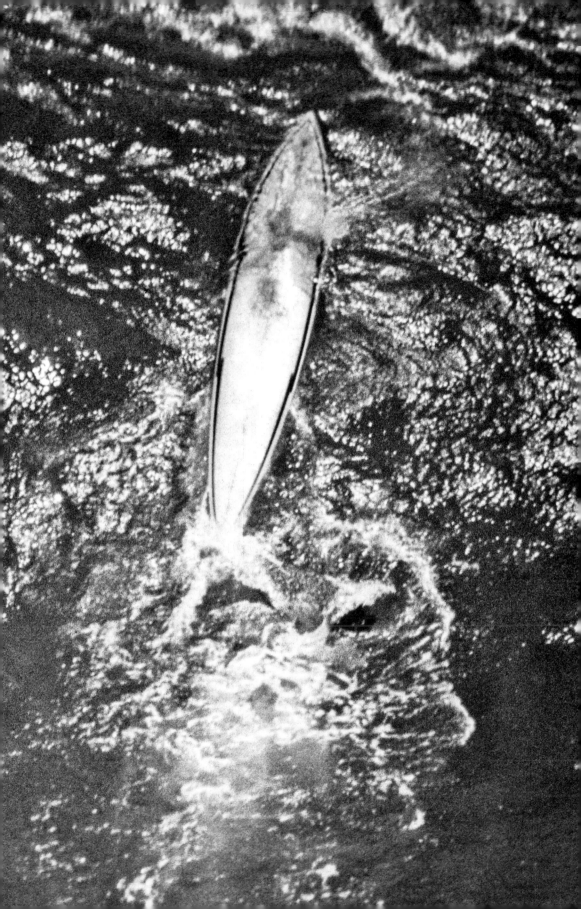

Incident at Eke Moku

My generation of surfers in Hawai'i grew up with two big fears about surfing. These fears were born of stories from the generation of surf pioneers before us. They were the first of the modern generation of surfers to challenge the big winter surf of the North Shore. There were ancient Hawaiian surfers before them, but no one was there to take pictures or to tell us the stories afterward.

The first, and biggest, fear came from a tragic incident involving Woody Brown and Dickie Cross. They paddled out late one afternoon in the early 1940s to surf Sunset Beach on a rising swell. There was no one else out—or even on the beach—to witness their go-out. The swell began to rise dramatically and before long they found themselves paddling rapidly out to sea to escape the crashing sets. Soon they were too far out to sea with the surf too big for them to attempt a return to the beach, and it was starting to get dark. They decided to paddle down to Waimea Bay several miles to the west in hopes that they might be able to get to shore in the deeper water there. They got to the bay in total darkness only to hear a giant set breaking outside of them. Woody made it to shore somehow, found himself face down in the sand, his surfboard and even his swim shorts gone. Dickie Cross was never seen again.

Twenty years of surfing the North Shore, as well as the big winter surf on all the other islands, gave me an understanding of the basic mechanics of how waves are created and how quickly a swell can rise and fall. A healthy respect for the surf—and Woody and Dickie's terrifying plight lodged firmly in my memory—kept my senses attuned to changes in the surf conditions, with a ready escape plan back to the safety of the beach if necessary.

The other big fear that we all lived with was from the stories the older guys used to tell us, about being held down for two waves. A big wave has more than enough

When living on Maui and the summertime south swells
rolled in, the only place I wanted to be was on the long
left walls of La Perouse Bay. Photo: Erik Aeder   195

power to hold a person down for the fifteen- to twenty-second interval before the next wave of the set rolls in. I was careful not to get caught inside when I was out in big surf. We were all in pretty good swimming shape in the days before surfboard leashes. A half dozen swims in through the rip of big Sunset, chasing after your surfboard, were considered routine and didn't bring even the onset of fatigue. But the chance of being held under for several waves was always in my mind. Breath-holding for long periods and the ability to relax during a wipeout were practices I took seriously.

Summer surf is usually playful surf, and I would often let my guard down then. The whole attitude changed when summer came. Girls, kids, sometimes even dogs jumped in the water, laughing and having a good time. On occasion a big south swell arrives, and the seriousness goes up a notch, but never to the level of the winter surf mentality. Big summer surf is still fun.

La Perouse Bay is one of the last frontiers of summertime surfing on Maui. Appropriately, it is found at the end of the road. This area saw a great deal of ancient Hawaiian activity. The King's Trail begins at La Perouse, crosses the last lava flow from Haleakala Crater, and wanders through numerous house sites and stone corrals as it heads toward Kaupo. In 1786, the Comte de La Pérouse, a famous French navigator and the second European after Captain Cook to visit Hawai'i, found a safe anchorage in the small bay. Although he only stayed for a few hours before sailing away, the bay still bears his name. Its rugged lava shoreline is far less attractive than the beautiful white sand of nearby Big Beach Makena, but the pounding surf lures the surfers like a picnic lures ants. How long it will remain a frontier is anyone's guess, but for the time being it stays preserved.

Before surf leashes, La Perouse was seldom surfed, as the sharp lava shoreline destroyed any lost boards. Yet its attraction was undeniable. The stark black lava shore flanks azure blue water. The wind-whipped 'Alenuihaha Channel lies outside, and beyond that sits the Big Island of Hawai'i with the majestic summit of Mauna Kea in the far distance. Throw in some pounding surf with the blue-green waves marching in, cascading whitewater, and windblown 'ehukai and it is a sight to behold.

On a south or southeast swell, La Perouse would produce waves twice the size of any other south shore surf spot in the rest of the island chain. There were numerous times when we would hear of a tiny south swell in Lahaina and take a chance on the long drive to La Perouse. There we would be rewarded with clean four- to six-foot waves and nobody else even thinking that this kind of surf could be happening.

On a sizeable summer swell, this bay could, and usually would, create surf of serious intensity. Beyond that, the place had what the Hawaiians call *akua*, or spirit power. There always seemed to be a strange presence around, a feeling that someone else was there even with no one else in sight. On many occasions, we would arrive to find the surf very small and crowded with a group of loud-mouthed surfers bitterly complaining of the long car ride and the lack of waves. Cursing the spot, they would pack up to leave. Once they turned their backs on the surf and started walking out the rough lava trail to where they had parked their cars, a nice set would roll in. As soon as they were gone, the surf would start pumping, and we would have a great session. This occurred too many times for it to be written off as a fluke. We actually came to rely on this happening whenever we arrived.

The area is what the Hawaiians called *Eke Moku*, meaning a place where everyone is equal, where there is no difference between *ali'i* and *maka'ainana*, royalty and commoner, where one cannot cast a spell, where no evil is. Eke Moku was the ancient Hawaiian name before La Perouse came. We treasured the place and were careful to show respect at every opportunity, cleaning up after ourselves and often after others who were sloppy with their trash. Eventually we would be at La Perouse for every single south swell, only going to Lahaina for the annual Kimo's Longboard Contest at Mala Wharf.

This story begins with the excitement a good-sized south swell would stir up in our little La Perouse group. My brother Victor, Brad Lewis, Chris Vandervoort, Mark Anderson, and I all made plans to meet early the next day.

We got to La Perouse to find a big swell, clean trade winds, and a whole day ahead of us. Timing our jump off the jagged lava rocks, we paddled out to meet what the day would bring. When it's working well, like it was that day, the wave starts way outside in a huge peak at the far left corner of the bay. It can be a short hollow right off that peak, but the better ride is the long, lined-up left that peels into the bay. A good wave will come all the way across from the outside peak to end right in front of our jump-off rock, a good 500 yards distance. It is a long ride in anyone's book and critical all the way, forcing the surfer to drive hard to make the few sections that pop up over the shallow reefs inside. Each of these inside reefs is a takeoff and surf spot in itself, but the good ride is when we linked them all together from the peak outside.

The waves were great that day, the sets plentiful and the rides long and thrilling. As the tide started to go out, it seemed the sets were less consistent, but I noticed that they seemed a little bigger. The outside peak is difficult to line up, as it is so far out in the bay. The sets appear rather suddenly with little or no warning. During a long lull, we started talking and paying less attention to what was coming. Before we knew it, a set snuck up on our group. Everyone started paddling to the right toward the shoulder. I was sitting deepest and saw no chance in that direction. There seemed to be a small chance to get around the left side, so without hesitation, I headed that way. I managed to duck-dive through the peak and escape the pounding that the others took. The set swept them all the way inside, and I rode several waves while they made their way back to the lineup.

Brad Lewis, whom we affectionately called 'Butt Jammer' because of his unique surfing style, noticed this. He asked me how I had evaded the set and I told him that around the left side was an easy escape. Brad was one of the best surfers on the island and a longtime partner of Victor's and mine in our pioneer adventures in big outer-reef waves on Maui's north shores. Big-wave experience teaches a person to pay attention to any little thing that will help prevent one from getting caught inside.

When the next set loomed up, again we were too far inside. Brad and I went to the left. Jammer was a bit further out when the first wave stood up tall and pitched out and over. He was in a position to duck-dive, while I was right where the thick lip was going to land. I had no choice but to abandon ship.

I bailed off my board, expecting to let the leash take the punishment and dove for the bottom. Waiting for the wave to pull my board, I was ready when the leash went taut and rolled over on my back underwater, waiting for the wave to pass.

A surfboard leash is designed to keep a surfer from losing his board so it usually is an asset. Sometimes in bigger surf, it can become a liability. When the wave is strong enough to pull the board far away from its rider, the tension on the leash is tremendous. With the surfboard on the surface and the surfer underwater, the lateral pull of the leash keeps the surfer from being able to swim up to the surface. It's as if he is anchored to the bottom.

It took me a few long moments to realize this was happening and that I wasn't going to be able to get up before the next wave. Immediately I quit struggling and tried to relax, settling down to wait for the number two wave to go over me.

Holding your breath underwater when trapped has either a very calming effect or causes panic. If panic begins and the surfer is unlucky, he may drown. Surfing in big surf makes all surfers think a lot about situations like this. They know the stories about the guys being held down for two waves, and they know most of the guys in the stories end up having to be rescued. Guys who ride big surf figure out sooner or later that they are alone; no one can really help when a set crashes through the impact zone. The surfer trains himself to relax in these tense situations.

So I held on, tried to stay relaxed, conserving air and waiting for the next wave. I figured I would make my move as the next wave rolled over me.

When a wave goes overhead, from underwater it looks like a big carpet rolling up. The backside kind of rolls back toward the surface, and I thought I could use this energy and ride it up. From down on the bottom, I felt more than saw the next wave go over. I remember thinking, "Wow, that didn't take long." I tried to go up, but the tension from the leash was still too powerful. I wasn't going anywhere.

Desperation started to creep in. I could see the surface above me. There was light shining up there, but it was dark where I was. I couldn't get away from the bottom. I was swimming upward as hard as I could, but I was still being pulled sideways and could make no progress toward the surface. I knew I had been down a while and would need to breathe soon.

I imagined what happens in these situations is that the mouth opens underwater trying to suck air and then it's all over. I kept my mouth clamped shut.

Finally, on the edge of despair, I clawed my way up and just managed to break the surface when the third wave broke over me. I can't remember if I got a sip of air or not, but the exploding wave pushed me in and I felt that horrible tension on my leash slacken. I finally made it to the surface, sucked some air, and pulled in my surfboard. I got a grip on it just as the next wave hit me like a dump truck.

After what I had just been through, nothing was going to get my board away from me now. I held on fiercely. The set kept coming and I could feel myself being pushed in toward the jagged lava shore. Everything about me felt weak and I couldn't find any power to paddle through the incoming waves. I knew the shoreline was getting closer, so I stole a glance behind me to see where I was.

I couldn't believe my good fortune. I was directly in front of a very narrow beach of smooth rocks, perhaps some remnant of the old King's Trail, which had utilized smooth river stones to line the floor of the trail over the rough lava. It was no more than eight feet wide along a mile-long shoreline of sharp jagged lava. I was right in front of it when I needed it most.

Afterward when I had time to think about it, I would believe that it was just more akua or Hawaiian spirit power at work, taking care of those with respect for the manakai, or life of the sea.

It was the only smooth access into or out of the water on this whole side of the bay. I turned around and quickly scrambled ashore. I was sucking hard, filling my lungs with sweet air, thinking about how I had somehow managed to survive being held under for not just two waves but three. I was also thinking that despite the heavy breathing right then, it hadn't been that bad. A feeling of lethargy seemed to weigh down my entire body, but I figured that was a result of having held my breath for so long. There also was a weird tension, a tightness inside my body that I felt was some manifestation of fear. I didn't like it. I remembered stories of other surfers who had ended their surfing careers after a traumatic wipeout, and I began to understand why.

After what seemed like only a few minutes, Butt Jammer walked over and sat down next to me. He told me how he had successfully ducked under the first wave but got blasted by the second one, breaking his board in the process. He swam all the way into the bay, got out, put on his slippers, and walked all the way back out to find the other half of his broken board. This must have taken at least twenty minutes, maybe more, but it seemed like only moments to me.

We had a laugh about being caught inside, and he walked away to find another board to go back out. I knew I was stalling, worrying about being so freaked out by this heavy wipeout that it might affect my approach to surfing from there on out. I realized that I needed to get right back on the horse that threw me, or I might never again. I jumped back in and paddled out to the lineup to face my fears.

I had learned a great lesson. Hold on to the board at all costs; it is a surfer's salvation. I had also learned that letting go of the desire to breathe allowed me to hold my breath much, much longer than I ever thought possible. I'm certain that the greater lesson was of letting go of desire in general.

My inner compass had steered me to that release point only for the time I was underwater. I am still working on that lesson of letting go, as it seems to hold the key to all possibilities. Surf realization has a way of sneaking up on you not only in the surf, but even more so in daily life. Pay attention, because the lessons are fleeting but the rewards of "getting it" are great indeed.

G-Land

G-Land was the most challenging wave and also
my favorite spot of all the places that I've surfed.
Photo: Erik Aeder

GETTING OUT

Many of my close encounters with my inner self while surfing have taken place at the surf spots I like and frequent the most. G-Land is one of my favorite places. Every time I return, I feel a definite warm feeling permeate my entire being the moment I set foot ashore. This feeling is hard to describe. It's a stronger feeling of home than I get when I go back to my real home. This feeling says to me: This is where I should be, this is where I belong.

But as familiar and comfortable as G-Land feels when I first get there, there is a different feeling I must face every time I paddle out on a big day. It is a feeling of trepidation and great apprehension. G-Land is incredibly long and fast breaking, and it is very tricky to line up and pick a good wave. Even the paddle out is a hard and treacherous process that requires perfect timing, strong paddling, and a bit of luck.

The way G-Land is set up to receive the swell is a miracle in itself. The beach faces straight west, a wonderful direction to view the spectacular sunsets. The easterly flank of Grajagan Bay rolls around to become the southeastern tip of Java. It is ideally situated to catch the southerly swells as they march in.

A submarine canyon lying just offshore further assists the waves. This undersea trench is one of many in the area. Some, like the Lombok Trench and the Java Trench, are among the deepest in the world. These underwater canyons allow the swell to expand its energy in the deep water. When it exits the trench, the energy is then compressed as the swell moves into the shallow water near shore. This magnifies the size and power of the surf. There are always bigger, stronger, and more consistent waves at G-Land compared to Uluwatu and the Bukit on Bali just sixty miles to the east.

This is an interesting phenomenon as the west-facing aspects of both spots are the same and only a short distance apart, yet the surf at G-Land is always larger. Not only are the waves at G-Land bigger but sometimes certain waves in a set will be quite a bit larger than the average set wave that day.

A NEW SWELL

A new swell arrived the morning of a particularly good day and the boys were stoked. Not that the surf before had been bad, but a new swell is always a cause for rejoicing. This new energy, reinforcing and reintensifying the surf energy already in abundance there, put a giddy feeling into the pit of every surfer's stomach.

The present surf camp at G-Land is comfortable and accessible. Often surfers without the skills to match the surf fill the lineup. No longer the hard-core surf camp it once was, G-Land has become a regular stopping point on the Indo surf tour circuit. There can be over a hundred people out on a crowded day. A good-size swell has the effect of tempering the enthusiasm of the less skilled, keeping some of them out of the lineup to watch from the safety of the beach.

But for even the most adept, the paddle out is preceded by a moment of mental preparation for the ordeal of breaching the surfline to reach the lineup. Not penetrating the surfline can have disastrous consequences. The long lineup and the strong sweep of the waves wrapping in can pound even the most skilled surfer all the way from Kong's through Moneytrees and finally down onto the barbecue grill of Speed Reef, almost before he can come up for air. The sets move down the line and if his timing is bad, a surfer will be dragged all the way down the unforgiving reef.

The worst aspect of this experience is that the further down inside a person gets swept, the shallower and more dangerous the whole situation becomes. Inside Speed Reef is not only shallow, but it also has big outcroppings and jagged coral fissures, unlike the relatively flat reef inside Moneytrees and Kong's. On a low tide, inside Speedies can be sheer terror and lots of bloody cuts.

Even with water on the reef, it's no picnic. The surf grows in size and power on the lower end of the reef. Those unfortunate enough to be stuck inside in that area better have their wallets open because they are going to pay in one form or another.

To be caught in there after riding a wave is one thing, there is adrenaline in the system and some power to deal with the situation. But to be dragged all the way down there while attempting to paddle out is utterly demoralizing. The only hope is to somehow hang on, and if lucky, get dragged down to the boat channel without getting ripped apart or hung up on a coral head.

If this is a person's fate—if he does end up in the channel, terrorized from the ordeal, out of breath, energy, and everything else—one of two things will happen. He will wish he had started from the boat channel in the first place, taking the longer but easier way out. And if the pounding was bad enough, from then on, he will always paddle out from the channel, and be safe rather than sorry.

Or he will really study the paddle out and figure out how to do it correctly. Years of doing it, with the attendant bad moments tossed in, have taught me the value of doing it right. Patience is key. Waves always come in sets with lulls between them. One never knows how long a lull will last; it's all about making one's move at the right moment. Sometimes it's a sweet paddle out with no drama. Yet, twenty feet behind a guy who's having it easy, another surfer might be on the edge of terror, skirting disaster by only inches.

The next step is the tricky task of lining-up, trying to find a good position to start from on this long and challenging wave that appears to have no beginning place. After resolving that comes the most difficult part: paddling into the first wave of the day.

The very first time Peter McCabe and I went to G-Land was by boat from Bali, long before any surfers camped onshore. We started from outside the waves and spent the entire week paddling up and down the surfline looking for something to line up on. It was frustrating; we never did find a good place to catch a wave. It wasn't until we stayed on the beach and watched the waves from the inside that we saw the spots where it looked like the wave had a good beginning.

One spot was right in front of a small tree on the beach with leaves that were shiny and the same colors as the Indonesian currency. We called it the Moneytree and set up the mess hall there with a bright orange tarp for a roof. We could see the orange tarp from out in the surf; this really helped our positioning. We later became familiar with the reef and wave and didn't need it anymore.

Top and Bottom   **The early days at the surf camp were right on the edge ... of the jungle taking it all back. Photos: Don King**

The other spot was further inside; it was a definite peak that we named the Launching Pad because it would launch us into the run at Speed Reef. There were several tall trees in the jungle that we could use to line up on the Launching Pad once we could recognize them at a glance. A definite lineup to position on is critical in any surf, but at G-Land it was paramount. To take off too far back and have to straighten out often meant a long trip around the horn. The whole set would peel off outside with us trapped inside, helpless to do anything except watch, take the pounding, and hang on until it was over.

THE LOW-TIDE LIGHTBULB

In the early days we didn't surf at low tide; no one had booties to walk over the dry reef. We timed all our trips to coincide with the new and full moon tides. We would wait until there was enough water to paddle out and would have to come back in before the tide ran out too much. Of course we began to overstay our tide window, and eventually we discovered a soft, mostly sandy trail in over the reef. Here we could walk slowly without cutting up our feet after paddling in as far as we could on our boards turned upside down.

Tom Parrish came with us one time and liked the solitude of the low-tide lineup, when the rest of us were resting on the beach. The second day he came back cut to shreds by the reef. It took us hours to bandage all his wounds. No one went out at low tide again for the next several years.

Scott McClelland, a friend from Maui, and I were there by ourselves a few years later. He kept watching the waves at low tide. I hardly looked out there until there was enough water to paddle. But the waves, indifferent to the tides, peeled perfectly.

I was reading a book, not paying any attention, when finally he looked at me in exasperation and said, "You see how good those waves are, why the hell are we just sitting here?"

I looked up at the still dry reef and said, "Relax, the tide's still too low, just wait for the tide."

"What do you mean relax? The waves in Maui never get this good, I'm going out," said Scott. He put on his slippers, grabbed his board, and started walking out over the reef.

"What are you going to do with your slippers?" I yelled after him.

"Stick them in the back of my shorts," he yelled back, already well out on the reef.

"You'll lose them," I said.

"So what," was all I heard, and he was gone.

I couldn't concentrate on my book anymore. I got out the binoculars. Scott got to the edge of the reef, waited for a lull, and slipped out quicker than I'd ever seen it done. I watched him get tuberide after tuberide until I couldn't stand it anymore, got my slippers and surfboard, and followed him out.

I remember watching him ride a good-size wave not more than fifty feet from where I was standing on the edge of the reef. He gave me the sign as he went by, middle finger extended.

The whitewater from his wave dissipated to a trickle as it got to where I was standing. I jumped off the reef and paddled out without getting my hair wet. It was the easiest paddle out I ever had. We discovered that the waves were breaking in about the same depth of water that they broke at high tide. The lesser volume of water inside made the waves thinner, cleaner, and more defined—lining up was much easier.

All Scott kept saying was, "I told you it was good."

He was right. We both lost our slippers but found there were little cracks in the reef that we could ride up into with the whitewater. It was high and dry on both sides. As long as we stayed in the crack, we could stay afloat until the whitewater stopped. Then we could climb up on the reef well inside of where the waves were bashing. It was a startling discovery that refuted the low-tide myth. We were both shocked by the discovery. It was a slow walk on bare feet over the dry reef back to the beach but we didn't mind.

We further discovered a high-tide cache of rubber slippers back on the beach. The high tide had swirled in and deposited a pile of lost slippers above the high water line. They must have come all the way from the ferry town of Banyuwangi and the Bali Strait. Here was a treasure trove of slippers that we could pick from everyday to walk out over the reef, discard, and then paddle out to our new low-tide spot.

Later we would bring booties to walk out to the low-tide surf. Once in deep enough water to paddle, we took them off and shoved them down in our wetsuits or Speedos to surf in our bare feet. Coming in was just the reverse. We surfed up into one of the cracks, which were smooth from centuries of surf washing through them at low tide, put the booties back on, and walked in.

Over the years and countless sessions, we learned these small things that made it all a little easier. That is the thing I find so stimulating about surfing: that learning process never ends. Every time I go out, if I can stay open and aware, something I didn't know before or maybe I've forgotten reveals itself. Often these lessons can be applied to life in general. When the light goes on, these lessons can have a profound effect on one's life. This is the process of surf realization, and the more we are aware of it, the better our lives will be.

THE EDGE OF PANIC

The surf was up at G-Land and we had successfully negotiated the treacherous paddle out. We always started out up the beach to give ourselves plenty of room to be swept down in case we encountered a strong set due to poor timing. Once outside, we relaxed as the current drifted us into our lineup spot.

I caught a few waves at Moneytrees. On one particularly good one, I rode right through the Launch Pad and all the way to the end of Speedies. I paddled back out to the crowd that was waiting at the Pad and pulled up to see what the sets were like there. If Moneytrees is surfable, I usually assume that Speedies is not consistent or big enough. I have a hard time sitting down there, watching all those great waves break up the line at Moneytrees with nothing much coming down to Speedies.

It was no different this day. Beautiful waves were pouring in at Moneytrees, but by the time they got down to the Launching Pad they were less than half as big and pretty much dissipated. The real wave at the Launch Pad is an entirely different set than what comes in at Moneytrees. The Launch Pad sets swing far to the right and are often missed because everyone is watching up the line to the left. The wide arc of the set that peaks at the Launch Pad is what gives Speed Reef its formidable size and power.

I sat in the lineup talking to Betet, one of the great young surfers from Bali. He had come over with Rizal Tanjung, the first Balinese professional surfer, to visit and surf with us in the surf camp. Like the rest of the crowd, we too were looking left when all of a sudden there came a big set at the Pad. As soon as we saw it everyone started paddling like mad to escape, but too late. The wave broke in front of us and we had to duck-dive underneath it.

Betet with his small board got down deep, but with my bigger board, I couldn't penetrate enough. Underwater I felt the wave pulling me back in. I wasn't in any danger on this wave, but I lost ground as the surge got a grip on my legs. I surfaced twenty feet inside of Betet, but at a glance, I could see the next wave was smaller. I paddled furiously, got a good duck dive this time, and felt myself come cleanly through the other side. The sight that greeted me when I surfaced is one I don't want to see again.

Outside, I saw what had to be the biggest wave that had come through all day. I saw at a glance that I was caught. I was way too far inside to attempt to paddle out. I was dead center of the huge, wide Launch Pad peak; I was flanked on either side, so there was no escape around it. I quickly looked toward shore and saw that I was still in pretty deep water but was on the edge of where it starts to get shallow. Meanwhile, the wave was moving in, gathering steam as it came.

My mind was ticking like a time bomb as I ran through my options. I found no solace in any of them; there didn't appear to be any escape from this imminent pounding. Cold fear washed through me as I realized that I couldn't even abandon ship and dive underwater. It was just deep enough that this much whitewater was going to tumble me for a long distance down the point, into all the pain and suffering that lay that way.

For a moment I wondered where this wave could have come from. It was half again as big as any wave that had come through at Moneytrees, and twice as big as what had been hitting the Launch Pad. It was a rogue wave, a one of a kind. But as that thought crossed my mind, it dawned on me that it could be a rogue set with maybe more of the same behind it.

I groaned with helplessness. I had no options. I was in the worst place anyone could be. That thought made me weak. I was still sitting on my board, I hadn't moved since the first sight of this monster. And this monster was coming to chew me to pieces. I knew that even trying to paddle further in was only going to make it worse because it got shallower and the hungry reef got closer. I was frozen in place, not doing anything, just sitting there dead in the water.

My mind was on the edge of panic. I was seriously worried about surviving this mountain of water that was poised to slam into me. And the whole time the wave just marched in toward me. I didn't even see anyone else; it was just me and the wave. Closer and closer it came and I still didn't have a plan.

What do I do? What do I do? That question was echoing through my mind, but no answer came. I watched the wave break, exploding with a detonation that I felt deep down inside me. The whitewater was a boiling cauldron headed right at me. It was like the maelstrom of the ancient mariners, the whirlpool of death from which no one escapes.

The moment before impact, without any conscious thought, I turned my board toward shore, facing away from the monster wave. I sat there gripping the rails with my hands and legs, and waited for the impending collision. I took a deep breath, I think I even closed my eyes. Despite expecting the crash, I was shocked by the power. It was like being hit from behind by a train traveling at full speed.

The blast knocked me and my board up in the air and out ahead of the wave. My surfboard was immediately gone from under me, and I tumbled over and over. I realized that I wasn't getting ground into the bottom, and by the lack of pressure on my ears I could tell I was near the surface. Over, under, sideways, down I went until I felt the power easing up a little. I grabbed my leash and started climbing up it. My surfboard was afloat, and I pulled myself to the surface using it as a buoy. As I broke through, I quickly sucked in some air and looked behind to see what was next. As I feared, the wave behind was just as big and coming hard. I had time to climb on my board.

I thought that sitting on the board, facing shore, worked so well the first time, I would try it again. I turned away from the wave and hung on, but I felt better than I had with the first wave. The impact was as bad as the first time and the scenario was the same. I tumbled through space, climbed up the leash when it started to calm, and before I knew it, I was back up above the surface. I looked outside as I climbed on my surfboard and realized that I was far enough inside that I could safely duck-dive the next wave. I dove under the rest of the set and then I was down near the boat channel where I could easily paddle back out.

Once outside the surf, I stopped and started thinking about what had just happened. At first I started giggling and then I was laughing out loud. Other guys paddled by me; they must have thought I was crazy the way I was laughing to myself. They had no idea what I had just experienced.

As I thought about it, I understood how near the edge I had been. Total panic was just around the corner, but somehow I didn't go there. When there were no options available, when I absolutely didn't know what to do, I did what a total beginner would have done: I sat on my board and turned to face the shore. I kooked-out, but it certainly turned out to be the right thing to do.

It made me think that maybe sometimes we have to go back to the beginning to find the answers to the questions we have at the end. The answer may be so simple that it is easily overlooked. If one believes that the truth lies within, faith dictates that it will reveal itself when it is most needed. It's there, so keep paddling where it leads.

The Mother

of All

Pipeline Swells

I was awake for an hour when the phone call came, but Darrick's words made me think I was still asleep and dreaming: "Surf is up, brudda. You need to be here."

This from the most reliable wave-caller I know. I was awake enough to know that it was September 2. My mind tiptoed around the sound of that message at this time of year. "Where are you?" I asked.

I was looking out the window of my home in Olinda. I had a sweeping view of the north coast of Maui. I couldn't see any whitewater. Maybe Darrick was on the South Shore.

"I'm right in front of my house and the sets are already ten feet," he replied calmly. Darrick is always calm with anything surf related.

Darrick lived on the point at Sunset Beach. My brain stirred toward clarity. Still, looking down the hill, the north shore of Maui was devoid of any surf at all. I lurched back toward confusion: Is he seeing things, or am I? The coast looked just like it always looks during the summer: flat.

"Brudda, this is a serious swell, straight out of the west with a twenty-six-second interval and lots of waves in the sets; it has Pipe written all over it," he continued.

That explained why nothing was showing on Maui's north shore. A straight west swell is blocked by Moloka'i and West Maui. An interval of twenty-six seconds between waves, however, is significant, and rare.

The earth's atmosphere has regions of high and low pressure. Typically an area of low pressure, a weather disturbance, will slide off of the coast of Siberia and head eastward into the North Pacific Ocean. Wind from the high-pressure areas surrounding it flow into this depression. As the wind blows over the surface of the ocean, it creates ripples. The ripples allow the wind to get a better grip on the surface, making bigger

The outside Second Reef at the Pipeline
showing signs of life. Photo: Jeff Divine

209

ripples. If the wind continues to blow, the ripples grow into small waves or wind chop. If the wind increases, it drives the chop ahead of it and piles the chop on top of itself. In this manner wave trains are formed, grow, and acquire a direction of travel. If the wind continues to blow, eventually they form huge waves. The waves are a result of a transfer of energy by the wind from the air to the water.

The distance between waves, known as the wave interval or period, is determined by the amount of energy transferred from the wind to the ocean. It is an important factor in determining the strength and size of the waves when they reach shore. The wave period is also a determining factor in the wave speed. A long interval indicates a lot of energy, and these swells are able to travel long distances before their energy dissipates.

These weather disturbances are constantly photographed by satellites and tracked by meteorologists who monitor them. As the storm tracks eastward across the Pacific, it enters an area where the winds are aimed directly at the Hawaiian Islands.

As swells pass under the National Oceanic and Atmospheric buoys anchored in an arc several hundred miles from Hawai'i, the buoys record their passage as well as their height and wave period. Buoy reports are broadcast on weather band channels mainly to keep ships and boats apprised of current weather conditions for ocean safety. Although reports of rising swell activity are at minimum an inconvenience for ship captains, for surfers listening, both heights and wide intervals are welcome news.

An interval of sixteen to seventeen seconds indicates a swell of significance, regardless of the swell height. Surfers know this is a ground swell with wave energy deep in the water; the waves will be big when they break. Conversely, the energy of a wind swell runs mainly on the surface. The storm generating the swell is much closer; there is less energy in the swell to travel any distance before it dies out. The wave period of a wind swell is shorter and the wave power is not as strong as that of waves coming from ground swells. A buoy report of a twenty-six-second interval comes as a shock to most surfers, especially the ones who pay attention.

This report spurred me to action. I phoned my brother, Victor, to give him the surf report. We decided to get over to O'ahu as soon as possible. We were in a frenzy from that moment forward, but we had a clear goal in mind. We both had visions of solid North Shore waves after a long summer of dinky surf.

By 10:00 a.m. we were ready to drive to the airport. We lived high up on the side of Haleakala and it took a while to get to the bottom of the hill. We picked up Junior on the way to the airport. Victor and I have known Chris 'Junior' Vandervoort since he was an infant. He grew up into a fine young man and a great surfing partner in our surf adventures around the Valley Isle. Of all the surfers on Maui that day, possibly only Junior, Victor, and I knew there was some serious surf to be had on O'ahu, a short hop away.

We arrived at Kahului Airport, unloaded Chris's and Victor's boards, parked the car, and checked in for the flight. My boards were on Oahu where I had left them at the end of last winter's surf season. Here it was early fall, just out of summer, and the excitement of winter surf was on us once again.

Flying out over the reefs off Kanaha Beach, we remained surprised by how few waves were showing there. We knew that a westerly swell wouldn't show on this part of

Maui's north shore, but that only heightened our excitement. A swell from 270 to 280 degrees is one of the best directions for Hale'iwa, Sunset, and the Pipeline. There would not be even a ripple at Kanaha, and the sets could still be ten feet at Sunset.

We could hardly sit still for the twenty-minute flight to Honolulu. We became even more antsy when we saw faint corduroy lines of swell marching down the Moloka'i Channel heading straight east. At last the jet lined up for the approach into Honolulu airport, and we had to settle back into our seats for the landing.

We collected our baggage, got a rental car, loaded up, and headed for the North Shore. Once clear of Pearl City, the roads were less congested and we pushed the speed up as high as we dared. We didn't want a policeman to pull us over for speeding, but we wanted to get there fast. We passed through Wahiawa and climbed the last grade at Helemano, then the road headed back downhill through the pineapple fields.

From that vantage point we could see the North Shore; there was the whitewater, and like in the dead of winter, we got that funny feeling in the pits of our stomachs. Avalanche, outside Hale'iwa, was breaking and the wind looked perfect out of the east. We were stoked. Up until that moment we had been going on the eyes and word of another person and traces of what we wanted to believe. This was different. We saw for ourselves that there was indeed surf of substance and we were going to get some of it.

We headed straight for the Pipe house, barely able to contain our excitement. The drive was unusual. Normally on a swell like this the road would be teeming with cars all carrying surfboards stacked on top. The highway was empty, so I supposed the surfers just hadn't heard about the swell yet.

We parked and ran to the front gate. It was strange: The right-of-way was empty and the house looked deserted. I unlocked the front door and went through to open the sliding door on the beach side. I guess I expected the yard and bench to be full of surfers like any normal Pipe day, so I was surprised to find Sato-san and Garrett McNamara the only ones there. Looking out toward the lineup I saw only one guy out. Maybe the waves were no good.

"How is it?" I asked them.

"Pretty good," answered Sato-san.

"How come no one's out there?" I asked.

"Only Liam could get out," Sato replied. "Too many sets."

Then I noticed all the guys with their boards at the water's edge waiting for a lull to paddle out. Twenty guys were poised to move at the first sign of a break in the relentless sets. I quickly changed into my surf trunks, grabbed my board, and headed out the gate.

From the top of the right-of-way, aided by that little bit of elevation, I saw what looked like a lull in the sets and ran down the beach. As I jumped in the water I figured everyone else had seen the same lull coming as they all dove in as well. Some of the surfers were launching way up the beach from in front of Off the Wall.

I noticed that the beach was gone. The big, wide summertime beach that piles up in front of the Pipeline had already been eroded away by this swell. Ordinarily during the first swells of winter the beach is huge. This causes a backwash problem in the lineup

of Pipe. Each winter it takes several big swells to wash out the sand. But this swell had likely started sometime late the night before, and in about ten to twelve hours already had moved many thousands of yards of sand. That, combined with the reported twenty-six-second interval, meant that this was a particularly powerful swell.

The paddle out at the Pipe on a ten-foot day is a combination of timing, paddling power, and a lot of luck. The surfer waits on the shore anticipating a lull, jumps into the rip running down the beach like river rapids and tries to breach the shorebreak before the next set comes. The rip takes him down the beach toward Sunset. If he can't slip through the little channel between Pipe and 'Ehukai, there's little likelihood he'll make it out into the lineup.

At the moment I hit the water there were two dozen surfers paddling furiously to penetrate the shorebreak. A successful technique requires the surfer to paddle up to the oncoming whitewater and duck-dive underneath it without losing forward momentum. Emerging beyond the wall of foam, he starts paddling madly again as the suction tries to drag him backward. One trick is to get a good jump when entering the water by running fast down the beach and launching as far out as possible. Another trick is to make balanced, clean duck dives.

Everyone was paddling as hard as they possibly could, ducking under wave after wave and paddling some more. I must have gone under at least a dozen waves. I

Top   Photo: Jeff Divine

Bottom   Looking for a break in the sets to time a successful paddle out is never an easy task. Photo: Jeff Hornbaker

should have been somewhere in that lull I thought I had seen. Instead, the whitewater coming in didn't seem to be letting up. I was hoping for a break, just one smaller wave that didn't break so I could go over the top and gain some ground. That's the purpose of timing the lull just right, to pass through the shallow inside shorebreak when the waves are at their least frequent.

After more than a dozen waves without any lapse, I stole a glance back in to get my bearings. I was completely shocked to find myself only ten feet from shore. Added to that, the rip had taken me all the way down past the lifeguard tower at 'Ehukai. I hadn't penetrated an inch in that sideways sweep beyond what I acquired from my initial launch jump off the beach. All that paddling had gained me precisely nothing. When I saw that I was almost down to Pupukea, I knew I had no realistic choice other than to turn around and go in to the beach.

On the beach strung out ahead of me I saw all the other surfers who had tried to paddle out. No one had made it. I saw 'Adam 12' and joined him. We started the long walk back to the Pipeline, where we would try to paddle out again. He said this was his fourth attempt and if he didn't make it this next time he was giving up; the long walk in the soft sand was wearing him out. He told me some other guys had been trying to get out for more than an hour and hadn't been able to.

Liam, Adam 12 said, had made it out during the only lull in the last two hours and was still the only guy out. Just as we were in front of the beach park, I thought I saw a lull in the sets and told Adam that I was going to try again from right there. He looked at me like I was nuts; no one paddled out to Pipe on a big day from there.

I dove in and started paddling hard. I got a break and managed to penetrate somewhat. Finally, I made it. I was all the way down past Pupukea at Gas Chambers, but I was outside the surfline. I began the long paddle back to the Pipe watching the tubes that lured me onward.

When at last I reached the lineup I paddled over and sat next to Liam. "Where is everyone?" he asked.

"No one can make it out; they can't get through the shorebreak," I told him. "I just barely did and had to paddle up from Gas Chambers. So don't go in 'cuz you'll never get back out."

"OK," said Liam. "There's way more good waves out here than you and I could ever ride, so we might as well stay out till dark."

A set was stacking up on the horizon, so we both paddled for position. I got into the right spot and started paddling for the first good one I saw. It was a good ten- to twelve-foot wave and looked clean. I stroked hard to catch it. It jacked up like only the Pipeline can, and I found myself in a bad place, hung up on the lip and not penetrating down the face. I slammed on the brakes, sat up, and back paddled to stop myself. I only just managed to keep from getting sucked over as the lip pitched and threw out.

I turned around, saw what was behind me and nearly panicked. Another ten- to twelve-foot wave was bearing down on me. I paddled like crazy, hoping I wasn't going to be too late. A sense of dread engulfed me; I could think of nothing worse than being caught inside at the Pipe with a big swell like this. I stroked up to the base of the approaching wave and very carefully made as perfect a duck dive as I could, concentrating completely on sinking the board on a level plane. I knew one slip would end in disaster.

Duck-diving through the Pipe wave is a lesson in the necessity of perfection. The base of the wave is so thick and powerful that any small flaw in penetration leads quickly back into the roaring pit. The sheer terror of those few moments when one is pulled back against all hope is the worst thing I've felt. I had been there too many times. I didn't want to ever be near that place again. Thankfully, my duck dive was clean.

I surfaced on the other side only to be confronted by another wave of equal size and bearing down on me in the same remorseless way. I had the advantage of being slightly farther outside, but I was still not in a safe place. I paddled for my life again. The duck dive pulled me through once again, but there was still another wave behind coming at me. I managed to paddle over the top of this one, but I was shaky and out of breath. Cresting that wave, I could see not only one more wave as big and perfect as the others that preceded it but also, to my astonishment, what seemed like an infinite number stacked up behind that one.

My confidence began to come back as I paddled over the next two waves and looked for a good position to attempt to catch one of these beautiful waves. I saw my wave, took a deep breath, spun around, and started to stroke hard to make the takeoff. It was a repeat of the first try. I couldn't penetrate the lip and had to slam on the brakes again, pulling back at the very last moment.

Knowing what was behind, I didn't hesitate. I put my head down and paddled as hard as I could. It was an instant replay, exactly the same scenario I had just endured. Again I experienced the terror of almost getting sucked back as I dove through the next few waves, then the increasing relief as I gained ground and could paddle over the top of the waves behind.

Then spotting my wave and seeing I was in position, I spun around and was determined to catch it. Once more I found myself hung in the lip and not getting into that wave either. Again I had to paddle like mad, duck-dive through several waves, get back outside only to find yet more waves coming.

Twenty to twenty-five waves had already passed me. I couldn't remember experiencing a set like this at the Pipe before. I saw yet another perfect wave coming and was absolutely determined to catch it. I paddled early and finally felt myself slipping into the wave. What a feeling of relief that brought. The accumulated fear from all those previous desperate moments had stacked up to take away my sense of identity. I began to come back into myself.

I stood up into my usual takeoff crouch and took the drop. It was the typical Pipe drop, late and thrilling. I carried my speed into the turn at the bottom, cutting the corner as the lip came down. I pulled up into the spinning barrel. All that effort to get there from Maui, the struggle to paddle out, the frustration mixed with terror of missing those first waves and having to escape the others behind, all of it paid off in that instant of slotting myself into the tunnel.

In that moment I had entered another realm. The roaring sounds of the wave crashing were suddenly silent. My fears and worries slipped away like droplets sheering off of glass. My sense of awareness became so acute in that nearly frozen timelessness I could see individual drops of water falling from the ceiling above. I was at one with the universe. A smile spread across my face as the wave shot me out of the barrel in a mist of spray that tickled and stung my face and back.

Paddling back out to the lineup I was amazed that the set was still going. I stroked hard thinking maybe I could get out there in time to catch another wave. Instead, after what must have been more than thirty waves, the set finally took a break. I paddled out to Liam and asked him if all the sets were like that. He answered that they were. We agreed that this was as pumping a swell as we had ever seen at the Pipeline. We were happy. We knew we were blessed to be sharing something special together.

It was a long lull, and we soon saw a few guys finally make it out. They were a little shell-shocked from the pounding they had taken just trying to paddle out. Some commented that they were already worn out before they had even caught any waves. It made me wonder which situation makes a surfer more fatigued, when he is catching the waves or when the waves are catching him.

We all surfed until it was too dark to see, not knowing if the swell would still be there in the morning. We wanted to make sure we got enough today in case it was gone tomorrow.

When at last I went in and walked up to the house in the twilight, I could still hear the waves booming behind me and feel their impact through the sand under my feet. I found my brother and Chris back from a great session at Sunset with Dennis Pang. They had found nonstop sets there as well and had surfed their fill. I don't even remember dinner, just a sleep that night filled with visions of endless sets stacked up to the horizon.

The next morning was, if anything, bigger than the day before, and the sets had as many waves as the previous day. On the first day the sets were pounding into First Reef, on the second day the sets had grown bigger and the outside waves were stacking on Second Reef Pipe. A takeoff at Second Reef could set up a surfer for a nice run through the inside First Reef. Coming into the regular takeoff section from outside and behind running at full speed is the ideal situation to ride Pipe. The outside takeoff shifts around and is hard to line up; the drop is also bigger and longer but not as critical, so there is time to find the ideal position at full speed.

The problem at big Pipeline is that a surfer sitting on the First Reef will discover that the bigger sets will flank any takeoff position. These sets then generate a current into the pit that makes sitting near the shoulder almost impossible. The only forgiving factor is that the Second Reef waves are, relatively speaking, a little mushy on the outside. There is a chance of diving underneath them without worry about the shallow reef.

The surfer who gets caught outside and dragged back into the First Reef is in the worst place possible at the Pipeline. With ten- to twelve-foot sucking barrels pitching out as far as they are tall and not a lot of water between the surfer and the reef, the only recourse is to throw oneself on the mercy of sea. At this point the choices are limited. Arms wrapped around the head offer some feeble protection. Eyes open or closed makes little difference. The surfer is virtually powerless to do much more than curl up in a ball and hope not to hit the bottom headfirst. This is not a situation to take lightly. The chilling specter of death haunts the Pipeline reef. More surfers have been killed there than at any other surf spot.

During Darrick's epic west swell, Max Medeiros and I got caught way too deep and too far inside on one set. We had no choice but to try to paddle around the left side of the Second Reef peak. We made it under the first few waves. Then we came up on the other side of a wave and found the next one had already broken outside of us. I didn't even try to duck-dive under the mountain of soup coming at us. I just jumped off the side. Max tried a duck dive, and when I came up he was gone, whisked away by the powerful whitewater.

I was helpless, dead in the water with my leash stretched to its maximum. I dove down when the whitewater of the next wave approached and tried to let myself be pulled by the leash. If I had tried to anchor myself, I would have found myself stuck on the bottom, held there by the tension on the leash while my surfboard was pulled by a wave on the surface.

Each wave was carrying me further in and away from the safety of the deeper water on the Second Reef. My leash looked like a spaghetti noodle, stretched so far I couldn't even see my board when the wave was already thirty feet past me. Each time I went under, I could see I was being drawn further inside.

I was running out of breath after going under so many waves. The thought of being sucked into the inside reef was something I didn't even want to consider. I was running out of options.

Finally I came up from one wave and was surprised to find there wasn't another mountain of whitewater bearing down on me. As tired as I was, I got my board back under me and started paddling hard back out. I duck-dived under the next wave and a few more after it. At last I found myself far enough outside and in the channel where I could stop for a moment and catch my breath.

I looked around and saw that the set had wreaked carnage on the lineup. Most of the pack was gone, washed away and inside. A few of the guys who had been sitting far enough on the shoulder had managed to escape around the side of the set and were laying on their boards as I was, gasping for air.

When Max eventually paddled back out, I asked him what had happened. He just shook his head and said, "Oh man, that wave just dragged me almost to the beach before it let me go. Eh bra, I thought I was going to drown."

Again we surfed almost until sunset, but this time I made the right choice and went in before it got too dark. There is a danger in waiting too late to go in on west-facing shores, especially when the waves are big. Looking out to sea for the last wave, one faces where the light is brightest. There is still some light after the sun sinks below the horizon. Visibility is worsened when one turns back toward shore and faces into the darkest part of what little light is left. I have paddled right over the falls in such situations. With the waves at serious size, that is not a wise move.

Victor and Chris had gone out and surfed at Makaha with Dennis Pang that second day. Sunset Beach was closing out on the big sets. The west direction of the swell was a good angle for Makaha. They had a great time with epic West Side waves.

The next morning the swell was still holding at full strength. There may have been a bit fewer waves per set but only by a little. The size was still the same. Where the first day the wave size had been a conservative ten to twelve feet, the second and third days were easily ten to fifteen feet. Likely some waves were bigger. That is big Pipeline by anyone's standards.

It was the strongest west swell I ever witnessed at the Pipe. I had seen some bigger and some better shaped, and some that lasted longer, but never in my memory was there a swell with so many waves per set. The wave interval on the buoy reports held at over twenty seconds for all three days.

This was a result of a very large fetch a long distance away, and nothing between the storm center and the Hawaiian Islands to confuse the swell train. With the direction and size, it was too big for Sunset and almost too big for Hale'iwa, although I heard there were some good waves there.

It was a perfect swell at the Pipe. All the local Pipe guys were there: Max, Derek and Michael Ho, 'Johnny Boy' Gomes, 'Larry Boy' Rios, Liam, Tony Moniz, everyone, the North Shore guys, the West Side guys, the Town guys, the East Side guys, you name 'em, they were there. None of the out-of-town people were in the Country yet. It was a local-boys-only swell.

This was the Mother-of-All-Pipeline swells. I was glad to have been there from beginning to end.

A Good

Day

to Die

I like big waves. I was called to them not out of machismo but instead from practical necessity. As soon as the surf rises above what in Hawai'i we call ten feet, the crowds jockeying around in the water decrease by 90 percent.

My brother Victor, a couple of friends, and I pioneered quite a few outer reef-breaks on Maui during the 1970s. Those occasions when the surf was up with the right wind conditions were memorable. But there was a price to pay. There usually is in big surf. Positioning is difficult, especially at outer-reef spots with vague lineups and few other surfers to mark a starting place. During most ten- to twelve-foot swells, occasional sets in the fifteen-foot-plus range appeared suddenly and forced us to dive for the bottom. At twelve to fifteen feet, the twenty-foot sneaker set could have serious consequences.

The few waves ridden were always great, but too many got away, and there were plenty that required immediate payment of big-water dues. With Mother Nature firmly in charge, we learned to expect these situations. Some days were better than others, and everyone hoped it wasn't his turn to be the unlucky guy.

The best return for a full day of traversing a vast blue-water arena might be six or eight successful waves. I went to sleep those nights with brief recollections of a nice drop or a good section. Still, my mental playback could not exclude the waves that had marched through our picket line that day unridden, the wonders we never knew. Big waves are the most frustrating and elusive part of the entire surfing experience. The effort is daunting because the waves are there to see in all their grandeur, but paddling into them requires as much luck as skill.

Assisted takeoffs have been part of surfing since Hawaiian chiefs used their outrigger canoes to help them into waves moving too fast to catch on a board. Standing on the outrigger while his strongest paddlers stroked their mightiest, a chief used this momentum to launch into the wave. In the 1970s Jeff Johnson attempted to tow Flippy Hoffman into a wave at Ka'ena Point with a boat. In 1987 Herbie Fletcher used his first-generation Kawasaki Jet Ski to tow Martin Potter into a nice Second Reef wave at outside Pipeline. Those early attempts did little to encourage further pursuit into the realm of assisted takeoffs. Big-wave riding remained as it always had been: a lot of effort for a limited return.

A corner was rounded when in 1992 Laird Hamilton, Buzzy Kerbox, and Darrick Doerner found some small success with a Zodiac inflatable at Himalayas. All three surfers were driven to expand their experiences of big-wave surfing. There were too many guys in the lineups, on boards growing longer and less performance-oriented, to compensate for the crowded takeoff zones. That first foray at Himalayas revealed to Laird an epiphany. The prevailing big-guns-for-big-waves theory was more about paddling to catch the wave than about riding it.

Laird responded. For his next time out with the Zodiac, he fastened some windsurfing foot straps on his 7'2", a board believed by the experts of the big-wave surfing world to be much too short for the waves he wanted to ride. Laird zipped into a big wave at Outside Backyards with his feet in the straps. On that first wave he knew that his experiment worked. The shorter board was faster, more maneuverable, and much easier to control than a big gun. But Laird was a solo spontaneous mind against the long years and strong currents of the slowly evolving theory of big-wave surfing.

Laird enlisted my help, and on our first attempt to build a tow-in specific board, we agreed that 7'10" was short enough for the waves he had in mind. By then much more had evolved in this new surfing direction. A surf spot at Pe'ahi Bay on the north shore of Maui, aptly named Jaws, had a perfect setup for towing into waves that appeared to be substantially larger than Waimea Bay or any of the other existing big-wave locations.

Yamaha WaveRunner jet skis were substituted for the trusty old Zodiac. The skis were fast and proved to be much more efficient. The skills and teamwork required to attempt Pe'ahi developed quickly and improved at a rapid pace. The reaction from the rest of the surfing world, however, ranged from cold to hostile. Big-wave purists scoffed, expressing disdain for the notion of riding a wave without paddling into it under the surfer's own power. They said it wasn't real surfing.

I saw what Laird and his close-knit crew were doing, and it looked like surfing to me. Lack of interest afforded Laird and his group the advantage of empty lineups in which to try new techniques, sharpen skills, and build on their strengths. By the time anyone else recognized the merits of the program, Laird and team had already refined their expertise.

Immediately, the specialized tow-in boards were a vast improvement over conventional boards adapted for the new environment. I was stoked to be working directly with Laird during a quantum leap in surfboard design. Narrow outlines made the tow-in boards much faster. Laird swept across the faces of gigantic waves at breathtaking speed. The speed alone took surfing to a different place.

For decades surfboards had been built as light as possible to enhance performance. Tow-in boards had to be different. They needed to be stronger because with foot straps they were more like a windsurf board than a regular surfboard; they could be jumped. Landing jumps on a lightly glassed board usually resulted in two pieces. That only had to happen a few times before we beefed up the glass jobs.

The need for more weight in the boards also became clear when lightweight boards skittered out of control, falling down the faces of huge, very bumpy waves. Heavier boards cut better through the chop and had more momentum. Tow-in boards and Ferraris don't feel heavy when they're moving: like a race car designed to hug the ground while speeding above it, a tow-in board is designed to slice with control into a wave face that is never as smooth as it appears. Tow-in boards opened the door to bigger waves than anyone ever before had ridden.

All of the members of Laird's crew were expert windsurfers. Laird, Buzzy, and Darrick were also very experienced big-wave surfers. The others—including Dave Kalama, Mike Waltze, Pete Cabrinha, Mark Angulo, Rush Randle, and Brett Lickle—were not. Wiping out or being caught inside by huge surf is always terrifying, but the jet ski proved to be a reliable rescue tool that became increasingly more efficient as the crew learned how to master it in big waves. Being in the big surf began to be less scary.

A windsurfer myself, I had discovered something extraordinary while wave sailing. A windsurfer was able to ride a much bigger wave than a surfer, simply because

the windsurfer could catch that wave before the surfer could even try. Laird's group had been the first to pioneer the break at Jaws on their windsurf boards. Through windsurfing, all of them had experienced riding into waves from far outside where the waves were actually breaking. This was a crucial skill.

Most surfers seldom had ventured beyond the lineups. Apart from diving and spearfishing, there had been no reason to go. A surfboard couldn't catch the waves except during a short moment before they actually broke. The appearance of a wave well outside the takeoff zone is much different from the steep crest where paddle-in surfers catch them. If the ocean is deep where the wave of energy passes, it may be difficult to discern on the surface. Coming toward shore through deep water at Pe'ahi, a wave just doesn't look like much before it gets into the area where it is ready to break. The ability to differentiate between one wave and another out beyond the break takes a lot of practice, and this skill was an advantage that windsurfers had over surfers.

At first I thought these guys were nuts. As I watched them get better, however, they made it look easy. Almost effortlessly, each one of them could select the wave of his choice in any set, ride into it at speed already standing up, and maneuver into any position on that wave that he wanted. They became so good that every one of them was capable of riding several waves in a set without getting his hair wet.

I was sold. I suffered no purist reservations about this not being surfing. I wanted to get in on the action and ride waves. The end of winter and the big surf didn't preclude Laird and company from continuing to learn what jet skis could do. They took me out to Mud Flats on the south shore and taught me the quick water-start, as well as how to drive the ski to do the pickup. I paid close attention, knowing I would be in a

Coming into the wave from the shoulder gives a false
sense of security at Pe'ahi; the wave quickly becomes
a fire-breathing dragon, and the only real safe place is
sitting in the channel. Photo: Sylvain Cazenave

desperate situation at some point, down in the water, waiting for my partner to bring me the towrope for one quick chance to get up and get away from the next impending huge wave. Tow-in surfing was a partnership, a two-man team. The two took turns, with one guy driving while the other surfed.

My first few times towing were in relatively small waves of little consequence. I needed those training runs. A quick pickup is not as simple as Laird made it look, nor was it as easy in breaking waves as it had been in flat water. There were a number of fumbled attempts that could have been disastrous had the surf been serious. Also, the tow-in boards were not as easy to ride as they appeared under experienced tow-in surfers.

The high speed off the towrope required me to adjust. I outran almost every wave I caught during my training sessions, ending up too far on the shoulder, where I lost speed and bogged down. Again, that would have been bad in big surf. The foot straps were difficult to use on a surfboard where a surfer is accustomed to shifting his feet around constantly. My years of windsurfing again proved invaluable, and I soon figured out how to surf strapped into one position. To windsurf without foot straps imposed limitations on speed, jumps, and other maneuvers. As I gained more experience, tow-in surfing proved to be the same. The tow-in board straps offered the same advantage as they did on sailboards. I kept practicing, thinking about how it would be when I got out into the big waves, concentrating on things I knew I needed to improve.

I went out in some medium surf in the ten- to twelve-foot range at a spot I knew well. Immediately I marveled at the ease of wave selection, takeoff positioning, riding a shorter board, going much faster, and especially the quantity of waves taken in a short period of time. At once I understood that this was a very efficient way to ride big waves. The tables were turned—it was a huge return for little effort. I was convinced that big-wave riding would never be the same.

One evening I flew into Maui from my home in Central Oregon knowing a big swell with prime offshore Kona wind conditions was imminent. I woke the next morning to a sight most surfers love, corduroy lines stretching out to the horizon. The crew gathered at Maliko Gulch to launch from the small boat ramp there. I had made Laird a new 7'4" tow-in board and myself a scaled-down version in the same length.

The banter among the boys was light and carefree, but while watching the set waves pour into the narrow bay I began to experience the first stages of anxiety. The sets were bigger than any I had seen there before. The biggest sets broke across the entire mouth of the bay, sending whitewater far up onto the normally dry ground of the parking area. Launching the skis was tricky, impossible from the boat ramp, which was being pounded by breaking waves. We dropped the skis off the trucks and trailers onto what normally was high ground to wait for a big surge of whitewater to float them away seaward.

Eventually we got the trucks secured far from the surge inundating the shore. We loaded boards and people onto the skis and began the twenty-minute journey up to Pe'ahi Bay. The surf was huge and unruly near the shoreline, the sound thunderous and the 'ehukai hung like a fog in the still morning air. We motored well out to sea to avoid any of the sets that were breaking farther out than we had thought possible. I was very familiar with this area, having fished and dove there during the summers. It seemed crazy that waves were breaking where I knew the water to be impossibly deep. Yet swells marched in, steepened, and crashed over in the blue water.

Laird appeared indomitable, a mountain of muscle and strength. I could sense this was exactly the kind of day he waited for his whole life. Dave Kalama was stoic, secure in his own strength, skills, and experience, calmly following Laird's lead. The others, Waltze, Angulo, Rush, Brett, and Pete exhibited little outward apprehension and looked well composed in spite of the enormity of the surf. The fact that we were headed for a place where we would be entirely at the mercy of the waves with no one but ourselves and these often temperamental two-stroke machines didn't seem to faze them.

On the other hand, I was almost soiling myself. I couldn't remember ever feeling so anxiety-ridden. I tried to break it down in my mind. What was I afraid of? I hadn't been out to Jaws before, but I had plenty of experience first-timing waves this big at other new spots. Why was I feeling so uptight?

In most situations, a surfer checks the surf before he goes out. From shore he makes a conscious decision to go or not. Even if he is unsure but game, his normal routine follows a pattern that offers the surfer a number of fall-back options. If the surf is too much for his ability, there is a good chance he won't be able to penetrate the shorebreak and will be driven back to the beach where he belongs. Should he somehow manage to make it out to the break, there is always the channel where the closer vantage can help him make the decision to engage or retreat. After that it is still possible to take a small bite by staying out on the shoulder, catching the edge of the wave, relatively safe from the dangers of the main peak.

Thinking about this, I began to understand my anxiety. Tow-in surfing leads straight into the power of the wave, launching into the swell even before the peak forms. There are no little bites, no half-hearted approaches from the shoulder. When the surfer releases off the towrope, he gets the whole wave. I knew from my early training runs that too far out in front was very far from safe. There is a zone in or directly in front of the curl to safely ride a wave. Too far back is disaster but too far ahead can be bad as well. Losing speed risked allowing the curl behind to catch the rider before he regains speed to get away. Even worse would be to lose the wave in the impact zone and have to deal with the wave behind, fumbling around a quick pick-up attempt with a surprised jet ski driver who had expected his rider to take the wave until it ended. Thinking about what can happen during the worst situation in big surf is a deep, dark alley.

I looked around me; it was a magnificent day for surf—a magnificent day for anything. The sky was clear blue and cloudless. Apart from the latent energy of this huge swell running through the ocean's surface, it was smooth and calm, a result of the still wind conditions. The forecast was for early light and variable winds turning to Kona, ideal for this entire stretch of coastline. Glancing at the other skis and their riders, I had a sense we were all on a great mission, even though it was one entirely of our own choosing. I remembered a line from an old favorite movie *Little Big Man*. A sigh escaped me as I said the line out loud: "What the hell, I guess this is as good a day as any to die." And somehow, I understood its absolute reality in that moment.

I must have meant it because suddenly all apprehensiveness, anxiety, and fear left me as though they had been washed away. I had a little chuckle to myself and realized I was ready for whatever.

We always joked about our reason for chasing big surf: We ride to succeed or to die. Other than the acknowledgement of each for the other, the only thing to get was some small personal glory. There is no tangible reward from surfing, no antlers to take home and hang on the wall. Eventually even the memories fade. And we risk our lives for this? Well, none of us wanted to die, and except for Laird, we never really went that close to the edge anyway. From an outside perspective, death was a possibility, but from our perspective it was actually pretty damn safe. Statistically, we would be much more at risk in a car on a Maui road.

I had been watching the break at Jaws since a day in the late 1960s when a friend took me out there to see a wave he called the 'Atom Blaster.' From high on the hill above, the empty waves look much smaller than they actually are. An unusual optical illusion forms to diminish the appearance of waves breaking when seeing them from up above. And without surfers in the water to provide scale, the illusion is even greater. At first glance, the waves looked very surfable.

During the 1970s I relocated from O'ahu to Upcountry Maui. I made an effort to regularly check out the wave at Jaws on big west swell days with Kona winds. Several times on exceptionally clean days, Victor and I tried to get up the nerve to paddle out there. After climbing down the steep trail to the rocky shore below, however, we changed our minds. From the rocks near sea level the place was utterly forbidding.

At sea level the waves revealed their true heights. A clean peak broke well outside, peeling left in a long wall while hooking hard right into a vicious bowl. That bowl is what we called the Atom Blaster. At what we conservatively estimated to be fifteen to twenty feet, it went thickly cylindrical with immense force. The blasts of spit out of those cartoonish barrels hung in the air for minutes afterward. We heard and felt the compression even up on the cliff where we watched in open-mouthed awe.

The magnitude of force didn't abate even after the wave had passed. The immediate aftermath was a cauldron of freakish whitewater boils as high as four feet, an impossible place to swim or stay afloat. The broken waves appeared to flatten in deep water again, leaving an indistinct surf-free zone before they reformed into a slamming shore pound. But even this moment of relative calm was unreliable because sometimes a bigger wave would push the churning whitewater right through without stopping.

The shorebreak was horrendous. The average wave was six to ten feet high but easily four times that thick. One after another they exploded onto the shore of huge boulders and slippery rocks that were rolled and tossed around like so many pebbles by the heavily surging shore pound.

We figured we might get lucky and ride a surge out safely—maybe. But getting up the beach would be a nightmarish gamble at best. The rocky shore was steep; a mistimed approach would likely result in the unlucky person being sucked down into a hole between the boulders. The slippery, rolling rocks were big enough to break any leg. Then, there would be the next wave pushing in to pound and pulverize.

Every time we climbed back up the cliff trail, all of our brave talk was silenced; we felt beaten, our tails tight between our legs. But fear never stopped us from watching, and letting our imaginations soar.

What had seemed impossible to Victor and me during those years before tow-in boards and jet skis not only was possible, but Laird and his crew had done it. And now my day had come, it was my turn.

As we sped along over the rolling swells, the ride up the coast took us past the lighthouse at Kuiaha Bay where, on a small north swell, a great surf spot lies hidden. But on this day, the waves broke far outside the narrow entrance, cascading up and almost covering the lighthouse tower, turning the little bay into a torrential washing machine.

We passed angry waves erupting in water I knew to be fifty feet deep with no bottom contours to promote such a thing; they were driven only by the size, power, and speed of this incredible swell. Just before Pe'ahi, Laird pointed out a left he said he was watching as another potential surf spot. One look was all it took to know I wouldn't be joining him; the wave looked deadly, breaking with full power into the rugged rocky shoreline.

A short way past that spooky left we motored into the deep channel that allows Jaws to be the ideal tow-in surf spot that it is. Shutting down the skis in the safety of the blue water, we sat ringside a short distance from the gargantuan end bowl section. One set was all the crew needed to see. They began loosening the tow-in boards and talking about who would ride first.

I had watched many times from the cliff above or the inside shore, but this was my first opportunity to be so close and still be a passive spectator in safe waters. I was content to sit out the first session and take some notes from the channel. Both the waves and skill of the tow teams were impressive. Up close the guys still made it look easy, but I could see that the wave faces were not as smooth as the placid surface conditions suggested.

The power of this northwest swell was very evident to me. I understood how it hooked first on the tip of West Maui at Kahakuloa, refracting off in a slightly different direction. Imagine swinging a wad of chewing gum. The hand holding it would be the tip of Maui, the long skinny string would be the refracted swell, and the thick gob at the end would be the wave at Pe'ahi. As a function of the refraction process, all the power of the swell slid down the line to amass precisely on the lineup at Jaws. As big as the waves had seemed on the ride up the coast, they were more than double that size here at the end.

The smooth waves I had watched for so many years from the shore reverberated through the channel like steady, continuous thunder. At close hand, the appearance of blandness without obstructions dissolved like a vapor. Power and violence surged beneath the surface. Although difficult to see, the potent energy was impossible to contain, creating wave faces bursting with subtle impediments. The crew encountered rough going as they bounced down what should have been smooth drops. It was like a ride on a wild killer bull thirty feet tall and trying his hardest to buck off the puny human on his back.

'The Strapped Crew,' as these windsurfer/tow-in surfers became known, were all marvels of athletic ability. Even in those monster waves, they made the rough riding look easy. No one seemed disturbed in the least as they continued surfing wave after wave.

Laird and Kalama often rode together on the same wave with Blue Angels-like precision, swooping around each other and the huge bowling sections. The other crew members rode as if they were surfing gentle Hoʻokipa rather than tempting fate at deadly Jaws.

I carefully watched the water boil up in the wake of each wave, the aftermath of power so violent and obvious that it made me feel sick thinking what it would be like to be trapped in there. In all respects, Jaws was the heaviest break I had ever seen. But watching the crew have fun was infectious. I began to formulate a plan.

Eventually some of them tired and returned to rest at the Zodiac we had anchored in the channel. Dave Kalama got on one of the skis and motored over to where I sat. He cut the engine, looked me right in the eye and quietly asked, "Are you ready?"

It was a simple question without pretense or expectation. I knew Dave was rock-solid, like the eye in a hurricane, ever calm while others might be losing their heads around him. With him as my partner I felt confident. "Why not?" I replied.

"Well, let's do it then," he said smiling.

He handed me the ski rope handle while I put my board in the water and my feet in the straps, still sitting on the Zodiac's pontoon. When he had idled the ski out to the end of the rope, Dave looked back at me.

"OK?" he asked.

I nodded, and he gunned it, pulling me up off the Zodiac, and we were away. In that tense moment the small ironies of life's journey made me laugh. Here I was on the way into my first wave at twenty-foot-plus Jaws and I wasn't even wet yet.

A set approached as we got out near the peak. Dave watched the waves, looking for a good one, and watched me to see whether we had selected the same wave. He pointed and I nodded. This was it. The ski swept around in a smooth arc and aimed back toward the others in the channel. I watched the swell well up and felt it pick up my board, the tension in the rope beginning to slacken.

Dave was driving with one knee up on the seat, halfway turned around so he could watch me and the wave ahead at the same time. He gunned the engine one more time as he turned off the back of the wave. This was my signal to pull on the handle, sliding out to the side of the ski wake to catch the whip off the rope as Dave turned away.

The slingshot effect just about lifted my board out of the water as my hull speed seemed to double instantly. I was in, standing up, with speed, not even wet and still far outside on the swell before it became a wave and raised up to break. It was just like I had dreamed. Wow!

The plan I had formulated while watching all the videos during the preceding months, and finally in the last hour sitting on the edge of the channel, was simple. I would play it safe by staying on the shoulder of the wall, well ahead of the heavy section. As I sliced into the huge mass of water, I had difficulty even estimating its size. My entry was far out beyond where the wave would encounter the shelving ocean floor, slowing the energy at the wave's base, pushing its top higher until it curled over. By then I would already be safely into the mid- to lower-section of the wave.

That thought brought a smile; this was going well according to the plan. Gently changing my angle of attack, I redirected toward the channel. I was careful not to bank too much, nor to push water and lose speed. Staying loose and playing it very safe, I rode across the whole wall ahead of the curl. It was no sweat. The guys sitting in the channel marked the goal line and I knew I had made it. The wave tapered down and I exited, easing over the back while Dave swooped in around me on the ski.

Grabbing the handle as it came by, I nodded to Dave. He gassed the ski, pulling me back out of the water. He had a huge smile on his face, and I suppose I probably did too. The guys in the channel hooted as we went by heading out to do it again.

Dave's smooth driving and uncanny wave selection put me into several more easy rides, and my confidence began to climb. Emboldened by my success, on the next big wave I decided to fade deeper toward the curl. Feeling pretty cocky I took my time as I pulled my bottom turn around, trying to stall closer to the barrel than I had on the previous rides. This was easy. With all the speed and extra time to choose positioning, there was nothing to it. Standing tall and casual at the bottom, secure in my line, I turned to look back at the curl behind me. That was almost my undoing.

Only inches away, hot on my heels was the gaping, swirling maw of a real monster. That roaring, collapsing tunnel was so utterly enormous as to be almost beyond my comprehension. The sight of it was so immediately and wholly frightening, I felt faint. I was completely stunned, humbled, and spooked by its close proximity. I was sure that if the thick, powerful lip landed on top of me, I would shatter instantly into a thousand pieces.

My confidence faded like a light going out. My body abandoned its jaunty stance and instinctively folded into a survival crouch, wishing to be further away no matter that I was already safely ahead of this potentially devastating curl and firm in that position. The wave ended like the ones before: without incident except for my horror flash. It was a good thing a lull happened when we got back outside.

I climbed up to sit on the back of the rescue sled and told Dave about the scare I had on the last wave. He nodded understanding, a serious look on his face.

"Yeah, it can go from good to bad in a hurry here; this is a seriously heavy wave," Dave replied.

I got a couple more waves that day and felt that I had definitely pushed beyond the previous limits of my big-wave experience. All said and done, it really wasn't that much different than any of the other first days in the past had been. The waves looked bigger and scarier from the channel, but after riding a few, I felt it had been about the same as always. In the snowboard world, mountains always look a lot steeper and hairier when at the top looking down. From the bottom looking back up, they don't look steep at all. I continue to wonder why that is.

Such is the life we can know. Living in the past and in the future—in recollection and in anticipation—creates a less clear picture of the present. By being in the here and now we understand that the past and future only exist in the present. That's all there is, but speaking for myself, I couldn't ask for more.

iv. TRAVELING FOR SURF

Bali in the mid-1970s was as laid back
and inviting as any surfer could hope for.
Photo: Dana Edmunds

229

Tales   of Indonesia

THE FIRST TIME TO BALI

I get a lot of credit for being a pioneer of the surf in Indonesia. I really don't deserve it. If not for a good friend of mine, I would not have had the good fortune to arrive there so early as I did.

Jack McCoy and I had grown up surfing together during the early 1960s on O'ahu's eastern coast near Aina Haina, Niu Valley, and Kuli'ou'ou. We traveled to Australia together for the 1971 World Surfing Championships as members of the Hawai'i State surf team.

We loved Australia. The place was spacious and inviting. The people were friendly and imbued with that particular essence of rugged individualism for which they've become justly famous. The surf exceeded our expectations. When it came time to leave, Jack calmly announced that he wasn't coming. He decided to stay Down Under.

Well, I supposed, why not? It was a great place. We left and he stayed. Jack and I kept in touch. I began doing some business with my surfboard company in Australia, and we enjoyed catching up during those visits. Several years later, when professional surfing contests began to happen, Hawai'i and Australia were the two main venues. Australia became a regular stop on the surf circuit and a very agreeable one at that. In Australia, surfers were regarded as legitimate professional athletes. That was a big step up for us. At home, surfers were marginalized, regarded as outcasts who disdained the core values of the larger society and lacked any form of work ethic.

Jack perked my interest in going to Bali. He deserves most of the credit as one of the premier Indonesian surf pioneers. Jeff Hakman and I were staying with Jack down in Torquay for the annual Bells Beach Easter Surf Classic. The little beach town of Torquay is a cold, gloomy part of Victoria during Easter, but sometimes the surf can be pretty good.

Jack had a great health food restaurant he owned with a couple of friends. On the wall there was a black-and-white photograph that intrigued me from the moment I first saw it. It was just a small four-by-five print of a water shot Jack had taken, or so I thought.

Among his many talents, Jack is a first-class surf photographer and a formidable water cameraman. The picture was of Wayne Lynch up high in the lip of a sweet-looking left. In response to my eager questions, Jack revealed that the wave was indeed even better than the photo could show. It was at a place called Uluwatu on the exotic island of Bali. I found out later that it was not Jack who took the picture, but his film partner Dickie Hoole. They had bought a new Nikonos water camera in Singapore, and Dickie swam out their first day in the surf to give it a try. Surf photography is never as easy as it might seem. Out of twenty-four exposures, twenty-three were blurry, white-out total misses, and the twenty-fourth was almost another except in the upper right hand corner was the image of Wayne.

As a child I had a thing for Bali after seeing the movie *South Pacific*, where Bloody Mary sang a haunting song about a mysterious place called Bali Hai. I barely knew about the island, but as soon as Jack said "Bali," I was certain I was going.

Jack and I went to work on getting Hakman excited about it. Eventually we got him to agree that after the next contest, the Coca-Cola Surfabout in Sydney, we would all go check it out. Jeff was not wholeheartedly enthusiastic about the place because when Jack related the story behind the photograph, there were some reasons for concern.

The year before, Jack, Wayne, and Nat Young went up there on the first Bali trip for all of them. The surf they found was great, but there were too many late nights, too much sunburn, a few hairy motorcycle crashes, and Wayne came down with malaria upon their return to Australia. Neither Wayne nor Nat wanted to go back again.

Jack, however, was a Hawai'i boy born and raised. He'd had no trouble acclimating to the steamy equatorial weather. The surf there had something that he hadn't seen

Uluwatu in 1975 was a surfing paradise with few people to share it with. Today it still is paradise, and everyone knows it. Photo: Dana Edmunds

anywhere else. Jack broke out the Alby Falzon film *Morning of the Earth*, which had a section of Steve Cooney and Rusty Miller riding the long, winding left at Uluwatu. The waves looked terrific. Finally Jeff said OK.

The flight from Sydney to Denpasar is a relatively short one. With the long twelve-hour haul from Honolulu to Australia still fresh in our minds, the five-hour Bali flight was a breeze. With Jack as our amiable and well-seasoned guide, we were headed toward great waves in a warm place where surfing was still new.

We flew into our final approach to the island winging in from the south. Out the side windows we could see long lines of surf wrapping down a rocky headland. Even from that altitude the waves looked good. Later we learned that this headland was called the Bukit. The west side of it, where we would find Uluwatu, was all lefts. The other side had lots of rights, but the prevailing southerly winds blew onshore. That same wind was straight offshore on the Uluwatu side. Those wind-combed, beautifully peeling waves beckoned to us right from the start, while we were still flying in on the airplane.

After landing on a runway—built on the reef straight out into the surf—we taxied to the small terminal. When the crew opened the door, a blast of hot, humid air hit us like a breaking wave. We filed out as if we were passing through the portal to a dream. Beyond the airport, everywhere we looked were coconut trees, thousands of tall, beautifully shaped trunks capped with fronds that swayed gently in the tropic breeze.

Bali in 1974 had a sleepy village atmosphere. Everyone and everything moved at a languid pace. The tourist trade, consisting mainly of European travelers, had been directed to the east side of the island, near Sanur. Two main hotels, the Bali Beach and the Bali Hyatt, handled most of the island's guests. There were excellent reefs in front of both hotels with fast, peeling rights, but the prevailing southerly trade winds blew onshore by late morning.

Sunshine is the only real enemy in Indo for anyone who likes to spend all day outdoors in the surf. Sunscreens for the skin got better but the eyes didn't have that luxury. My first attempts at eye protection were swimming goggles. Photo: Dana Edmunds

We were headed for the side of the island where the winds blew straight offshore. It was not far from the airport. Our destination was Kuta Beach, where small losmen, or bungalows, were intended for tourists who wanted to rough it a little. Compared to the international hotels of Sanur, the Kuta Beach accommodations were a bit primitive.

Jack had stayed at a place owned by a Mr. Kodja, who greeted him upon our arrival like a long-lost relative. The unexpected friendliness of the Balinese people was completely genuine. After five minutes, we were all treated as though we were family. Kodja's losmen were nestled in a coconut grove a short walk from the beach. It was an idyllic spot, cool in the shade, quiet and peaceful.

I was stoked. We dropped our bags inside and headed to the beach for a look at the ocean. Our first sight was a wave crashing in the shorebreak. It was a perfect wave, swept clean by offshore winds. Following behind it was a seemingly endless procession of more just like it. The water was a clear blue-green and was beckoning us to jump right in.

Jack and I looked at each other, peeled off our shirts, and raced down to the water's edge. We were like two kids loose in a candy store. We spent the next few minutes bodysurfing the thumping shore pound, pulling into spinning barrels, and squealing in complete delight.

"I told you, didn't I?" Jack gloated.

"And I believed you too, didn't I?" I replied.

We slipped into another bodysurf where I slid up on Jack's back and rode the big man like a bodyboard. Giggling, we popped up together from the closeout.

"Come on, let's get out, I've got to show you something better," Jack announced as we waded in.

From higher up the beach he pointed out a wave breaking on an outer reef to our left. "See that? That's a perfect left just like Ala Moana. I say we get our boards and paddle out, what do you think?"

The candy store was getting bigger all the time. We got our surfboards and walked about a half mile to where the crescent-shaped beach curved out toward the outer reefbreaks. There were a couple of hotels along the way, built just back from the beach; one called the Kartika Plaza looked like the biggest hotel in the area. Another smaller one that seemed to be about ten bungalows built around a courtyard was the Sunset Beach hotel. This one was right in front of the end break on the outer reef.

This outer reef ran for about a half mile before it intersected the airport's reef runway. It was a long paddle out to the surf, but with nothing better to do and all day to do it, we jumped right in. As we got closer to the waves, they got bigger and better, and we paddled harder. No one was out. Jack informed us that this break was called Kuta Reef. It was indeed very much like our home break of Ala Moana; a long, peeling left with a big, hollow bowl about midway, then another whole inside section that tapered down and finally ran out of gas into the deep water channel.

It was heavenly and Jack kept saying, "I told you guys. Didn't I tell you?"

He did and he was right. I was never so stoked to be anywhere in my life, and it was only the first afternoon. Our tickets were booked for a month's stay, but Jack had assured us that we could extend them if we wanted.

The next day, Jack declared we would look for the real waves out toward the point we had flown over on our approach to the airport. Kuta Reef was just an appetizer.

Uluwatu was the main spot, and the waves there were quite a bit bigger. The candy store seemed to be turning into a shopping mall and I couldn't wipe the grin off my face.

ULUWATU UNVEILED

The first time to Uluwatu began with aspirations of a well-planned, precisely executed Special Forces assault on the surf. It quickly deteriorated into a fool's mission right from the start. It was our second day in Bali, and we had seen few other tourists where we stayed in the sleepy village of Kuta Beach. There were a couple of hippie backpacker types, some older Australian couples, but no other surfers. Jack McCoy, who was a veteran of another trip here a year earlier, knew he could hire transport for us down on bemo corner.

As I followed him on the dirt road fronting our losmen accommodations, he explained that a bemo was a little Datsun or Toyota pickup truck with a canopy built over the bed and bench seats. Private cars were scarce. The occasional taxi was a late 1950s or early 1960s Chevy, painstakingly maintained but most likely still running on the original factory parts. Engines wheezing, rods knocking, mufflers shot, shocks long worn away. The American vehicles were lovingly cared for and polished at every idle moment to a high gloss, but they were much too big and overweight for the narrow, pot-holed, mostly dirt tracks and lanes.

Denpasar and the more built-up Sanur tourist areas might have been different, but in Kuta Beach time seemed to stand still. The few private vehicles we noticed were motorbikes of miniscule engine displacement but kept immaculately clean even after years and many miles of use. The consummate family ride featured father sporting an antique motorcycle helmet offering little or no protection doing the driving; mother in traditional

The local mode of transportation was the bemo and the drive out to Ulu was slow and bumpy, but in every village all the kids would run out laughing and cheering us on.
Photo: Dana Edmunds

sarong, wearing a construction hard hat offering much less protection sat side-saddle behind; with a youngster or sometimes two squeezed in between. It made quite a picture but the lack of traffic and the sedate pace of ... well, everything, kept their world safe.

Bemo Corner was a busy place. Three bemos, their drivers and assistants, plus a half dozen bystanders, made for a huge crowd. Jack, towering over everyone by a foot or two, spread them apart by his immense presence and high-volume talk-show-host voice.

"I want to hire bemo all day," he boomed.

His dad, 'Big Jack McCoy,' was a much-listened-to radio personality in Hawai'i and young Jack had inherited the voice. Two of the drivers immediately found they were busy, but the third, with the oldest, most beat-up bemo perked up with interest. Jack and he put their heads together and exchanged a rapid-fire dialogue with much sign language, which I couldn't follow but soon realized was a spirited negotiation. Jack came back to me, all smiles and shaka signs.

"Yeah man, we got him to take us out to Ulu and wait for us all day for 4,000 rups. He's going to get gas and will come by our place in half an hour," Jack informed me.

At 400 rupiah to the U.S. dollar and 600 to the Aussie dollar, I guessed ten bucks for a car all day was a pretty good deal. We went back to wake up Hakman, who was a late sleeper by nature, to tell him the good news and get our gear together.

We loaded our surfboards, some food, water, and ourselves into the back of our ride and off we went. It was early enough that most of the shops were still closed and the roads empty. The exhaust fumes blew directly into the back where we sat but we were too stoked to care. We passed the turnoff to the airport and were into new territory. At one point, shifting down into low gear, our little truck strained up a fairly steep hill. Looking out the back, a veritable sea of coconut trees stretched as far as we could see. On the left we had a brief view of a beautiful bay of jade-green water, with the airport runway on the far side and a wave breaking off the end of it. Jack informed us it was Jimbaran Bay and the high ground we were now on was the southern tip of Bali called the Bukit. At the end was an ancient temple inhabited by monkeys. There we would find the surf of Uluwatu. We had surfboards, we had food and water, we had plenty of stoke, and the waves were stacked to a horizon yet unseen.

We rolled through several little villages where everyone smiled and waved. We smiled and waved back. We saw a couple of other bemos headed the other way, their backs crammed with people. A few times we slowed down or stopped to let a man, or sometimes a very young boy, herd beautiful cows across the road using a long stick. The cows were golden-brown and white and looked more like beefy deer than bovines. No one seemed to be in a hurry except us.

Back then there weren't many surfers around, and there were no signs or in-dications of where we would find Uluwatu. We drove to the end of the road and walked out to the deserted temple perched on the sharp point. It was a sheer drop to the water below, maybe 800 to 1,000 feet straight down. The temple must have been hundreds of years old and was deserted except for the occasional monkey flitting through the shrub-bery. The surf looked great but disappeared out of sight around the point. Jack said he wanted to show us this place first, the southern-most tip of Bali, but that we needed to backtrack down the road to get to the surf spot of Uluwatu. An occasional track led off into the shrubs but they all looked the same. Jack had been here a year before but couldn't remember which was the right track. Our driver and his assistant were no help, as neither had any idea what we were looking for nor was there anyone around to ask.

Finally we came to a track leading off the road that looked good to Jack. Our driver wanted to know when we would be back, and we guessed at about four to five hours. Except for us, the chirping of the birds, and bugs, there wasn't anything else. We looked at Jack, shrugged our shoulders, grabbed our gear, and started down the track. The terrain was rugged limestone, full of hills and gullies, and the track was steep, crooked, and rough. It was a single track bordered with a thorny cactus-like plant that grew like a vine. We just followed where the track led. Up and down it went, back and forth, never in a straight line for very long, if ever. The thick walls of thorns didn't allow much view, but the track seemed to be going somewhere. We came to an intersection and debated which turn to take.

Figuring the main road we came in on was more or less parallel to the coastline, we decided we needed to move at right angles to that. But the trail had twisted so much before the intersection it was hard to tell which way that was. We chose one and moved off. Soon we came to another trail crossing; again, neither way seemed headed toward the ocean. We took another guess and continued on. Before long it became apparent that we were headed back toward the road so we backtracked to the intersection and took the other way. After following this track for a while, it didn't seem to be going where we wanted either.

Jeff climbed a nearby tree to get his bearings. It was a small tree, but I climbed up behind him. From this elevated view we could see the ocean in the distance and clambered back down with enthusiasm. Suddenly Jeff let out a screech, lifted up his shirt, searched himself, and plucked off a tiny, black ant. Then one bit me rather painfully, I peeled off my tee shirt and Jack jumped in to help us brush the ants off. Jeff held one of the tiny creatures up between his fingers, exclaiming, "How can such a small ant have such a large bite?"

This was our introduction to the insect life of Indonesia, a study that would fascinate us over the next twenty-five years of discovering and marveling at the many strange types.

Knowing which way the ocean was didn't seem to be much help, as the trail wouldn't head that direction. I had the idea that we should breach the thorny trail boundary and cross-country it. This met with the approval of both Jack and Jeff, since we sure weren't getting any closer the way we were going. We walked along until we found a light place in the thorns, moved some aside and slipped through.

The other side was a huge, open space, like a pasture except without much grass. It was an empty field, so the going was easy, and we happily headed the way we wanted to go. This didn't last long, as we soon came to the end of the open area and met with another thorn wall. Finding an opening to get through was more difficult, but after breaking our way past the thorns, we were on another track headed somewhere, but not toward the ocean.

We had been walking for over an hour and a half, and were hot, sweaty, ant-bitten, and out of patience. Going back wasn't an option either; we had to admit we were lost. Just when it seemed like we might start going for each other's throats, we heard someone coming. Around the corner came three surfers who looked like they knew where they were going. Introductions made, we found ourselves with three Maui boys, brothers Mike and Bill Boyum and Fred Haywood. It was a chance beginning to a lifelong friendship and many shared adventures.

Finally, with the new leadership, we arrived at the cliff overlooking the waves. It was as magnificent a sight as any surfer could behold. Perfect lines swept by clean offshore winds rolled in, peaked up and peeled off, occasionally hollowing out, spitting spray and continuing to peel off further. Jeff, Jack, and I blinked our eyes, blinked again, looked back, and realized we weren't seeing things. This was real and except for Mike, Bill, and Fred, there wasn't another soul around. We had just walked up to the gateway of paradise.

We followed the Maui boys down a makeshift ladder into a sea cave. In contrast to the searing temperature up above, it was refreshingly cool. The sand was coarse and clean. Mike had a Balinese boy who worked for him carrying an Igloo cooler jug. He brought it down the ladder and handed it over to Mike who beckoned us over to take a swig.

"Fresh pressed cane juice with lime," he explained.

It was ice cold and delicious. There were some white things floating in the juice that he said were mangosteen. They were even tastier. We left our shoes and gear with the boy, whose name was Ketut, followed our new guides' lead, and paddled out the cave entrance.

When we burst out into the sunlight, a sight right out of the best wet dream greeted us. As great as the waves looked from up above, they were even better up close. The surf was awesome. Punching through the inside whitewater, we timed our paddle out and slipped through the surfline. Outside we could see a wedging peak that looked like a nice beginning to a long, fast peeling wall.

Bubbling with barely contained excitement, I stroked out toward the peak, saw one swinging wide, paddled to intersect it, and dropped in. It was a steep takeoff, but the wave face was so clean and beautifully textured by the light offshore winds that I could have made it with my eyes closed. I stalled my turn, timing it to slip under the pitching lip, and tucked into my first tube at Uluwatu. A feeling of complete satisfaction washed over me as the wave curled around me. A smile spread across my face and I let out an unrestrained hoot. I knew this was some kind of surf heaven—and I was only on the first part of my first wave here.

We surfed hard for the next several hours. The sets were consistent with more than plenty of waves for everyone. It was a steady five to six feet with an eight-foot set steaming in on a regular basis every third or fourth set. The peak shifted around but bowled nicely, allowing a perfect backdoor setup right off the takeoff; then it was a race down the line as far as we wanted to paddle back out.

Eventually the tide began to go out, and the waves went into a transition mode, still good but not as defined in the peak takeoff. The Maui boys suggested we go into the beach and rest a little, let the tide go out, and come back out later. Ketut had brought our gear around to the front beach where there were some little caves at the base of the tall cliff offering cool shade. We crawled in, drank more of Mike's cane juice, and tried to close our eyes.

They wouldn't close, or if they did, images of perfectly peeling waves reeled off behind our eyelids. An hour later the tide had dropped dramatically, exposing the reef all the way out to where we had been surfing. Some local villagers in their bare feet walked out and began poking around the dry reef. It seemed the lower the tide got, the better the waves became. The takeoff seemed to be farther down the line from where we had surfed at the higher tide. It was an unusual wave that started small and then grew as it peeled down the line.

We picked our way over the dry reef carefully so as not to slice up our bare feet. Not far from the edge, the wave stood up, crashed over, then quickly died down to a gurgle where we stood not thirty feet away. It was the most amazing thing; the wave was powerful and hollow where it broke but dissipated down to nothing in a short distance. But getting to it was going to be tricky without getting our bare feet all cut up on the reef.

I noticed some cracks in the reef that seemed to lead out and were deeper. I put my surfboard in one with the fin up, carefully lay on it, keeping my full weight off by pressing down on the reef with my hands. When the surge washed in underneath, it floated my board, and I was able to ride back out with it. As soon as it was deep enough to paddle, I could make better speed and left the others behind doing their rock dance. Eventually there was deep enough water below me that I could roll my board over the right way and paddle full stroke. The rollover was a maneuver that I had down pat, having practiced many times during long waits in the lineup. I could do it in a flash without even getting off the board. Before long, I was in position to catch a wave while the others were still inching their way on dry reef.

A wave about four feet came toward me and looked good. The takeoff was easy, and I flicked a turn up onto the wall. The wave stretched out ahead of me as I raced it down the line. It seemed to grow not only in height but also in girth. I could see a section looming ahead of me that was twice as big as where I had first caught the wave. With good speed and a good line, I flew into the backdoor of the section and found myself deep inside a serious tunnel. A few more pumps and I shot out the other end, easing over the top as yet another even bigger section loomed ahead.

My heart was pounding, my breathing rapid, with both increasing when I saw the next wave. I put my head down and paddled hard to get out of the way of a full-on eight-foot, top-to-bottom, thick barrel. Angling for the shoulder with a good head of steam, I slipped around the wave but not before I had a chance to look deep within its bowels. I saw that it was hollow and clean enough to ride thirty feet back in the barrel. I was shaking like I had a fever, realizing how lightly I had taken my first wave. I had to be careful pulling into these thick inside waves as they broke very hard in very shallow water.

Fred Haywood was on the third wave. He had made it out pretty quick, maybe his feet were toughened by the sharp, low-tide Shark Pit reef in Lahaina, Maui. Riding backside, he approached the heavy inside section I had backdoored a few waves earlier.

His wave was much bigger than mine. As I sat up to watch how he planned to negotiate this difficult section, he hit his turn perfectly and projected high on the wall just as the whole wave threw out over his head. Bent over at the waist, he eased a turn back down, somehow held his edge, and blew out of a tunnel big enough for our bemo to fit inside.

We named the inside section the Racetrack that day because it was exactly that, with high-speed, full-throttle runs that you raced to win or die on the razor-like reef waiting below. To this day, I remember pulling into a backdoor that I was watching break three sections ahead, ducking late into the first one as the second one was already pitching over, and seeing the third section in the distance getting ready to throw. Somehow I slipped through all of them and squirted out safe and sound.

The surfboards we brought to Bali that first trip were our contest boards for Australian events at Bells Beach and the North Sydney breaks. I had a 7'8" diamond tail, a 7'4" wing swallow-tail, and a 6'8" that I only remember as wide, thick, and fat. The 7'8" was too long and didn't get much use. The 7'4" was the best size for what we were riding, but not one of my boards worked as well as I wanted. I got so frustrated with the 7'4" that I brought it back to Kuta one day, took a Surform tool, shaved off the wings, and reglassed over the bare foam. At the end of our trip, I gave it to Kim 'The Fly' Bradley of Avalon who was with us in Bali. I never wanted to see that piece of crap again. Kim hung on to the board, and recently Jack acquired it, showing it to me last winter on the North Shore.

Jeff's boards didn't work any better, and he ended up riding a board I had made for Jack in Torquay right before we left on the trip. Jack is a big man, so the 7'4" I built was a big board. But Jeff liked it and rode it every day. Able to knee paddle because of all the flotation, he had the added advantage of seeing the sets first. One time he also spotted something swimming toward us. As I looked where he was pointing, we both realized at the same time that it was a huge sea snake.

We both turned and bolted for shore, paddling right through the Maui boys sitting further inside. They didn't bother to ask what we were running away from, they just turned and joined our flight, all of us knocking each other over trying to get away. Of course, the commotion we made trying to escape chased the snake away but we didn't know that.

This trip was the first time that Jeff and I had worn surf leashes; they took some getting used to. They had been around for several years, but I guess we were old school and felt we didn't need them. The rocky shoreline of Uluwatu at high tide was death on lost surfboards. Everyone else used a leash so Jeff and I gave it a go. The leashes of the day were black surgical tubing with a length of nylon inside. The theory was that the tubing would stretch out until it reached the length of the nylon, stopping the board from going any further, then rebounding it back to the surfer. The only trouble was that the waves at Ulu didn't stop pulling when they reached the end of the cord inside, and they easily snapped the nylon. The wave kept pulling, stretching the rubber tubing to the thickness of a rubber band, at which point the rubber broke, or worse, it recoiled the board back like a rocket.

Unless the surfer was aware of this and ready for it when it happened, he would surface after getting tumbled by the wave to find his board flying back at his head. If he was lucky he might get his hand up in time to stop it. If not, he could get nailed right in the face. I fell off my board a lot so I had to put up with all the crap that went with using a leash. Jeff, on the other hand, gave up on the leash and concentrated on never losing his board. The only time he lost it was one time when Mike Boyum bailed off right in front of him and it was either let go or get nailed by Mike's board. The attitude was different back then. When someone lost his surfboard, the guy riding the next wave surfed in and retrieved it.

I loved everything about Bali—the surf most of all—but the people were special too. I think the Dutch realized that when they colonized the region because they left Bali much as they found it while exploiting the heck out of Java and Sumatra.

Uluwatu was a world-class surf spot. Jeff and I would go out there four or five days in a row until its intensity just wore us out, then we would stay in Kuta for a few days surfing a much tamer Kuta Reef. A day or two of that and we would long for the power, the size, and the sheer magnitude of Ulu. We got a little motorbike; I would drive while Jeff held both boards behind me. Often we would be the only ones there.

Boyum lived right across the street from where we stayed, and we would try to get him to go out too, but Ulu was a heavy place. Nobody wanted it too much. The days we wouldn't go out there weren't because of a lack of surf; it was just a lack of motivation on our part. We were weary from all that surf. Jeff would sleep all day long on those days. It seemed the surf never stopped. Ulu was never less than six feet for the entire six weeks. It was utterly relentless. We would give it a miss just to come down from the high energy. By contrast, the people and the pace of life in Bali were languid.

There was a period in my life—the previous six or seven years—when I had no desire to be anywhere else than the Ala Moana parking lot during the summer season. Missing a south swell at the Bowl was an anathema to me until I went to Bali. Then all I wanted to do was go home, work, make some money and new surfboards, and get back to that idyllic island as quickly as I could.

Life is quite a journey; we find something we like and immediately build a fence around it to keep it the same. Then something else comes along, and we are over that fence in a flash with hardly a look back, chasing off after some other pipe dream.

A typical Indo local, the deadly poisonous
coral sea snake. Photo: Dana Edmunds

d. GALLERY

Above   Photo: Dana Edmunds

Right   Wayan, my board carrier, waited
for me each day with a patience I could only
envy. Photo: Dana Edmunds

A bottom turn at Uluwatu, before anyone had any ideas of building hotels on the hill in the background. Photo: Dana Edmunds

Above   Photo: Jeff Divine

Right   Enjoying the ambiance of a luxury beachfront
suite at the G-Land surf camp—just 10 steps from
the water—with Sidesy and Hosko. Photo: Art Brewer

Mike Boyum, who had the vision to create the first surf
camp and see it through the headaches of getting it going,
walks in after a long surf session. Photo: Don King

Left   Having board carriers at Uluwatu allowed us
to jog in to the beach for a pre-surf warm-up. They
would carry our boards for twenty-five cents each
way; most used what they earned as start-up capital
for bigger business ventures. Photo: Dana Edmunds

Above   The shape of a big-wave board in 1975,
standing just outside my shaping room next to the
chicken coop in Olinda, Maui. Photo: Dana Edmunds

Treasure

Islands

Samudra is a place of dreams, untold riches, and natural wonders. The name Samudra comes from an ancient Sanskrit word, meaning ocean. Early traders from India gave it that name a long time ago. However in 1292, a European traveler named Marco Polo, coming from the court of Kublai Khan, visited this beautiful place for five months. In his reports back to his own people in Italy, the name Samudra was misinterpreted as Sumatra, and Sumatra it has been ever since.

It is a paradise of many sorts. Home to early man as far back as 4,000 years ago, it hosted the development of a number of diverse people and their unique cultures. Many of these people are still there; some, like the indigenous groups in the Mentawai Islands, remained untouched by outside civilization until only this century. Others, like the Bataks, are not far from their days of headhunting and ritualistic cannibalism.

This island, the sixth largest in the world, is also home to a variety of wonderful animals, including tigers, rhinoceroses, elephants, and sun bears, as well as numerous species of monkeys, apes, and giant lizards. Its natural resources include oil and natural gas in great supply as well as vast forests of valuable timber. The fertile soil and plentiful rainfall make the cultivation of rubber, palm oil, tea, coffee, cocoa beans, tobacco, cloves, and black pepper a bountiful and lucrative proposition.

Divided neatly in half by the equator, Sumatra is a land of diversely beautiful terrain, from its lush islands with stunning white sand beaches to the magnificent Bukit Barisan mountains, the regal volcanic lake Danau Toba, and around one hundred volcanoes of which fifteen are active. The country of Indonesia is, in large part, supported financially by the wealth of Sumatra. It is indeed a treasure island. For a surfer, it is a place where dreams come true, because another thing Sumatra is rich in is good waves.

Ours is a group of old friends who have made a life of surfing and of seeking out new surf spots far from the beaten path. Most of us were there in the beginning when surfing first came to Bali. We were there in the beginning when G-Land became the world's first surf camp. And we were there throughout it all when both places, as well as almost everything else in the immediate area, became so popular that we thought paradise was lost forever.

A brilliant equatorial sunset somewhere in the
Mentawai Islands off Sumatra. Photo: Kimiro Kondo

Surfing being what it is, one can always find solace in the waves no matter how many other people are there, but like meditation, the fewer the distractions, the easier the task. So we set our sights on new horizons, going farther afield than ever before, foregoing the tried-and-proven areas in search of new breaks. We knew we could get skunked and find nothing, but we believed in ourselves enough to know that whatever we found, it would include enjoyment and fulfillment as well.

The average age of our group is fifty years old. We've been through a lot, most of it hard and some of it downright miserable. Some would say we've become spoiled; I would call it refined. We want to do everything as enthusiastically as ever, but why rough it when it's possible to go in style and comfort.

We all have families now, others to answer to. The days of intense surfing are still here, but the motto of "damn the torpedoes, full speed ahead" has been replaced by the more mature approach of pacing ourselves. We surf so we can surf again tomorrow, not like there is no tomorrow. Pacing ourselves isn't just when we're in the water; it's the complete lifestyle. It includes healthy food, rest and recuperation, and good sleep. It also includes being vigilant in protecting ourselves from malaria. This area is a red zone for malaria, a deadly disease carried by a tiny mosquito. It can kill a person; it has and, with great regularity, still does kill unaware or ignorant surfers.

Traveling to find surf can only be done effectively and efficiently by boat. With the growing interest in finding uncrowded surf, especially in this area, there is a multitude of boats for hire. We've always gone with Martin Daly on his *Indies Trader* fleet. For this season he had a new addition, the *Indies Trader III*, and it was available to us.

The *Indies III* is a beautiful ship. For surfers hunting waves, it's more of a floating palace. Built originally for conducting surveys on the ocean floor, it has become the number one surf ship on the seven seas. With a 7,000-mile range and full-time water-making capabilities, we would probably run out of food before we ran out of fuel or hot showers. Completely air-conditioned, it was, especially for this old G-Land crew, as first class as it gets.

We went from ten- to twenty-plus-hour flights on our respective airplanes straight to this wonderful paradise afloat. We started in Padang, where Dutch traders

The *Indies Trader II* was a luxurious way to travel around looking for surf, not that one had to look far in the Mentawais. Photo: Kimiro Kondo

settled in the early seventeenth century among the local Minangkabau tribes. Here in this seaport that traded with ancient kingdoms and forgotten civilizations, our journey begins. Once our gear is aboard and stowed away, we shove off into the setting sun.

Our team leader and benefactor is Tommy 'Tuna' Pfleger, a professional sport-fishing operator, environmental crusader, and full-time champion of preserving and managing the oceans and all the life within it. Head lifeguard and big-wave scout is Darrick Doerner also known as 'Double D' or 'DD.' Regular foots include Victor 'Daddy' Lopez and 'Brother Bill' Boyum from Maui. From Australia come the goofyfooters Peter McCabe of Newcastle and ex-Kiwi Allan 'AB' Byrne of Queensland. Kimiro Kondo is here to photograph the moments, and I am here to write about the events.

A log of our surf experiences over the next two weeks reads like a fairy tale. Even reading back afterward, the record of it seems too good to be true, but that's how it is sometimes: Surf is where and when you find it. Our first day is small and easy—the best way to break into the whole rhythm of Indo surf in the equatorial zone. Sunburned eyes for Allan and a quick roll over a dry reef for Peter are our first casualties, relatively minor but a price to be paid. We jump back aboard ship with the jet lag washed off and head off to find more surf.

Day two is a mild surprise after the two- to three-foot surf the day before. Sets look like they might be eight feet. But it's offshore and peeling, and we find ourselves completely alone on the outside lineup. The other surfers here seem to be surfing the inside peak, which, while it may be more hollow, is also a lot smaller. We have fun for several hours until we notice the sets are growing bigger.

Our Aussie cook rings the lunch bell, and we come aboard for a gourmet lunch while we cruise over to the next island where a good left awaits. As we motor up to the left, the onshore wind miraculously dies, and the sight of this fast long left reeling down the reef rallies the whole crew for an afternoon session that lasts until the sun sets. The left is six foot, fast and fun. The sunset explodes colors into the darkening sky and dazzles us after an already dazzling day of surf.

We spend the night and on first light are rewarded with the sight of a golden morning set of very large waves peeling down the reef. We are in the water quickly and find the surf to be an excellent eight to ten feet, very fast, very long, and ending in what the locals call the Nuclear Zone, a suck-out disaster on a dry reef. DD finds himself locked into a big one, and I watch helplessly from the shoulder as he tries to dive off in the barrel. He gets slammed straight into the reef, shredding his back. Darrick is our strongman, the youngest and fittest member of the group. The sight of his raw, bleeding back is a sobering reminder to all of us of the dangers we face. We surf from dawn until late afternoon, when a sea breeze finally comes in, not enough to wreck the waves but just enough to ruffle the faces from the earlier perfection. We take this as our cue to leave and ship out for our next destination.

We awake somewhere else, and as beautiful and perfect as yesterday's wave was, today's wave is even better. Nobody has a name for it; as far as we know it's only been surfed a few times. We dive into the surf as quick as we can. Breakfast? Who said anything about eating food when there are waves like these to feast on. Maybe it's just that surfers have short memories of great surf past, but I keep pinching myself to see if I'm really dreaming or not.

This may be the most user-friendly right I've ever surfed. Long and fast, with a surprisingly workable face and several hollow sections that are textbook backdoor setups. We end up calling this place the Bank because every wave we get is like money in the bank; there aren't any bad waves at all, only better ones. We spend several days surfing ourselves silly on this place before another boatload of surfers show up and we turn over the Bank to them.

It's been a week of this; again we wake up in someplace new and beautiful. There is a small right off a little point. Peter dives right into it. A couple of surfers come out from the island and are as surprised to see Peter as he is to see them. We notice other signs of life: A small airplane takes off from what looks like jungle, we see telephone poles through a gap in the trees, a car drives down a road—we move on.

We unlimber the jet ski for the first time and tow out to a big mushy left for a trial run. Moving on to the next island, we see a right that as we get closer, turns into something unbelievable. Perfectly peeling round right cylinders lure us quickly into the lineup. It looks six feet, but as we get into the water, the waves appear to be bigger. A set rolls in and we paddle for our lives.

A wave of epic proportions confronts us, perhaps only twelve feet tall but all of sixty feet thick at the base. It sucks down all the water for ten yards in front of the wave, making a giant trench. The first set we just paddle away from as fast as we can even though the wave stands and breaks in a huge perfect peak that immediately funnels into a fast-peeling wall.

A few sets more, a little less gun shy, and a little closer to trying to catch one, it becomes increasingly apparent that our boards are too small to paddle into any of the big ones safely. We consider the small ones, but reason that it would be disastrous to get caught inside. No one wants to wait inside, and we dance around the sets outside until it is evident that we can't catch any.

We fool ourselves for another hour before Daddy gets smart and goes for the jet ski. While DD changes the foot straps over to regular foot, Daddy tows me into a set on my 7'0". I realize too late I've made a mistake. I get in early but way deep so I draw a fast line toward safety. But it feels like my board is dragging a bucket. I look down to see if something is wrong with the board. It looks fine. Next, I look back and see that I'm way too far out on the shoulder; no wonder the board feels funny and slow moving.

But as I turn back, the curl behind not only catches me, but suddenly I'm deeply locked in. I grab my rail and pray for daylight. I know I don't want to fall here so I hang on for dear life. Faster and faster, my board accelerates through the tube until I slowly get ahead of the curl enough to ease over the lip. I make it, but the wave behind is bigger and I'm trapped. Thinking I'm finished, I surrender, dive off my board, and start hyperventilating in anticipation of getting creamed. I failed to realize that by making the first wave, I rode far enough into the bay to escape the heavy grinding barrel. Down here on the end, it's a thin-lipped spinning tube, much less severe than the deadly pit out on the point. I try to get back on my board and paddle, but it's too late. The barrel is still superhollow but

thin and nowhere as strong or violent as the beginning of the wave. I easily dive under, and Daddy is there with the jet ski for the pickup. I have him tow me right back to the tin-boat where Kondo is shooting from and DD is waiting for the rope.

The next hour we are all treated to a spectacle. First Daddy pulls DD steadily deeper into wave after wave. The lines he draws and the speed he travels makes it seem like he is toying with this wave that seemed so deadly only a few minutes ago. He comes in from so far behind the section that it appears unmakeable from our vantage. One turn later and he's too far ahead, the wave not fast enough for his speed. He continually out-runs the tube, turning the grinding barrel into a playground for on-the-face maneuvers, cutting and slashing up, down and back around. It is a stunning display. Daddy finally gets his turn on the rope, a few sets, more high-speed carving, and before we know it, the sun begins to set and another great day comes to its close.

Day eight finds us traveling back to the Bank, but the swell has dropped, and compared to the last time we were here, coming back is a letdown. We drop anchor just around the corner at what looks like a small left. DD and Daddy are still running on yesterday's juice and take it easy, but the rest of us paddle in to a fun, fast left. So fast in fact that one slip and it passes the hapless surfer by. But when we pump it perfectly, we zing down the line, covering ground in big gulps, slipping through, but only barely. Some waves are perfect and easy to make, but others are like whirling dervishes, leaving us behind like we're standing still. We surf from noon till sunset. Today's spot is small boards, large maneuvers, and big fun. We don't even have a name for this place.

We're back the next morning. It's bigger and even harder to make but the per-fect ones are ... well, they're perfect. Some look good and we pull in only to get mugged. There are lots of waves, the whole gang is getting plenty, and everyone's spirits are soaring. The only problem will be trying to remember just some of what is becoming a total sensory overload. When so many good waves come, one forgets to remember any

The tin boat was a nice way to paddle out
without getting wet. Photo: Kimiro Kondo

but the most outstanding. We try to savor the moments—the events preceding the wave and the whole ride from takeoff until end, the afterglow paddling back out—but facing the sight of another perfect wave is just too much. Pacing ourselves, there is enough energy to paddle out for another one even though we will almost certainly forget it as soon as the ride is over.

The sun is the real enemy, and we use any and all protection: sunscreen, long sleeve rash guards, hats, goggles, staying underwater as much as possible. We can always surrender to the air-conditioned lounge with an ice-cold drink. But we can do that when the surf gets shitty. It just seems like that never happens. Three days of this same left and every day a little bigger, a bit different, and somehow even better.

The third day, everyone seems to have found their groove, applying the lines they feel best with, revealing this canvas as being wide open to any style of surfing artist. Impressionistic, art nouveaux, classical: anything goes. We surf ourselves into a sunburned, sated state. Finally we drag ourselves aboard the ship to a hot shower, hot meal, and a cool bunk.

Day eleven would have to begin with some more thoughts about day ten. I remember Brother Bill bailing out when we found ourselves too far in on a big set. I was out ahead and duck-dived under it, but only barely. Billy got creamed. There were some hall of fame tubes but mostly just high-speed racing to stay ahead—an extremely challenging wave and the nature of each wave entirely its own. The most common trait was that the water was wet; from that point almost everything else was different. It was a hard wave to make, too fast to get out over the lip. The only escape was a Hawaiian pullout and to hope there wasn't a bigger one behind. If the one behind planted us, it was a long although quick wash all the way in. But that was yesterday, and today we are back at the Bank and it looks worth a go-out.

The wave at the Bank is forced to wrap in quite dramatically, draining a lot of juice from the swell, but the peel is near perfect. The wind comes onshore and some of us take a much-needed rest from the sun. We haul anchor and motor into another small group of islands with several lefts and another perfect right. DD and AB find the right to their liking and kill it all afternoon while the rest of us watch movies and sip ice-cold drinks.

We are all daydreaming about what we've had when we pull up next to the best-looking left we've seen in days, hours—well, at least since the last left anyway. There are villagers fishing out of their little canoes, and they come over and stare at this giant ship parked in their little backyard. Some French surfers come out from the village and surf with us. They have been here the past four days, and it's been just like this, perfect, four to six foot and totally ripable, sometimes tubing, but all the time peeling.

We are the first surfers they have seen while they've been here. Another perfect setup and we are all tuned up and feeling very comfortable with our boards. With lots of waves to choose from, we surf composed and sure-footed. Everyone gets a memorable wave or plenty. Tommy Tuna says some are the best waves of his life but he has been saying that everyday.

Kondo sets up from the water and fires off some great shots. At one point, he, Peter, and I get ourselves trapped by the biggest wave as Tom rides by. We get planted.

The fact that we were all in it together makes it OK. After we all get plenty of waves, we ship out again.

A few hours later and we are back at the first big right and it's really big now. Breaking out in the deep blue water with the thick rolling whitewater, it looks absolutely magnificent. We dash out to find it a solid ten feet, but thick and roly-poly. There are some fun drops on big, rolling mountains of water. It is a fitting end to another epic day.

Day thirteen starts out uneventful; everything looks mushy or rough. Finally, in the afternoon we end up at the same little left we started out on thirteen days ago. It's much bigger and breaking in a lot more places. We go out to the innermost break, and it's eight feet on the sets. It is fun, long, and fast rides on the most startling blue-colored waves. Everyone gets more than a few waves and then we get called back aboard: It's time to ship out. Our final stop is Padang and the end of the trip.

Anytime I go surfing can be a religious experience if I let it. It is an up close encounter with one of our world's greatest natural wonders. Out here on the edge of the known world, far from the distractions of civilization, I can more easily find this space. But in reality any of us can find it anywhere because we carry it inside us everywhere we go. During the course of our ordinary day, information from the senses bombards one's mind. This pulls the mind outward. It is only when we still the mind that we are able to turn it inward where joy and wisdom lies. In this inner space we find how to live in peace and harmony.

Surfing teaches us about this inner space and these inner moments because they occur regularly during the surfing experience. Crowded waves, dirty water, and bad vibes can distract us from those magic moments to the point of being unaware even while those moments are upon us. Surf trips like the one I've just described do wonders for reacquainting us with that inner space. The moments of enlightenment are pure and personal, but better when they are shared with good old friends. And the most amazing thing is that every time it gets better than before, it makes me wonder how long it can continue to do so. That we will be here doing it all over again next year goes without saying.

The Mile-

Long Rides

I got a phone call from a woman in New York who said she was from the *60 Minutes* TV show and was putting together a program on tow-in surfing. She said she was Lesley Stahl's assistant and that they wanted to do the show on Maui sometime in the fall. This was in late summer. Braden was her name, and she said she had seen the Laird video and thought there might be a good show for *60 Minutes* in it.

She asked if I would be interested. I said maybe after I heard more about exactly what they wanted to do. A month passed before I heard from Braden again, but when she did call she was very excited. Lesley Stahl thought the show was a good idea. She was all for it.

Lesley Stahl is a very well-known TV news correspondent who covered the White House during the Reagan and Carter years for *Meet the Press.* She has been with CBS and *60 Minutes* for as long as I can remember. In addition to her interviews with U.S. presidents, I had watched her interview such world leaders as Margaret Thatcher, Boris Yeltsin, even Yasser Arafat. Now she was going to be interviewing a bunch of surfers. I definitely wanted to be in on this.

So another month went by before Braden called again and said they finally had settled on mid-November for the shoot. I had missed my fall Indo trip but had managed a quick surf trip down to San Jose del Cabo instead. With the start of the fall surf season in Oregon, I had a lot of surfing under my belt and felt in pretty good shape.

Darrick called a few times to tell me that he would have my tow-in board and everything else ready when I got there so I didn't need to bring anything. I started to look forward to the trip even though the snow had begun to fall and it looked like we might have an early snowboard season. At the same time, I started to have second thoughts. My wife Toni reinforced those thoughts. "If it's big Jaws, you better just sit in the channel," she warned.

Being physically in shape may be one thing, but being mentally in shape for big Jaws is something altogether different. I reassured Toni that I would be careful.

For someone who has spent a great deal of time traveling the world, I found the trip to Maui a lot longer than I ever remembered. I found out how out of shape I was for a five-hour plane ride. I shuddered when I thought about the long trip down to Indo, which is five times longer than the short one to Hawai'i.

I finally arrived in Kahului late Thursday night, and as I was wandering through the airport looking for my baggage and rental car, I ran into Sonny Miller, who had just arrived as well. He said Nelson and Janey were outside waiting for him and I should just hook up with them instead of getting a car of my own. Nelson is a good friend who takes care of Laird's Kaua'i property and was there to drive the camera ski for Sonny.

Janey is Laird and Gabby's business manager; she put together our side of the whole *60 Minutes* deal almost single-handedly. I went outside, jumped into their car, and off we went into the warm Maui night. We ended up at Laird and Gabby's house while Nelson and Sonny went to stay with Darrick. It felt good to go to sleep with the window open. I can't do that during the cold winter in the Pacific Northwest.

I woke in the dark to a low, rhythmic throbbing. At first I thought it was jet lag, but as I came awake I realized it was a sound as well as a vibration. My God, I thought, is that surf? To a long-time surfer, it's an unmistakable sound. Laird's house is on the mauka, or mountain, side of the highway, at least several miles from the ocean. As I got up and made my way through the dark house toward the kitchen, I noticed the garage light was lit. I went into the garage to find Laird ripping open the packaging on the new tow-in board I had brought over for him.

He came over, gave me a hug. "You hear that?" he asked.

"Yeah, is that the surf?" I asked him.

A huge smile lit up his face as he went back to unpacking the board. "Yeah man," he answered.

His cackle exposed the glee he was feeling. The winter so far had been a big surf dud, and the boys had spent too much time sitting around twiddling their thumbs. I was already feeling the energy of the booming surf, and now I could feel Laird's energy like a heat wave.

"So what do we have here?" he asked.

He peeled away the last bubble packaging from the little peashooter that would be his vehicle on waves that are beyond most people's imaginations, mine included.

"Well, as near as I could remember, I think that's what you told me you wanted the last time I saw you," I told him.

Last time had been when I jetted down to LA to do some narration work on another movie Laird and Janey were putting together called *The Ride*. That had been a quick trip, and we only had a brief chance to talk about new tow-in boards. I watched him go through the typical surfer new-board checkout and waited for his reaction.

First he hefted the board, feeling its weight and balance. Then, holding both rails, he hoisted it in front of him, at once looking at the nose section and getting a feel for the rails. Next he put it under one arm while running his other hand up and down the rail from midsection to the nose. Finally, he grabbed the one rail with both hands, holding it down by his knees, and checked the rocker and the foil.

"Beautiful ... and perfect," he said to me with a big grin. "This is going to do the job."

I let out a big sigh of relief. As a shaper I never know what to expect when I present a surfer of Laird's caliber with a new board. This first-encounter bonding ritual is a crucial part in the acceptance cycle. It's the first step in the mating dance that goes on with every new board because if there is any negative reaction in this initial encounter, it will carry over into the first go-out or, worse, may relegate the board to the back of the garage where it won't even get a chance in the water.

Laird said, "OK, we need to strap this thing up, rally the boys, and get going. I know we're going to get some good waves somewhere."

It was still dark as we piled into Laird's truck and drove the short distance over to Darrick's house. DD was already up and running.

"Coffee's hot in the kitchen," he called out from the garage where he was getting his equipment ready for the day. "Swell is six to ten degrees out of the northeast; interval is not great but it sounds pretty big to me," he announced. "GL, your 6'6" is right here; we just need to change the foot straps around to goofy. You want me to get you a cup of herb tea?"

"Yeah that sounds good. I need to rig up Laird's new shooter—you guys got some Astrodeck?" I answered.

"Oh yeah, we got everything, but let's take a look at this new stick," DD replied.

No one is more tuned-in to the equipment side of surfing than Darrick is. It is a pleasure to make boards for him because not only is he very appreciative and makes good use of all of them, but he also constantly gives me feedback on every aspect of each board. One time he and Laird called me on their cell phone from their jet ski in the channel at Jaws after some particularly great rides on a brand-new board.

Laird, his ski and boards lashed to the sled,
loaded for bear or anything else that the ocean
might throw at him. Photo: Tom Servais

"Oh baby, that's what I'm talking about," he cooed.

He went on lovingly fondling the new board. In addition to keeping me informed of his own equipment needs and wants, DD also feeds me, in great detail, relevant info for Laird's boards as well.

"Look," said Laird, taking the board from DD.

Handling it as gently as he does his newborn daughter, he set the tail down lightly at his feet and pressed the board to himself. "Six foot, two inches, same size as me; this thing is just raring to go."

We got busy getting it ready to use, putting the Astrodeck down, drilling out the inserts, and screwing in the foot straps. Laird and DD debated over which fins to use and finally settled on some special G10 shapes personally done for them by Curtis Hesselgrave at Future Fin Systems. Soon we were ready to go. Janey came by to say she would go coordinate the *60 Minutes* people while we went to get the jet skis from 'The G-Man,' their personal super-duper mechanic in Ha'iku.

Kawasaki USA had come through with two brand-new 1200cc, four-stroke models for the boys. Apart from some minor test-running and fine-tuning, they had never been bloodied in action yet. This would be their debut. They looked ready for it all shiny and bright.

G-Man gave us the scoop on the trick tune-up he had done the night before and some last-minute advice on running the new skis. We hooked up the double trailer and were off.

As we drove by Ho'okipa we saw a set that was gigantic. This is the stuff Laird lives for; he couldn't stop giggling with excitement. I was glad we were headed to the west side where I knew the waves would have to wrap almost ninety degrees and likely would be quite a bit smaller than the monsters we saw between Maliko and Ho'okipa.

Next stop was the gas station in Pa'ia where we ran into some other jet ski teams all headed for the other side, too. As we drove down the cane field road to Ilima's house at Baldwin to meet Dave Kalama, Laird started to think about his stomach.

"I need some food, what about you?" he asked.

Laird got on his phone, called Janey, and asked her to find him something to eat. I was a bundle of nerves by this time and the last thing on my mind was food. We pulled into Ilima's beachfront yard and there were the remaining members of the team. His son Dave, Sonny, and Nelson were busy hooking up jet ski trailers and tying down equipment and were generally in a white-hot, surf-fever frenzy. The surf was up, the day was young, and we were ready.

Janey arrived shortly thereafter with the *60 Minutes* crew in tow. The camera team jumped out to film the preparation action as it happened. Janey also had about twenty pounds of food for Laird from Anthony's, his everyday breakfast spot in Pa'ia.

We decided the surfers would all go to Honolua Bay first to check it out and figure out what to do from there, while the others would go get the rest of their stuff and meet us somewhere on the west side. Soon we were off and running, a convoy of jet skis, specialized tow-in equipment, and hot-to-trot surfers. Needless to say, the energy level was at a peak high.

We drove through Kahului and headed out toward the west side. As we rounded the bend by Thousand Peaks, I could see whitewater on Olowalu Point. Laird and I wondered if this was south swell and speculated that maybe it was north swell wrapping this far around the island. As we arrived at a vantage point where we could see the Olowalu surf break and Launiupoko Beach Park in the distance, we couldn't believe how much surf was there. At last we could see the direction.

It was north swell wrapping down a coastline that usually is open only to summer swells from far south. Puamana looked like a pointbreak. We watched a guy get a 200-yard right slide on a well-overhead wave. Cars were parked all along the road, and there were a ton of surfers out in the unusual but outstanding surf conditions.

When a north swell is big enough, it turns the whole west side into a series of pointbreaks as the waves wrap down the coast. Driving past Lahaina toward Honokowai, it's impossible to see through the trees and bushes as we could earlier on the road. Recent developments blocked the view at the former drive-by surf check spots of Rainbows and Osterizers. The entire Honokowai-Kahana-Napili area is so built up with houses and apartments these days that a person can't even see the ocean anymore.

Heading up Pineapple Hill I looked back and told Laird I could see lines of whitewater sweeping the coast. Coming over the other side of the hill, we both could see all the way to the outside of Honolua Bay. There was definitely a lot of surf. Maybe too much, a condition neither of us had experienced on this side of the island.

Going by Stables and Slaughterhouse Beach all we could see were waves breaking further out than we had ever seen. Tourists were parked all over the place gawking at the huge surf. Driving down the dirt road above Honolua, we knew the swell was too big for the bay to hold.

The wind was a light northerly trade making the waves a bit sloppy. Not that it mattered; Subs, the outermost break at Honolua Bay, was breaking out in the middle of the Pailolo Channel and the bay looked like the ocean water in *Victory at Sea*. It was a mess.

Just then Laird's cell phone rang. The caller was Archie Kalepa, saying that he, Buzzy Kerbox, and Mark Anderson were going out at S-Turns—it was looking like J-Bay at six to eight feet. We turned our caravan around and headed toward Napili.

A local family has a homemade boat ramp next to their property on Napili Bay. Their ramshackle home is a bit incongruous amongst all the high-rise development in the area, but to us it is like a touch of old Hawai'i in the midst of *malahinis*, or tourists, and concrete. We asked the old man as he sat outside on his plywood deck watching TV whether we could use his boat ramp.

"Go 'head, but you guys betta watch out, the waves stay only big today," he replied.

We told him that was why we were there, and he just laughed. He said he would enjoy watching us.

The *60 Minutes* camera crew filmed us making last-minute equipment preparations, getting into our surf gear, and launching the jet skis off the sketchy ramp. The tide was coming in and the surge coming up the ramp made the launching a little hairy, but Laird, DD, and Kalama are probably the world's best, so they made it look easy. Laird

"Go 'head, but you guys betta watch out, the waves stay only big today."

and Kalama teamed up while DD and I got on the second ski. Sonny and Nelson got their camera equipment loaded up on the third ski and we were all ready to go.

As we motored out through the faint channel we saw that the sets were relentless. Getting out through the surfline would require precise timing and a little luck. DD and Laird expertly picked a brief lull, jetted out through the impact zone, and before I had time to worry, we were safely outside the lineup.

S-Turns is a pretty obvious but seldom-ridden surf break. Windsurfers like it when the north wind and north swell are up, but today the surf was too big and the wind too light for them.

"OK brah, you're up," DD said to me.

I took a deep breath and unpacked my board from the rescue sled while he got out the towrope and attached it to the back of the ski. Laird and Kalama were nearby, but Laird wanted to try out his foil board and they were getting that toy ready.

"Here we go, here comes the set," said Darrick.

He looped around me with the ski, presenting me with the towrope handle. I took another deep breath as he idled out to the end of the rope and gave him the nod. With a big smile on his face, he gassed it, and I was up and riding. We rolled over a few waves and then saw a pretty good-sized one coming our way. DD lined up the ski, looked back at me as he ran down the swell, and, when he gauged the timing was right, turned back out to sea, whipping me at full speed into the long, lined-up wave.

I flew into the wave, zipping along so fast that my board was skipping like a stone above the wave's surface. The first thing I noticed was that this wave was not six to eight feet; as the thick swell slowed, steepened, and began to grow in height, I glanced down the face and saw that this wave was an easy fifteen feet. And it wasn't even starting to break yet. I took an even deeper breath and planned my attack. I figured I would just stay near the top of the wave since it was lined up far ahead.

The 6'6" board felt small on a wave this size, especially going this fast. I stayed in the top third of the wave, pumping and weaving to maintain speed. I thought I must be covering a lot of ground going so fast, but there was no end to the wave. I kept going and it kept forming ahead. Finally it looked like a section too long to make so I eased out over the top. DD was right behind and swooped quickly around me as I glided to a stop. Just before I started to sink, I grabbed the handle and yelled go.

Again we were off. As we turned back in the direction from which we had come I looked shoreward and saw that we had traveled a long way down the reef. The hotel we had caught the wave in front of seemed a long distance back from where we were now. Funny how that is—it seemed like just a brief moment on the wave, but it must have taken some time to ride so far.

We motored back up north and DD looked back at me, pointing out another wave, several waves behind the one we were going over. I gave him the thumbs up, and he swooped into position for another nice launch into a choice wave. The wind was a little out of the north, making the waves a tad bumpy, but at least it was downwind in the direction we were riding.

This wave was slightly smaller and I began to loosen up. I faded down the face, turning hard and deep at the bottom, and snapping turns off the top. I was riding a 6'6" by 16" board on a twelve-foot-plus wave, so the board felt as slippery as a bar of soap. When I pulled out, DD was right there for another quick pickup and we zoomed back to the lineup. There was a momentary lull and I needed to tighten my foot straps, so once we got outside I gave Darrick the stop signal and let go of the rope.

"Where are Laird and Dave?" I asked when DD pulled the ski up alongside.

"Oh, they saw that first wave you got and decided to forget the foil board, they went in to get their tow-in boards," he answered, "They'll be back any second."

As if to emphasize the point, we watched a ski whip Laird into a wave way up the line. On his new 6'2" he was making these enormous leaps off the chop on the wave's face and flying twenty feet before landing, and then launching off another bump for another twenty feet down the line. By the time he got even with us, he had probably been in the air 80 percent of the time and on the wave only 20 percent. He gave us a huge grin and a big hoot as he flew by. My foot straps were repaired and ready, so we got up again as another huge wave loomed.

My strategy is always to catch the biggest wave in the set. That way, I figure, there isn't a bigger wave behind the one I'm riding to catch me inside. Starting off standing up gives a surfer a big advantage in spotting the waves coming in. When I gave Darrick the go-ahead, it was on what looked to me the biggest wave of the set. He slung me into it, and I took off down the line.

Far away in the distance I saw Dave still following Laird's wave. Laird had to have been riding that wave for at least a mile. He also must have been going a whole lot faster than I was. He made that long section, where I figured to exit the wave because it didn't look makeable to me.

As I came over the top of my wave, I saw there was a bigger one behind and it was already breaking. This was going to be tight. Darrick came flying in and put the rope where I could grab it. I didn't even wait for the handle when I saw the look of concern on his face. I knew he was looking at the wave behind me. I grabbed the rope short and told him to hit it. I didn't dare turn around and look, I needed all my concentration to not blow the pickup.

Once I was up and planing, I let the rope slide through my fingers until I got a good grip on the handle. Only then did I turn around and look behind. The biggest wave we had seen so far was right on the tail of my board. I held on a little tighter. We were going through choppy water from the wave in front and I didn't want to fall off here. I held on with a death grip while Darrick gassed it straight in and we pulled away from the wave. Now we were inside the surfline, but at least we were safe.

Darrick pulled me around inside while we waited for a lull to get back out. Pulling someone over whitewater is a tricky maneuver but DD had it down. He positioned the ski so both ski and rider went over the wave at the same time. If the ski goes straight out, the towrope drags in the wave and pulls the rider down.

We soon got our lull and were back in the lineup. I had already gotten about ten waves, so I signaled Darrick that he should go. We stopped out where Dave and Laird were changing riders too. They paused when I dropped off the rope next to them.

"Eh brah, we thought you were toast, did you see how big that wave was behind you? You did good on that pickup, that was close … real close. The last thing we saw when we went over the wave was you waiting for the rope and then we couldn't see anymore and didn't know if you made it or not. But guess you did," they were both as happy as I was that I hadn't taken a beating.

So with DD and Kalama on the towropes, we swung back into action. Darrick was riding the new 6'0" pintail I had made for him and Dave was on a little 5'6" Timpone shooter. It didn't seem like the sets were as big as when we were first out, but there were still plenty of great waves and the sets were plenty big for the boys on their tiny boards.

After a few medium ones, I pulled Darrick into a pretty good-sized wave and nosed up to the back of it trying to watch his track from behind to get an idea of where he was and what he was doing. He blazed down the line going very fast. I was almost at full throttle trying to keep up. I could see his track as a faint line on the back of the lip and Darrick just kept wailing down the wall. And then the wave sectioned and I couldn't see his track anymore. I slowed down wondering why he would straighten out instead of kicking out. I thought maybe he had enough speed to go around under the section. By then I could see the wave was closed out and still no sign of Darrick.

I slowed down even more, looking back up the line to see if I had missed him. No Darrick that way. I rubbernecked to the left and the right but he was nowhere to be seen. Finally near total exasperation, I saw Laird and Dave pulling back out and they were both pointing in to what I assumed was Darrick's position. I started heading in, and finally saw him inside and farther down the line than I expected. But I had delayed too long.

The next wave was breathing down my neck, and I could see that there wouldn't be time to grab him. I could go in front of the wave but would miss him, have to go all the way inside and work my way back out over the waves behind. It would be a while before I would get to him. The alternative was to try to get over this wave bearing down on me. Darrick would have to eat one more wave, but then I could get to him.

I decided to try to get over the wave behind. I raced down the line, pegging the throttle on that big 1200cc four-stroke. I was looking for an opening on the wave face that wasn't too steep so I could ease up over the top without catching too much air. It didn't look good, the wave was starting to section down the line, and once it broke, my chance to get over it would be gone.

I saw a small section where I thought I could slip over, but it was closing down fast so I had to act fast. I was hauling ass going parallel to the wave, and when I got to the open section, I turned the ski up the face and made my move. I was going way too fast, everything worked like I planned until I hit the top of the wave. Even with the throttle backed off, my momentum was enough to launch me a long distance in the air.

I guess I thought I was on one of the older, smaller, and lighter skis and that I could correct my angle once I was in the air. But that 1200 was a hog and I came down the same way I went up … sideways. Landing on the port rail didn't allow the jet to propel me out of the splash like I had hoped. I was pitched forward and jammed the end of the left handlebar straight into my groin—oof!

The ski bounced up and landed back on the starboard side this time. Again I was thrown forward into the other side of the handlebar. Somehow I held on, a little sore and out of breath but safely behind the wave and ready to swing in to pickup Darrick. I reached for the throttle lever but was shocked to find it wasn't there.

What the hell—I could see the next wave was big and bearing down on me. I glanced down at the throttle assembly and saw that the entire throttle lever was gone, sheared off at the base. The broken piece was lying down in the gunwale near my foot. I reached into the assembly with my fingernails, tearing them in the process, but somehow got enough of the throttle cable to pull on to make the throttle work. Moving again, I dashed in to get Darrick. I got the rope to him and pulled him up before the next wave could get us. Farther inside where it was safe, I slowed, dropping DD into the water, then circled back to him.

"What's up brudda?" he asked.

Showing him the broken throttle lever, I told him we were done for the day. I thought he would be angry since he only got a couple of waves, but he was more concerned if I was OK. My right hand felt like I had broken something, but it was only the unbreakable ABS plastic throttle lever that broke. My index knuckle was only bruised and sore.

I told DD about taking the handlebar in the groin, and, always the lifeguard, he said we should check for damage right now. So trying to keep our balance on the bobbing ski, he unzipped my wetsuit, and I peeled it down to take a look. It was already black and blue, but except for being a little sore, it looked pretty minor. Six inches lower and I probably would have been singing soprano. Except for taking the ski out of action for the day, I had gotten off light.

We motored in and beached the ski. There was a huge crowd of people along the road watching the action and traffic was backed up. My brother Victor was there with his tow-in board looking for a ride, but I said our ski was broken. He said there were about six skis out there. I remembered seeing some other skis off in the distance when we were out there but, except for Laird and Dave, had never gotten close to any of them. We figured they would be coming in to gas up sooner or later and someone would give him a tow.

A guy across the street offered his outside hot shower, which I gladly accepted. Nothing could have felt so good to my bruised and battered body. The *60 Minutes* crew had a room on the sixth floor of the Napili Shores Hotel to film from. I decided to go down there to watch the action and lick my wounds.

Laird and Kalama outclassed the rest of the field by a large margin, not only in their wave riding but in their entry and pickup techniques as well. It was obvious they were in a league of their own. From the vantage point above, I could see the action of both surfer and ski and watched Dave running the ski at full speed behind the wave while Laird on the wave appeared to be going even faster and would pull away. I know those Kawasakis are capable of fifty miles per hour in flat water, maybe a bit slower in these surf conditions, but Laird had to be going somewhere in the neighborhood of fifty. It was a sight to behold. Victor got out with Mark Anderson and had a good time speeding down the long-riding waves.

Finally, the sun got lower and the day began to come to an end. It seemed like it went by in a hurry, but time has a way of doing that when everyone is having fun. We loaded up the jet skis, said adios to all the people, and headed back to the other side of the island. It was dark when we got back and everyone was pooped. Laird and I dropped the skis back off at G-Man's. He chuckled about breaking the unbreakable throttle lever but said he would have everything ready to go again the next morning. We limped home, ate a quick dinner, and hit the hay.

Morning came quickly, and while the booming surf was not as loud as the day before, it was still there. A little weary, sore, and bruised, I dragged myself out of bed and into a wake-up shower. I knew we had a big day ahead. Lesley Stahl was going to be on location today. It would be my job to hang with her and explain what was going on while the other guys were out in the water. I shaved, combed my hair, and brushed and flossed my teeth, thinking I better look my best for one of the most famous news commentators in the world. Laird, his dad Billy, who had just arrived the night before, and I rallied DD, Nelson, and Sonny, gathered the equipment, and headed back to the west side.

The surf wasn't quite as big as the day before. Arriving at Honolua Bay, we could see that it had tamed down and was very surfable. We went back down to Napili and launched the skis at the old man's place. He was sitting in the same place, watching TV; he thanked us for the beer we had given him the day before. I drove back up to Honolua with Matt George, who also had come in the night before.

There was quite a crowd gathered on the point watching the action. Four skis were already in the lineup and the waves looked fun. The wind was still light northerly and the sets were an easy ten to twelve feet, but every once in a while a much bigger set would roll through. Laird, Dave, Darrick, Victor, Nelson, and Sonny finally arrived and they immediately went into action.

From the cliff there on the point, the view is about as good as it gets. Matt and I sat back and enjoyed the show while we waited for Lesley. The film crew showed up first, and I helped them find a good location from which to shoot. Finally Lesley, Braden, and the main group pulled up and got out of their cars. Lesley Stahl, who has interviewed world leaders, was completely stunned by the whole scene.

The vantage point from the cliff was similar to the best seats in any athletic stadium. Lesley didn't completely understand the game or know the players, but the action was undeniably spectacular. Like the pro she is, Lesley didn't waste a moment. She moved us into position in front of the cameras, where we could talk about what was happening out in the ocean, and her crew got it all on film.

The show was basically going to be about Laird. As if on cue, every wave for the next fifteen minutes came right to him. Everyone else must have been resting because for that time while Lesley and I stood on the cliff, Laird got all the waves. Ride after ride thrilled Lesley to no end. She had never seen anything quite like this, but then again neither had most of the crowd there on the cliff.

Tow-in surfing at Honolua Bay is something very rare. Usually the most crowded surf spot on the whole island, that day the waves were too big for the paddle surfers, so the jet ski teams got to have it by default. I was completely jazzed watching the action. Having surfed there hundreds of times, occasionally in similar conditions, I knew what an advantage it was to tow-in instead of paddle. I couldn't wait for my own chance. Finally, Lesley figured we had enough of this, and I was free to go surf. She would go up in a helicopter and follow along up above as Laird surfed.

I got on the two-way radio and told Victor and DD that I wanted to surf. They would meet me down at the old boat ramp inside the bay. In the old days at Honolua, everyone used to park down there and paddle out. Over the years the road has deteriorated and a locked gate was put up, but a person can still walk down the old road. It's an old creek bed and the trees are big and shady. The cliff has a great view, but it's up in the pineapple field. Up there the terrain is windy, dusty, dirty, and offers no shade. Down at the old ramp, it's cool and quiet.

I let all the feelings of the early days at Honolua wash over me as I walked down to meet Victor and Darrick. The west side is hot, uncomfortably so, but I felt cool as could be walking down that old road with my surfboard under my arm. The only sounds were the wind whistling through the trees and the birds singing. Victor was waiting at the ramp by himself. He said Darrick swam in at the point since that was where the car was. I jumped on the ski and we motored out to the waves.

Victor and I have surfed Honolua every time it's good for the past twenty-five to thirty years. We know the place intimately. The main break on a good north by northwest swell is called the Cave. This is the site pictured in most of the photographs seen of Honolua Bay. It's also so crowded on a good day that many surfers will take one look at the mob scene and not even paddle out.

Just out from the Cave is the Point, which is also a good wave but usually smaller and not as hollow as the Cave. Further out from there is the Coconut Grove or just Coconuts, which is good when the Cave is good and can be very hollow as well. The farthest outside spot is called Subs, named after a huge rock that looks like a submarine surfacing right inside the takeoff zone. On the north to northeast swell direction like that day, Subs is the place the swell hits best and biggest.

Victor and I love Subs because it will hold a big swell and always is the least crowded. To get to tow-in at the place is a treat beyond description. Victor had a great session with Darrick while I was up on the cliff, and he was stoked to get me into some good waves.

The teams who were there earlier must have run low on fuel because by the time we got to the lineup only Laird and Kalama were riding. They pulled up while we were getting ready and said they had to zip back to Napili to do some pickup shots. They said it shouldn't take long and they would be back as soon as they could.

Now Victor and I had the whole bay to ourselves. Nelson had let Sonny off and now had Billy Hamilton on his ski, but they were just watching from the channel. It was a beautiful day with beautiful waves. There were hundreds of people on the cliff watching us, but the water was empty. Victor saw a set approaching and told me to get ready. We motored out to pick up the biggest wave. The thing about towing-in at a familiar spot is that I feel very comfortable, I know the lineup, I know the wave, I know where I should be and what I should do. This makes the whole process smoother and easier.

Victor knew which wave he thought was best, but he looked back at me to get a final confirmation. I gave him the nod and he gassed the ski into position. Usually whenever we had paddle-surfed out here when it was big, the takeoff positioning was ultracritical; more often than not we would be in the wrong spot and would have to let the wave go by or, worse, be a little too far inside and have to deal with the anxiety of being trapped.

With the jet ski, it was the easiest thing in the world. Victor would flick me into the swell way outside of where it would actually start breaking, but I had so much speed that I could just swoop and glide into any position I wanted. The wave here going into the bay was much smoother than the waves yesterday out at S-Turns. It was like riding warm butter, slicing around, going anywhere I wanted to on the wave face.

My board felt solid and fast and, with each wave, I grew more and more confident and daring. A few times I turned up high and had the wave explode on my back blasting me into the air and back down the wave. With my feet secured in foot straps I could just ride it out. Without foot straps, I would have been knocked off by the exploding whitewater. Sections loomed ahead and started to break, but I had enough speed to go down and around them. Every time I finished a wave, a little out of breath, I asked Victor if he wanted to go in my place.

He laughed, shook his head, and said, "No way bra, you go."

On one particularly big wave I rode through Coconuts and into the Point where I had to pump the board a little to stay in the wave as it turned the corner. Before I knew it, I was backdooring the Cave section and still riding. Might as well go the whole way I thought and kept milking it right to the end of the Keiki Bowl. I pulled out of the wave almost at the boat ramp when Victor swung in to pick me up.

"How long was that ride?" he yelled.

A look of surprise and joy beamed from his face. I climbed on the sled instead of grabbing the rope for the long ride back out, and we talked about how great the waves were the whole way.

By the time we got back to the lineup, Laird and Kalama were back and ready to go. All afternoon we traded waves. Bigger sets began to show up, maybe a result of the lower tide. The rides were long. At one point, we all pulled over to catch our breath, and Kalama said that because it took four minutes going at least fifteen miles per hour to get back out to lineup, he figured we were getting mile-long rides.

Don Shearer showed up in his hotshot helicopter with Lesley Stahl hanging out the passenger window and zoomed around following Laird as he rode waves so she could get a sensation of the speeds we were riding. Then they were gone, and all of a sudden, we realized that the sun was about to go down. After one last wave each, we packed it up and giddy from the experience, headed back toward Napili under a radiant West Maui sunset. Leaving the sky a psychedelic red-and-orange light show, the sun sank into the sea between Lana'i and Moloka'i as we pulled into Napili Bay.

We got all the skis loaded up and headed out on the road home. It was hard to remember all that had happened that day, all the waves we rode, all the fun we had. Tomorrow would be another day and who could say what that would bring, but the thought of it was far from our minds at that moment. Flashes of waves or rides would flit through our minds and bodies like electric pulses, and we would talk about it, but mostly we would just savor those moments in silence, quiet little smiles on our faces.

The TV show had time constraints that prevented them from showing much more than the interviews with Laird, Gabby, and Billy. Most of us got left on the cutting room floor. But that was fine; the memories of what we had could never be cut from the film reels of our minds. I would go back to Oregon and a great winter of snow; the boys would do a lot more waiting for surf but finally in early January would get an epic day at Jaws.

Life goes on and the surf and snow continue to come on a schedule entirely their own and almost impossible to predict. Surf is where you find it, but it's always there, if not in the ocean or the mountain on a particular day then always in the mind and spirit. Ride the glide and let the spirit soar.

Chile

This tricky little paddle is the quick way out at Punta de Lobos.
That's me almost to the island, John McMahon about to jump, and
Yvon Chouinard hanging back, maybe wondering at the wisdom
of this approach. Photo: Jeff Johnson

Life is like riding a wave. There is no way to know what the ride is going to be like from the vantage point of the takeoff, but inevitably there is always more ahead. Sometimes the ride is fun and wonderful. Other times it's scary and dangerous. Anticipation gives rise to expectations, but more often than not there will be surprises along the way.

I had just started working for Patagonia, a company that I've admired and respected for a long time. It's a company that isn't just out there to make money, but one that is in business to be successful and do worthwhile things with that success. Preservation of our environment becomes more important every day, as the race goes on to save our planet before we destroy it with so many self-serving endeavors—most of them in the name of business and profit, of one sort or another.

Patagonia is a pioneer company in the relatively new lifestyle sportswear industry. They look for ways to give back instead of only taking. As the surfing industry continues to grow into land-based mass markets, Patagonia has become an industry leader in seeking ways to sustain civilization rather than contribute to its collapse.

My first week on the job was a dream gig. It was a surf trip to Chile with the charismatic and energetic owner of the company, Yvon Chouinard, and a group of surfers and photographers. We met at LAX, checked in to our LAN Chile flight to Santiago, boarded the plane, and all tried to get as comfortable as possible for the twelve-hour plane ride.

We had quite a crew. Yvon, John McMahon, Chris Carter, and I comprised the Silverback section. Keith Malloy, Jeff Johnson, Branden Aroyan, our still photographer, and Dave Homcy, the film photographer, made up the young buck contingent. Keith's brother, Chris, and Jack Johnson would join us a few days later. Landing in Chile, we were met by Jorge Montaner and Max Mills, two old friends of Yvon.

Jorge led us through the red tape of renting the cars we would need. We got the huge pile of surfboards strapped on the roofs, and Max led our caravan through the maze of Santiago; we headed straight for the coast. Our destination was the surf town of Pichilemu, where a strong south swell was in the forecast.

Once out of the capital city of Santiago, we drove by seemingly endless farms, orchards, and the occasional fruit stand along the highway piled high with displays of avocados, oranges, grapefruits, pears, apples, and other late-season produce. The countryside reminded me a lot of old Southern California when the orchards lined the highways, before the landscape disappeared under subdivisions and housing tracts.

Eventually we got to Pichilemu, a small coastal town that is very popular during the summer months of January and February when the weather is warm and everyone wants to come to the beach. We were there in mid-May. The late fall season had turned cold and the place was deserted.

Pulling over at the overlook of the main surf spot in town, we planned to get our bearings, meet Yvon's other friend Alex Soto, and decide what to do next. I immediately walked down the hill to the beach to stick my hands in the water to get a feel for its temperature. It felt like the midfifties, not bad compared to water temps where I surf in Oregon.

It was blustery and cold, but the sunset was spectacular. The dark, cloudy sky opened for a few stunning moments as the huge red ball of the sun slipped under the horizon.

I headed back to the guys to see what, if anything, had been decided. Decision-making by such a large group can be a slow process. When food was mentioned, however, everyone readily agreed that lunch was in order.

Alex and Max took us to a nearby restaurant. We were the only patrons on this off-season afternoon. A light lunch consisted of a big appetizer of fresh local *locos*, a Chilean abalone, and a main course of Chilean sea bass, lots of salad, and cooked vegetables. Obviously there was nothing light about this lunch.

I was fatigued from the long journey. While waiting for the fish course, I was already thinking about sleeping. However, after eating and paying what seemed to all of us very little for such a large amount of food, I regained some energy. We headed for the house Alex had rented for us. It wasn't far from the ocean and had plenty of room for our whole group.

We unloaded our gear, separated what we would need for a surf session, and headed back to the beach. There was a surf spot just outside the town called Punta de Lobos where we were told the surf would be the biggest.

The expected swell had not arrived yet. The waves were only in the two- to three-foot range, but the sun was out and the conditions looked good. Everyone jumped into their wetsuits and headed down the steep cliff to paddle out. I took one of the empty board bags and found a nice spot on the cliff top above the surf to do some yoga first.

As I went into my first asana, I noticed another group of local surfers with a small entourage climbing down the cliff. Four of the surfers went into the water while the other guys climbed a big rock that appeared to have a nice vantage point to view the surfing. Back in town we had heard that there was some kind of local surf contest the day before and that they had a final heat to finish up.

The thought occurred to me that I might be watching that final heat. I saw four surfers paddle out to where our boys were getting a few waves. They conversed, then our guys paddled further in and away from the local boys. The waves were infrequent but nicely shaped, and the four surfers proceeded to rip it apart.

The guys on the rocks seemed to be the judges for the contest. It didn't look like our guys were going to get any waves because the four hotshots were all over every wave that came. I saw our boys start to trickle in as the sun began to get closer to the horizon.

Keith paddled back out after a while assuming that the contest would soon be over, but he just sat there while the four Chilean surfers kept at it. It looked cold. Watching the sun sinking into the sea, I was certain Keith was shivering out there. Finally the sun set and Keith came in frozen. I was glad I had stayed dry.

An enormous and delicious sushi dinner, a night of trying to find sleep between the mosquito attacks, and the biting-cold wee hours of the morning in a house without central heating brought us to our second day in Chile. Unfortunately the bad wind from the north was there early. The anticipated swell had arrived but conditions were poor. We lounged around, ate another huge lunch, and idled some more until we felt the wind dying down.

It was still cold and cloudy, a gloomy afternoon by anyone's standards. Alex told us there was another spot to surf around the front of the point at Punta de Lobos, so we went for the hike to check it out. Keith and Jeff brought their boards, and Yvon brought his fishing equipment, but the rest of us just went to watch.

It was quite a setup, a steep cliff down to the beach and a powerful-looking shorebreak with quite a bit more size than the waves on the point. Keith, Jeff, and Yvon climbed down a talus slope to the beach while we watched from the cliff top.

The surf was not friendly. The boys had to be very selective in their wave choices. Even when they chose well, every ride ended in a closed-out section. They made it look a lot better than it was, but to us it seemed like an awful lot of work with little reward.

Yvon rigged his fly-fishing gear. Trying to keep his shoes from getting wet, he fished from the sand and off some of the massive rocks that jutted out into the water. Neither the surf nor the fishing was very productive, but they came back satisfied to have done it.

It was blustery and cold, but the sunset was spectacular. The dark, cloudy sky opened for a few stunning moments as the huge red ball of the sun slipped under the horizon. That evening we went back to the sushi restaurant, where again we were the only ones there. The gracious couple who owned it served us another fabulous dinner. This second meal was a different local fish in a choice of elegant sauces, followed by a myriad of gourmet desserts. It was a sophisticated meal that would have impressed the most demanding gourmand.

Back home, however, we faced another night of battles with the mosquitoes. The contrast between sumptuous restaurant meals and the squalor of insect warfare grew ever more stark. With the aid of more blankets to fend off the cold, we slept in anticipation of a day of surf.

Sure enough, a favorable wind-switch brightened an otherwise cloudy and grey morning. After breakfast and gear organization, we headed for the beach. Our first look revealed offshore winds, lines stacked out to sea, and a long, peeling left. No one needed a second look as we got into our wetsuits as fast as we could. The sets were consistent and looked relentless to paddle out through, but Alex told us of an easier way to the lineup.

On the outside, the waves broke off an island that was separated by a small channel from the point. Alex told us to climb down the cliff, paddle across the channel to the island, walk around to the front of it, wait for a lull, jump in, and we would be right in the takeoff zone. That sounded pretty straightforward. Watching wave after wave peel down the point, which would have made paddling out a formidable task, we looked forward to this easy jump-off spot.

Getting into a wetsuit may be a simple process for some people; it's a complete wrestling match for me. By the time I got my suit, booties, gloves, and hood on, everyone else was well on their way to the water. I wandered down the trail I had watched them take, followed it down the cliff face, and luckily found some guys just jumping in to paddle across to the island. I spotted the rock they were using.

The channel between the point and island must have been deep, because as big as the waves were outside, they didn't break where we paddled across. I jumped in and paddled to the other side. I had also seen where the guys ahead had climbed up onto the island. The surge was tremendous even without breaking waves, but I timed it correctly and it carried me right up on the rock shelf. From there it was a short climb up to dry rock.

The island was in two sections of tall rock spires. I couldn't see where the other guys had gone exactly, but following the upper dry sections I assumed this was the only way. There were a few tricky sections to negotiate that were slippery, and the surge was heavy; on the front side of the island the waves broke full force. I managed to get to where I could see the outside takeoff area where the guys were sitting. I figured I must be in the right spot.

The waves were a solid eight feet on the sets and consistent. Waiting for a lull, I inched my way toward the edge of the island. It was slippery and hard to see under the whitewater washing in. There was also thick, ropey kelp on the water's edge that reminded me of snakes or the tentacles of some sea monster. I had trouble walking through this stuff.

As I got near the water, another set came. I scurried back to the safety of a dry area of the small island. I tried several more attempts, but they only led to more retreats from waves. This wasn't getting me any closer to the great rides all the guys were having only a short distance away. During the whole time I had not found a good place where I could launch myself into the water. OK, I thought, I guess I just have to go for it quickly and decisively.

When the next lull came, I moved out determined to make it. The closer I got to the water the more it was like walking on a hedge, but I was going this time no matter what. Finally I got to where I could jump. Unfortunately, the tentacles of thick kelp not

only were wrapped around my feet and legs, but I also saw that I would have to paddle out through an area where they were really dense.

I had a brief vision of my leash tangled in them, being trapped in front of a set and slammed back on the island. I dove in and paddled hard, trying to keep my leashed foot high in the air so the loop wouldn't hook up on anything. A large wave came right as I jumped out and I raced to get to it before it broke. Lucky for me, my leash didn't catch, my adrenaline was pumping, and I managed to duck-dive under the wave just in time.

I came up clean on the other side and knew I had made it. The surge from the waves breaking over the exposed corner of the island carried me to the safety of the shoulder where Alex was sitting on his board with a shocked look on his face. As I sat up next to him, he was shaking his head from side to side.

"I have never seen anyone do that before in all the years I have been surfing here," he said.

"What do you mean—isn't that where you guys all came out?" I asked.

"Didn't you hear me yelling at you, I was telling you to come off the side of the island. You went right off the front into the most dangerous part. I was thinking that you had come to Chile for the first time and were going to get killed right in front of me," he explained.

Well, I didn't hear anything because the waves were crashing so hard. A near disaster, but surfing is like that, one close call after another. I was out and I would know better the next time. The waves were beautiful. I caught my first one and it was perfect for a long ride. I thought, "Yeah, I could do this all day."

I caught an edge on that first wave after riding what seemed like a long distance. I was surprised when I looked back to see how far I actually had traveled, even further than I thought. But looking down the point toward shore, I saw that I had only ridden about half the rideable length of the wave. I paddled back out determined to ride the next wave the whole way to its end.

That next wave took me for a ride. I was turning, cutting back, turning, over and over; it just keep lining up ahead of me. On and on I went until I started thinking about the paddle back. When I pulled out, there was still a lot of wave to ride. Looking back to sea, I was so far around the point that I couldn't see the island where I started. I could see it was a long paddle, but it was only my second wave so I still had energy for the paddle back.

Fifteen minutes later, not a lot closer to where I was headed, I was beginning to have second thoughts about doing this all day long. It took me more than thirty minutes of steady paddling to get back to the takeoff spot. With the current running around and down the point, it had been a long, hard haul.

Keith and Jeff were back in the lineup, and I asked them about the paddle back out. They laughed and told me that riding all the way to the beach and walking back was much easier. I rode the next wave to shore, found a path up the cliff, and got on the road. It was definitely less effort than paddling, and it only took fifteen minutes. The jump off the island was better this time since I knew the right spot.

It was an interesting surf spot. The long rides kept the crowd, which wasn't much anyway, circulating. A guy would be there for a moment, catch a wave, and be gone for the next half hour or so. Eventually the cold water began to take its toll, and after four hours, I noticed that none of our guys were coming back out anymore. I didn't want them all waiting for me so I went in on the next one.

Alex and the local surfers all agreed that the surf would be much better at low tide. They thought we should take a break until then. So we went back to town for lunch. This time it was a little place Yvon had his eye on that served local sandwiches. Anyone who thinks a sandwich is a light lunch has not experienced the sandwiches in Chile. The others' sandwiches were a pound of beef, mine a pound of fish. I wondered about surfing later with so much food in me.

The swell was still holding strong and the waves were a lot faster on the low tide. The jump off was also quite a bit less stressful, and we all got out with dry hair. The current coming around the point was fierce at low water: It was a battle to stay in the lineup. The inside section, if that's a proper description of 300 yards of wave, was zippering and hollow. Keith and Jeff came back claiming tuberides, but all I found were long rides that just went and went. That was perfectly fine with me. We surfed until dark and everybody came in buzzed. It had been a hall-of-fame day of surf.

This time we called and ordered our epic sushi dinner ahead. Platters of fresh sushi arrived even as we were sitting down. The terrorist mosquitoes back at our rooms were still problematic, but fortunately in Yvon's and my room I discovered their daytime lair in the closet. I had mashed them all in their sleep instead of allowing them to attack us during ours. Yvon questioned my small-animal hunting skills even when I showed him all the blood spots. He still lathered up with bug repellent, but I slept the untroubled sleep of the pure of heart that night without that dreaded buzzing of the blood-sucking mossies.

The next day the surf was the same, perfect and possibly even a little bigger. One of the day's highlights was Keith Malloy bodysurfing perhaps the longest ride ever. I happened to have ridden the wave before to shore, and I was just getting out when I looked back and saw what looked like one of the sea lions the point was named after slipping in and out of the barrel. It was quite a ride.

The rides were so long that it was impossible to get a whole one on a roll of film. Dave had to be very selective about when and how long to shoot. Chris and Jack showed up after our morning session and were eager to hit the afternoon low tide, especially after we told them about the great waves we were having. The late session was another memorable one and everyone went to dinner that night lit up from it.

The next morning we awoke to a slight weather change. It looked like we might have some sun but the wind, although not strong, had shifted back to north. Even without the offshore winds combing the faces clean, the waves still looked good. The size was a little less and there was some bump on the face, but the waves were long and peeling. Yvon and John, who had paddled out from the beach the last couple days, wanted to attempt the island jump off since they had been worked trying to come out from the inside.

There's probably nothing more fatiguing than getting caught inside. When it happens just getting out there, it saps one's energy for the whole session. So my tales of getting out without getting my hair wet at the top of the lineup had them willing to chance it. I drilled them on the whole procedure and then led them down the proverbial garden path. The high tide was working against us and the surge was worse. I described the first jump and the short paddle across to the island and told them to watch exactly where I climbed up.

So I went, got up on the island, took my leash off, put my board up high, and climbed back down to help if they needed it. John came first, got washed around by the surge, handed me his board, and got right up. I handed him back his board and got ready for Yvon. He came right across but when he started to reach the shelf I was on, I could see he was between the crests of the surge.

Being down in the trough made it a much longer and more difficult climb up, but the surge wasn't breaking so I thought there should be no problem. He was right there, the nose of his board no more than two inches from my outstretched hands. I glanced to my right to gauge the high point of the surge. When I turned my head back, Yvon was gone. It was the weirdest thing. One second he was there, and the next he had disappeared.

I stood up panicked. The area wasn't that big but he was gone. Then I heard the sickening crunch of fiberglass and foam smashing on rock. I could see John climbing down just around the corner no more that ten feet away, when suddenly Yvon's longboard washed out of a crack that I hadn't noticed before. I ran, and while John got a hold of Yvon, I grabbed for his board by the leash, but the plug in the tail block had been crushed and the leash was no longer attached. The board washed away.

A local surfer who was coming right behind Yvon dove back in and went after the loose board. I stood there feeling like an idiot but grabbed the longboard from the other guy when he got close. The nose and tail were completely smashed, and there were quite a few scrapes and dings on the rails and on both sides. Yvon was pretty shaken.

He had been slammed hard into that crack and smashed his upper leg on the rocks. We all climbed to higher ground where it was safe, but Yvon's surfboard was not in good shape and his leash was finished.

We couldn't go back the way we came. The only way was to paddle out and catch a wave to get back in. John and Yvon were probably wondering, "What has this moron gotten us into," but I just told them what we had to do next. I was thinking, "Here I am, my first week on the job, and I've just about lost the boss: I really am a moron."

The high tide was the real culprit, but there we were and the only way out was through the waves. Yvon's leg was seizing up, but he realized we had to keep going out to get back in, and he was still game. I said I was sorry a hundred times, but Yvon just laughed, telling me it was his own fault, not mine. Still, I wondered if I was going to have a job the following week.

We got out without further incident and got some waves. Yvon got one and took it in, his leg so stiff already he could hardly stand up. I felt like an idiot. I just stayed out and surfed rather than go in and face the jury. The waves were not great, the conditions were deteriorating, but it was still a long ride even if rough and bumpy. Finally I went in, the last one out of the water.

Everyone else had left and, still in my wetsuit, I piled into the car with Chris, John, and Yvon. Yvon's leg was badly bruised, and I apologized again for the rough treatment. John rubbed it in as much as he could, but soon we were all laughing about it. We were all old hands at this surfing game, which requires one to pay as often as he plays. This was just a case of the check coming before the meal.

Back at the house I wrestled out of my wetsuit, while Jack gave us a little impromptu concert. Everyone huddled around the single kerosene heater; it was noisy and stinky but gave out some warmth. John, Chris, and I were scheduled to leave the next day, while the rest were staying a few days longer; they planned to go up north to look at another surf spot that was supposed to be even better than the ones in town.

When I think about it, we didn't even surf the other two spots in town, preferring the bigger waves on the point. Still, every time we checked, the other places looked perfect too. It's hard to do it all, but I know I would go back again in a heartbeat. The three of us reluctantly headed out the next day, but with many memories of good times, good waves, good food, and great friends.

I think the next time Yvon suggests we go rock climbing, I'm going to say I can't make it. I know what they say about paybacks.

Yvon Chouinard and me about to launch
ourselves into the surf at Punta de Lobos.
Photo: Jeff Johnson

A long bottom turn on the 'Ski World Glacier' in the Cariboo Mountains of British Columbia, Canada. Photo: John Schwirtlich

v. SURF IS...

The Demise of the Ditch

Since it's gone, I guess there's no reason to keep the secret any longer. What we had was a pretty neat surf spot almost 200 miles from the ocean. For three years it had been double top secret. Even so, like everything else in the surfing world, the word had gotten out. That's why it was taken away. Too many people were having too much fun. Actually, the real reason wasn't about the fun but about too many people being where they weren't supposed to be.

How does a surfing wave occur in the middle of the desert? Well, I never would have believed it until I saw it. It starts with a long, cold winter season and lots of snow. Come spring that snow begins to melt, feeding the lakes and rivers, which are tapped for crop irrigation. Take a feeder canal transporting the water fifty miles away to a reservoir. Along that ditch are several features engineered to slow the gravity-fed flow of water. One of them is nothing more than a minor pinch on both walls combined with a slight drop in the slope of the bottom. Add the correct cubic feet per second of water discharged into the canal and somehow this combination works just right to produce a rideable standing wave.

My kayaker friend Ben, familiar with most of the standing waves in the various waterways in our area, told me he thought a surfboard could be ridden on this one particular wave. I laughed at first, but he persisted, and finally I drove out there with him to take a look. It was a hot summer day with temperatures in the midnineties, and I had been shaping surfboards for the past five hours. A break for any reason was a welcome distraction.

We drove through a subdivision on the northeast side of town and then down a dusty dirt road. Suddenly he stopped and turned off the key. I could hear the sound of rushing water but couldn't see anything. We got out and walked up a slight embankment, and there was the canal full of water. Directly below was—well—it was a wave. It was a glassy peak about two feet high breaking in the center of a concrete ditch.

Ben had an old Becker mini-tanker that had seen better days and was about to see worse. The sides of the ditch were sprayed gunite; they were rough, and they

A wave that is equally a right- and a left-hand break in clean fresh water that will give a surfer a ride for as long as he can stay on the board … too good to be true? Photo: Ben Moon

soon would be especially tough on the fragile fiberglass skin of a surfboard. He stripped off his shirt, grabbed his board, carefully stepped down the rugged wall, and launched himself into the water.

For anyone who hasn't seen a standing wave, it is a peculiar phenomenon. The wave breaks upstream against the current: The water moves while the wave doesn't. Ben took several quick paddles, and just like that he caught the wave. Slowly and deliberately he got to his feet and began surfing the wave. I stood almost close enough to touch him, but I was high and dry, perched on the concrete wall.

There have been times, on the edge of reefs, or on rocks, where I have been close to someone surfing. But the surfer would approach, go past and be gone, and I would have to deal with the crashing whitewater with varying degrees of success. Here I was right next to Ben as he concentrated fiercely on keeping the ride going, with the water madly rushing by. Although he moved from side to side on the peak, he stayed in the same place.

I remember the kids at Waimea Bay digging a little groove to open the river when it was full and much higher than sea level. Once they got the water flowing, it would cut a channel through the sand until it was gushing out into the bay. At a certain point, a standing wave would form that could be ridden on boogie boards. I had heard about some guys riding that wave with surfboards, but never saw it. I only remember that the stagnant river water—brown and smelly—wasn't anything I wanted to get my body near.

Here the water was fresh and clean, running from a high alpine reservoir, cool on that hot summer afternoon. I watched Ben from the bank, completely mesmerized. Finally, he caught an edge and the current whisked his board away from him. He swam after it, grabbed it, stood up, and scrambled over to the opposite side of the canal. Here the water eddied and the current actually ran back upstream. He walked slowly back with a huge smile on his face. When he got back to the wave, he paused, holding the board in both hands, then launched himself back into the peak and did it all over again. Still riding the wave, he looked over at me and said, "What do you think?"

"Let me try it," I answered.

He kept riding until he lost the wave again, chased his board down, stopped himself in another eddy on my side, and climbed out. I peeled off my shirt and he handed me his surfboard. I stepped down to the water's edge and jumped. The board had lots of flotation so it was easy to gain my feet. I was surfing, pointed upstream, and, like Ben before me, I wasn't going anywhere. Yet the dynamics of the fast-moving water created a sensation of great speed. At first I just trimmed, keeping the nose pointed straight upstream. Then I carefully moved back toward the board's sweet spot and tried some gentle turns. It felt just like a wave—a fast wave. Back and forth I turned. As long as I returned to the center of the peak each time, I stayed in the wave. Using the board's glide, I found I could go out pretty far on each side of the peak: It was a small wave with both a left and a right shoulder.

Eventually I stuck the nose and wiped out. I grabbed the board, put my feet down, and found the flat concrete bottom about two feet under the surface. By angling toward the side, I could step out of the mainstream current down the center and reach the eddy. There was no sweep at all along the wall. The bottom was flat and easy to walk on. I couldn't believe it: Here in the middle of the desert was a wave as refreshing as any on the ocean. I rode a few more times on Ben's board, but already my shaper's mind had gone through my own surfboard quiver in the garage at home. I couldn't wait until the next day to try out a smaller board.

Ben and I returned the following afternoon, and I enjoyed a much better session on a 6'2". But already, I had imagined a new, ditch-specific design. That's the beauty of having my own surfboard factory. It's something I've enjoyed throughout my entire surfing career, ever since I made my first board. Whenever I had an inspiration for a different type of surfboard, I could just go build it—which is exactly what happened the next morning. The first thing I did was shape the initial 5'6" Ditch Bitch. Using UV resin makes building a surfboard almost an instant endeavor, and by the afternoon, the Ditch Bitch was ready for her maiden voyage.

The first wave was a little tricky; I had never ridden such a short surfboard and surfing was very different on a freshwater wave. I was used to the buoyancy of salt water and needed to adjust. I tried to push myself up, but the board didn't offer much resistance and sank almost underwater. I adjusted to a lighter-footed approach, and once up, that short little board turned like a dream. It fit its intended wave perfectly.

Turning a surfboard back and forth as hard as one can takes a lot of energy. After about twenty-five turns at the ditch, my legs were pumped up and I was out of breath. While riding long waves like Honolua Bay on a north swell from Outside Subs all the way through the Cave, my legs would start to cramp. On an equally long ride at G-Land they never did. I had wondered about that and figured I was going faster and doing fewer turns at Grajagan, but turning hard and often at Honolua Bay. At the ditch, I could do turns to my heart's content, rest up to catch my breath, and continue until my legs were screaming. One afternoon I went alone and timed myself on one ride. I quit out of boredom after riding the wave for thirty minutes.

Ben and I vowed to keep it a secret, but the word, as always, slipped out. One day a group of high school kids showed up and soon became regular ditch riders. They promised to stay mum about it, but like any new wave, it was big news.

One day a guy drove up, parked his truck next to the canal, tied a rope to his front end, put his board in, and used the rope to water-ski into the wave. When he fell off, he walked back, introduced himself as Jesse, and watched how we were getting into the wave. "I didn't know you could do it like that," he said.

We got talking and discovered that he had never ridden a wave in the ocean. He had surfed a few other standing waves in the area and had just heard about this one. His old board was Oregon-made from a shop in Lincoln City. He had found it in a secondhand store here in our desert town and it worked well for him.

Over the course of hitting the wave daily we discovered that the trailing thruster fin was unnecessary; a twin-fin setup was much looser and easier to turn. We clued Jesse, our new ditch surfer friend, into this. He returned the next day, and before he got in the water he pulled out a cordless Sawzall and sawed off his back fin—a minor modification to better tune his equipment.

We had a cool thing going: Our small group would congregate after work, or after school, have a good time, try each other's boards, and go home revitalized from a great little surf session—two hundred miles from the ocean.

The collection of surfboards was interesting. Except for my little Ditch Bitch all were built for ocean waves and made anytime between the 1970s and the present day. The local secondhand stores immediately were cleaned out of the few boards they had that were sitting unsold for years and collecting dust. One of the guys had an aunt in California who found a cheap, used board in a surf shop and sent it up to him.

The Ditch Bitch worked best, and one kid offered to buy it. I had an improved design in mind and gladly sold it to him. I built two new boards, one for Ben and his 200-pound size, and the other a 5'6" twin fin in the sleeker and more refined design of the Ditch Bitch. The improvement was dramatic and our performance level went up. We were stoked.

My surf training before this had consisted of a two-mile paddle down river then a hard push upstream against the current with friends. We paddled on a beautiful section of the river, empty except for an occasional fisherman or mountain biker on the shoreside trail. Fish jumped, osprey wheeled overhead, deer grazed in the meadows, squirrels danced in the trees, and once in a while I heard the loud slap of a beaver's tail. But having a wave to ride was tremendously more exciting and a lot more action than just paddling. I went to the ditch on a regular basis and hit it with gusto.

But the word was out. More and more guys arrived. The lineup started to become exactly that: lined-up surfers standing along the canal wall waiting their turn. Yet like any surf spot, sometimes there wouldn't be a soul and I found myself hoping someone would come to share the moment.

In the fall, the water stopped. I arrived to find the ditch empty and dry. It was amazing that there had been a wave there at all. The bottom was just flat concrete. I don't know what I expected, but there was nothing there, just the slightly dropping slope and an insignificant squeeze in the sides. Water is a strange and wonderful thing, still and placid one moment, the next flowing fast enough to create a wave that can be surfed.

But it was all over for now. The ditch board went back on the shelf and the winter season rolled in. Snowboards and waves of snow were what we rode for the next six months.

When springtime finally arrived, ditch anticipation was at a fever pitch. A phone call came: There was water flowing again. Snow still covered all the mountains. The air was cold and the ditch water freezing. Full wetsuits kept the chill away for a while, but eventually numbness set in and the early-season sessions were shorter than we would have liked. The days became longer as spring moved into summer and the weather warmed up. New people showed up almost daily. Ben and I changed our timing, using the middle of the day, but others had the same idea. Our idyllic, secret little surf spot was becoming a full-on surf scene. Every new guy told all his friends, and sometimes there would be ten to fifteen people waiting in line for a turn.

It was against the law to be in the waterway, and we knew it would not be long before the authorities got wind of this illegal surfing. Sure enough, the sheriff drove out one day and told everyone to leave. That cooled things off for a short time, but before long the surf mob was back.

Dan Malloy came for a visit and I took him to the only surf in town. He was stoked and everyone was more stoked to watch one of the best surfers in the world ride our little wave. Jack Johnson, Donavon Frankenreiter, and G-Love came to town for a concert and wanted to see the wave. Ben and I drove them, and most of their band members, out for an epic session. Our town had a legitimate surf spot, and it was a good thing.

The following year, there were still occasions when no one was there, but more often than not it was crowded. Surfing attracts people and energy like honey attracts bees. It's always the same. It starts with a few guys who are happy to have others enjoy the fun, but soon their enjoyment begins to fade as the popularity increases.

There were small incidents of friction between some of the groups. Empty beer bottles and other rubbish appeared where once we had left no sign of our having been there. Ben and I got even better boards, as the precise design for this wave evolved. That kept our enthusiasm high, but we knew that something was going to happen. The sheriff returned several times, chasing the surfers away temporarily, but there were too many people, and nothing was going to keep the local surfers away from this wave. Fall rolled around and the water was shut off. Another desert surf season came to an end and the crowds went home.

Before the next season started, I ran into one of the original group having lunch. He surprised me by saying he'd heard a wall had been built across the bottom of the canal. Then another friend said someone flying a small plane overhead had seen a backhoe and concrete truck at the ditch. Information in the surf world has always traveled quickly—we used to refer to it as the coconut wireless. I passed the info on to Ben who immediately went out there and sadly reported that it was true. They had found a way to keep the surfers away.

Yvon and Malinda Chouinard were in town for an American Alpine Club conference, and we were touring around one morning. An avid surfer himself, Yvon knew about the ditch wave so we took a drive out there. The canal was still dry and the new wall was painful to see.

"Where was the Surfrider Foundation when you needed them?" Yvon said with his characteristic, hearty laugh. Both of us are old surfers, and the loss of any surf spot is a great tragedy that we've painfully experienced before, and will continue to do so in the future.

In Hawai'i, in the early 1960s, John Kelly and George Downing started Save Our Surf, the first organized group effort to protect surfing spots. Their mission is to gather and spread information regarding the beaches and shoreline where existing surfing areas are threatened by the state's development plans. Save Our Surf is an ongoing battle against those who don't, or can't, understand what a wave means. SOS's and the Surfrider Foundation's efforts continue to this day.

Riding waves, any kind of waves, is a very good thing; preserving and sustaining them is even better. Keep surfing.

A   Big

A standup paddleboard is just a big surfboard and another way
to ride a wave. All ways are fun, but sometimes the new way can be
a lot of fun in a different way. Photo: John Wrenn

Score

Yesterday I scored big. It was one of those rare days that left me so pumped up when it was over that I knew I was going to have trouble falling asleep that night. I figured I better write it down before the afterglow faded; that way I could savor it again and again. One of the sad things about surfing is that the best memories are fleeting. Before one knows it, the memories have all but disappeared, erased like they never existed. Sometimes when the focus of the ride is so intense, the concentration so great, it seems as though they don't even get recorded.

Many times I have finished a wave to find a blank space in my mind about what just occurred during that ride. Although peculiar, it happens with great regularity. By carefully recalling the few moments of actual thoughts, like the decision to catch that wave, or maybe an incident like someone in the way or a person yelling, or maybe working backward from that point at the end of the wave, I can piece together the whole ride. But often as not, if there is some distraction, like another set coming, or just not having that moment to reflect back, then that ride may as well be gone. It did happen, and how it unfolded possibly went into one of those many file cabinets of the mind, but the key to access that drawer is lost. Even as I sat there and wrote only a day afterward, recollections of those waves had begun to go hazy.

The easy part to remember is what got me there. In the buildup of most surf stories, the foundation is usually the waves. These days, with Internet surf forecasting, checking the surf has taken on an entirely new meaning. In the first several decades of my surfing career, I simply looked out at the sea and decided whether to paddle out or not. Now that I live farther from the ocean, things are more complicated.

Modern satellite imagery, storm information, and sophisticated marine buoys that monitor swell direction and height, wave interval, and wind speeds make amateur forecasting pretty simple. Of course, there are also professionals who make a business doing the same thing. For a fee, or even for free, one touch of the keyboard and the information to make that same decision days in advance is quickly available.

A big swell was coming, that much all the various forecasting services had agreed on. A storm in the Gulf of Alaska had made it a certainty. The wind and surface conditions forecast also looked favorable. Webcams make it easy to check current conditions, giving a picture of exactly the same view I used to have from shore. Whether I'm on the beach or 200 miles away, the decision is as it always was: Should I go or should I stay? This time I pulled the trigger, loaded up my stuff, and hit the road.

Less than four hours later, I had my first real look. My expectations were slightly deflated, but still the surf wasn't bad. It had size and the wind was enough offshore for the wave faces to be clean. The spot I was at, although the closest to my home, was my second choice. A friend reported an unfavorable wind at my first choice in an early-morning phone call.

I wrestled into my wetsuit and paddled out on my standup board. The waves were well overhead, but mushy and hard to catch, with an ill-defined lineup. On my standup board, I had better luck than the surfers on regular boards, but the session proved lackluster.

Three hours later, I had changed back into dry clothes and was ready to go somewhere else but couldn't decide where. I finally got through to my friend up north, but his report still was not encouraging.

Plagued by indecision, I ran through my options. The surf was coming up, and the wind should continue to come from a good direction (although the approaching storm would increase it dramatically). What the heck, I had nothing more important to do, and all the next day to do it. I headed north rather than head home.

The next morning, in the predawn grey, I strained to see what the waves were doing. First indications looked small. As it became lighter, it was obviously very small. This spot wasn't picking up the waves like the break I had been at yesterday. Hoping the swell would be coming soon, I suited up, got out my surfboard, took the long walk down the beach, and paddled out to join the other dawn patrollers at the outside lineup.

Six or seven surfers were already clustered in the lineup, but the only waves I saw were chest-high at the biggest and not very consistent. The anticipation was high and the crowd amped, but there was nothing to spend their pent-up energy on. Every once in a while a single wave, or maybe a set of two, would roll in, but that was it. Definitely not enough to go around for the growing number of surfers with expectations of a lot more than was available. Two hours later and only three weak waves to my tally, I surrendered. As I walked back with several of the guys who lived there, they all spoke of the buoy readings that morning of thirty-foot waves with fifteen-second intervals: significant indicators. We were all puzzled by the lack of surf.

I changed out of my wetsuit and put away my surfboard. Driving out of the side street I had parked on, I started to head away, but on an impulse, swung into the parking area facing the inside break for one last look. It had started to drizzle, but the wind was still lightly offshore. Some guys were surfing the inside on longboards and fishes, and as I watched, I saw a few of them get some nice long rides on waist-high waves. My morning had not gone as I had hoped, but with my standup board, I figured I could salvage something from the day. I wear a thinner wetsuit when I ride my standup board because I generally don't get as wet, and the suit was dried out from the session the day before. I slipped into the fresh wetsuit, unstrapped my big board, grabbed the paddle, and headed out.

The few surfers in the lineup were friendly and curious, having never seen a standup board here before. It was perfect for it; most of the waves hardly broke, but they stood up enough for me to catch and ride for a long way. Now I was catching a lot of waves and having a lot of fun; the dismal beginning to the morning was brightening up. The entire time, I kept an eye on the outside spot where one by one, the surfers there gave it up and got out for lack of waves.

Finally, the outer lineup was empty and I saw a nice-looking wave come through. It was probably only chest-high and there was only one, but it wasn't far to paddle on the standup board. I started to head that way, but just then, the wave I had seen on the outside moved inside and it was the biggest one yet. I turned my board, paddled hard, and caught it. I hung around the inside break after that, but every once in awhile, one at a time, a nice wave would roll through the outer spot. About a minute later it would roll into the inside as a bigger wave. The surf was good enough at the spot I was at, but I thought sooner rather than later I should take the half-mile paddle to the outside break for a closer look, and so I headed out. While the lineup I was headed for was mostly empty of waves, it was also devoid of surfers. It was also a nice morning for a paddle.

Just as I got close enough to really see what was going on, I noticed a single surfer who must have just paddled out. It let the wind out of my sails a bit: The local surfers here have a reputation of being very protective of their break. I didn't think this surfer would take kindly to a standup board in his lineup.

Right then, a significant-looking set loomed up outside. We both paddled to intersect it. The first wave was a solid five feet and nicely lined-up. The other surfer was too far inside and had to let it go, but there was another just like it behind. I waited and let him take first pick; I could see there was a third wave out the back. He caught his wave and I swung around for the next. Both were awesome waves, the best of the day by far. I rode mine for a long way until it petered out to nothing along the rocky shoreline.

I paddled out to where the other surfer sat waiting, said hello, and asked if he had seen any other sets like that one. I figured he would probably either ignore me or tell me to get the hell out of there with my big board. But he surprised me with a friendly greeting and shrugged in reply to my question, saying it was the first set he had seen. He went on to suggest that maybe it was indeed coming up, and we might be lucky enough to enjoy a brief window of good waves with no one else out. From my standing vantage point, I saw another set approaching and pointed it out to him.

The next set was better, slightly bigger, with more waves, and again we both caught great waves. As I paddled back out, another set loomed. And so it went, one set after another in rapid succession, the waves increasing in size with each new set. A very nice wave showed outside and I paddled hard for position.

Well outside of any of the previous waves, I did a quick turn around to set up my takeoff. It was the biggest wave so far and not one to take chances on. The wave here breaks very close to a rocky shore. One mistake on the big board and I would be caught inside and washed on to the rocks.

I glimpsed another surfer joining our twosome; it was my friend whom I had called the afternoon before. He had passed on the early-morning session, using better judgment than the rest of us, and had shown up now, at exactly the right moment. I carefully caught the next wave deep, turned hard at the top, and drove down the line. The wall reared up ahead of me threateningly, but my line and trim speed were good, and I flew down the line close to the curl but safely in front of it.

For the next hour, we all got as many excellent waves as we could ride. Those two paid some dues, taking off late and getting pitched, then eating the waves behind. But the interval between waves was long, even, and predictable; the sets and lulls were very defined. The wind continued to puff lightly offshore, combing the wave faces into a perfect texture. I kept thinking I should go in and exchange my standup board for a regular surfboard, but that would necessitate a forty-five-minute round-trip. I was having the time of my life right then and wasn't sure I wanted to sacrifice any of it for a surfboard and wetsuit change.

Other surfers came out, but everyone was friendly and more than a little awed by the growing surf, which continued to sprout taller with each new set. Some of the sets began to take on a serious demeanor. Ten foot, top to bottom, is about the maximum the place can hold; after that it starts to break on an outer reef and loses its form. At the moment, though, it was still in top shape and without letup.

The sets were lasting longer than the lulls. I would pick what I thought was the best and biggest one, well outside the surfers, ride it a long way in, and watch wave after wave peel through as I paddled back out. If any surfer looked interested in any of the waves I paddled for, I yelled for them to go and pulled back: There were plenty more waves coming.

My friend had to go to a meeting for his job and caught one final wave in. As he was climbing out on the rocks inside, I took a huge one from way outside. It peeled perfectly, and I just stood tall in the curl, dragging my paddle slightly to slow down. I pulled out even with where he was standing on shore and he let out a hoot.

On the paddle back out I passed another surfer paddling in. I could tell by the look on his face that he wasn't comfortable. I asked if everything was okay, and he answered that he was in over his head.

"Are you going to try and go straight in over the rocks?" I asked.

"No," he replied. "I'm going to paddle all the way in to the beach."

I told him to keep a watch over his shoulder so a wave behind him didn't pick him off.

For another hour the waves continued to increase in intensity. I was amazed that my big board was handling the waves so well. Of course, the waves were smooth, peeling, and pretty doggone flawless. Then a set showed almost on the horizon, much bigger than any so far. I looked at the surfers, but only one of them, a guy near my age, saw what I saw. We eased over toward the shoulder and moved outside. The younger surfers finally noticed the set and our outside position. They put their heads down and paddled hard for safety.

The first waves were good, but inside of us. Outside of where we waited, bigger ones danced, masked by the waves in front. Several waves went by, and we were finally confronted by one of the big ones. It had broken on the outer second reef, but I was far enough outside to make a move for it. I spun around and just managed to stroke down the face. The drop was endless and very bouncy. I hung on, using the paddle for balance and finally reached the bottom. I thought I had dropped down too far as the wave ahead started to break above me. I leaned into a turn, slicing the paddle deep for leverage, and swung around the section. Once back up on the wall, I could easily chase down the looming sections ahead. Far down the line, I pulled out and found myself shaking as though I had a fever.

I paddled back out. More sets kept coming. With the paddle, my takeoffs were clean, early, and easy. The clean surface conditions let me read what the wave would do, and I had plenty of time to react. A dark thought of what would quickly happen should I fall tried to creep into my consciousness, but I continued to push it aside. If I got trapped inside, I would be dragged along the rocky shoreline into a very dangerous situation where my only hope would be to abandon both board and paddle. I didn't want to even go there in my mind. I knew the board was maxed out; the fins were humming like crazy. Although it had gone fast enough to make all the waves, I had it redlined and could ask no more from it.

The waves still came, and from each set one would beckon to me like the Lorelei, and I would be drawn to ride it. Four hours had gone by quickly. The surf had grown faster than I had ever seen waves come up before while still holding perfect shape, even on the North Shore. I guess all those surf predictions and buoy reports had been right.

I began to think that maybe it was time to call it a day. Just as those thoughts were going through my mind, the set of the day appeared far out to sea. Suddenly outer reefs were breaking where none had shown before. I looked at the other old guy, and I sensed that we both had the same thought at exactly the same time. This was the end of it. The surf had surged up in a hurry but managed to hold its form up until now. Even at a glance I could see this set, still far out to sea, would be out of control when it reached me.

Once again I eased toward the shoulder and outside and the other surfers followed. The inevitable was upon us all. The surf was expected to reach the twenty-foot range, and it looked like it was doing just that with this approaching set. The wind suddenly increased and rain pelted down. Poseidon had stuck his trident into the sea and the storm exploded.

The set moved upon us, but we were safely beyond its grasp, well outside. The waves had lost all their previous good form. These were stormy and rough, full of boils and bumps. I wanted no more of it. Up until now, my big board and paddle had been an advantage over the small boards of the others. But I quickly realized, as the unruly set came on, the tables had turned and my advantage had just become a severe liability. I had an idea and paddled inside of the group. A smaller twelve-foot wave in the set came within reach and I paddled hard to get it. I just managed to pick it up and rode down the face, away from the rest of the set and the danger—if I could just keep my feet and wits about me.

As I rode down the line, it came to me that this was the biggest wave I had ridden at this spot. It kept going farther in and when it started to hit deeper water again, it started to back off; by paddling hard, I managed to stay in it. I realized I was far enough inside that I would be entering the in-between break. Here the wave hugs the rocks closely but peels along the rugged shoreline for another several hundred yards. I glanced over my shoulder and just about fainted when I saw a wave twice as big as the one I was riding right behind me. I hung on and paddled harder; to lose it at this point would put me right on the rocks.

The energy of all the surf on the inside gets channeled into a strong rip that runs back out along the shoreline in an opposite direction. I noticed several surfers as I streaked by, but I also was running into the rip current. The chop coming up the face of my wave was horrendous. The big board went airborne a number of times, but somehow I managed to stay on using my paddle for balance.

Suddenly, I wasn't going forward any longer. The wave had met its match against the rip and just stopped. I looked toward shore and saw I was actually going backward with the rip, back toward where I didn't want to be. On the other side of the rip, the inside break was completely out of control. It was breaking much farther out than where I had been happily and safely surfing only a few hours before. Fortunately, the set had just about run its course and the last waves rolled through.

I paddled across the rip, hoping to catch a smaller wave before the next set came in. Luck was on my side, a small wave popped up and I paddled into it. I rode straight in toward the sand. I made it up the beach and then it was over.

I put my board down next to my car and walked over to the public hot shower. It was raining cats and dogs, and no one was around. I stayed under that hot shower for fifteen minutes. Finally I got changed, loaded my board, and was ready to go. The ocean out front looked like the beginning of the old TV show *Victory at Sea*: stormy and completely out of control. Not a place anyone would want to be.

I was just making a U-turn to head for home when I noticed a surfer walking up the beach with a thousand-yard stare. It was the same guy who, two hours earlier, had said he was in over his head and was going in. I asked him if he was all right. He seemed to shake and nod his head at the same time. He said he was from British Columbia, and it was his first time at the outside break. He said he was totally freaked out and would just stick with the inside spot the next time. I told him with the way the surf had come up so suddenly, I was a little freaked out too.

He said the fear had almost overwhelmed him, and he had to reach down inside to something he didn't know he had. Even then he had almost given up. The strong rip current had nearly defeated him. Then he had seen me cross the rip and catch a final wave in. He had followed my lead and had finally made it.

We smiled at each other, both of us having had an extraordinary experience that day.

Paddling out in numbing-cold water, through a relentless shorebreak, and never knowing what one will find, but never despairing of doing it each and every time. Photo: John Wrenn

e. GALLERY

Above   Paddleboarding outside Big Beach Makena on the south side of Maui where the water is the bluest blue and the sand is sparkling white. Photo: Erik Aeder

Right   A fourteen-foot standup board ready to race, with the traditional ti leaf to honor the Hawaiian *eki*, or spirit power. Photo: Dana Edmunds

One beachcomber, four surfers, and an empty lineup with
perfect waves ... those were the days. Photo: Jeff Divine

Left   The 1974 Smirnoff contest at Waimea Bay offered the biggest purse ever in professional surfing at the time—I don't think I was thinking about the money when I took off, but I know I'm hoping it won't be as bad as this photo makes it look. Photo: Steve Wilkings

Above   Joe Quigg, Matt Kivlin, and Tom Zahn returning home on the Lurline after a splendid trip to Hawai'i in 1947. Photo: Joe Quigg collection

This photo of the Pipeline shows the end of the
wave still has a lot of zip left. Photo: Jeff Divine

Below   Coming in from the Second Reef takeoff   Right   Photo: Steve Wilkings
at the Pipeline, with still a long way to go before
its over. Photo: Steve Wilkings

Keep

Paddling

Paddleboard racing has been around the surfing scene for a long time. Big Dave Rochlen once showed me an entry blank to the first surf contest at Malibu in 1949. It was a paddleboard race, he said. As surfing events evolved over the years, there was always a paddleboard race included. Eventually it became all about equipment; some boards were simply faster than others.

In the 1966 World Surfing Championships, George Downing suggested holding a paddleboard race to determine a world paddleboard champion along with the surfing world champ. The California contingent readily agreed since they had Mike Doyle and Corky Carroll, both powerful paddlers with lots of experience and fast racing boards of their own. Australia, with a long history of paddle racing at their surf clubs, readily agreed. George Downing, ever a wily coach and a paddleboard champion in his own right, had an ace up his sleeve. On the Hawaiian team was Kiki Spangler, a formidable paddler whom George had taken under his wing to further develop Kiki's natural paddling talent.

The secret weapon, however, was the board that George brought with the Hawaiian team. A hollow balsawood beauty shaped by Dick Brewer when he worked for Hobie Surfboards, it was equipped with a rudder and tiller assembly operated by the paddler's toes. At that point in time, it was said, at least in Hawai'i, there was not another paddleboard that came close, and with Kiki aboard, they were an unbeatable combination. The story was, on the day of the race, Nat Young took one look at Kiki's board and said forget it. The race was held, and Kiki did win, but without Nat, the race never gained any international recognition.

One summer in the mid-1980s, my wife and I were relaxing at our Pipeline house for the Fourth of July. Dennis Pang showed up early in the morning and announced that we were going to paddle in the annual race from Sunset to Waimea. He said he had a fast paddleboard for me to use and it would be fun. I had never even paddled on a race board but imagined it couldn't be much different than paddling a surfboard, except easier.

Joe Pang, Dennis's dad and a strong paddleboard racer and beach boy in Waikiki during the 1940s, accompanied us to the start and gave us a pep talk as we unloaded the boards. The board for me was a Joe Quigg shape, twelve feet long, flat, narrow, and unlike any board I had ever seen before. Dennis had borrowed another board from a friend in town. It was also a peculiar shape, and he said it was called a Waterman. There must have been almost a hundred people paddling on a wide assortment of boards, mostly big surfboards, but also a few specialized paddleboards. Someone had a dog on his board, a few had their kids with them, there were a bunch of girls—it was supposed to be a fun event.

We lined up out to sea and a horn sounded to start the race. Dennis took off like a rocket, his arms windmilling in a blur. Caught up in the excitement, I began to paddle as fast as I could too. It wasn't long before I realized that if I kept up this fast pace I would pass out, so I slowed and tried to figure out the most efficient way to paddle my board. I trimmed my body forward until the nose began to go under, then moved back a bit. I kept an easy, smooth, long stroke going, regularly changing between alternate and double arm stroking. The field was spread out, and I could see Dennis far ahead, still maintaining his windmill stroke. Finally, rounding the point of Waimea Bay, I could see it was a short stretch to the beach and finish.

As we entered the Bay, I saw 'Surfer Joe' Teipel, a media personality and announcer of many local events, on a board similar to the one Dennis had, and he was passing me like I was dragging a bucket. He said something as he came by, but I was trying desperately to turn up the juice. I remember thinking that I should be able to keep up, after all I was in pretty top surfing shape, but Joe went right on by. Dennis was trying not to laugh as I staggered up the beach to the finish line. Later on he told me "it's all about the board," and the Waterman he had was the best board around.

With more information from Dennis, I tracked down the Waterman boards. A guy I vaguely knew in California owned the shape, so I gave him a call right away. Craig Lockwood, an avid paddler himself, had found designs from Tom Blake dating from the 1930s. He commissioned Steve Boehne, a well-known shaper and tandem surfing champion, to recreate Blake's board. He took the board to Foss Foam and got them to build a mold to produce a molded blank using matte glass in the foam.

This was an old technique pioneered in the late 1950s to make a molded board that didn't require shaping and would be stronger as well. It was one of those good ideas that didn't really work. The problem was the addition of the fiberglass into the mold disrupted the foaming process of polyurethane foam and left huge voids in the blank. This was a general problem with the early surfboard foam makers and resulted in a high reject rate. While Foss Foam spent a lot of time working on perfecting this foam process with the fiberglass, Clark Foam worked at reducing its reject rate. By the time most of the different molded surfboards had failed for one reason or another—mostly because they wouldn't stay watertight—there was a general consensus among the surfboard manufacturers that the custom board was a better way to go. Clark Foam, with the most advanced foam formula, soon became the most popular blanks for building surfboards for the next three decades.

Craig sold me two of his Waterman blanks and shipped them to Hawai'i. When I finally got them to my own shop on Maui and had a look, I was shocked. There were holes in the blanks that I could stick my whole hand into. This was the inherent problem with fiberglass in the foam mold and obviously Foss Foam had not come up with any solutions. I had no choice but to work with what I had. On the first one I attempted to fill the holes with a q-cell mix, but that ended up adding a lot of weight. For the second blank, I just glassed over the holes, trying to seal them as best as I could. Remembering that "fast" board he loaned me, I gave the first board to Dennis, and kept the other one myself. It was, as far as I know, the first Waterman on the island of Maui. It was also the first racing paddleboard to make the run from Maliko Gulch to the Kahului Harbor.

Rodney Kilborne and his Handsome Bugga Productions ran all of the surfing events at Ho'okipa Beach Park. He saw my paddleboard one day and suggested we have a race during the next surf contest. It was a good idea and the forerunner of many, now world-class, events on that windswept Maliko course. Rodney gathered a good field from the local Maui surfers. Laird showed up with a twelve-foot windsurf course-racing board. Kanoa Johnson, another local stud almost the same size as Laird, brought an Ole

paddleboard. Everyone else had longboards of different sizes and shapes. My Waterman didn't really attract any attention because, at that time, no one there had any experience with paddleboard racing or race boards.

It was a short course starting in Maliko Bay, down to Ho'okipa, a sharp left turn on the point between the rocky shore and the Pavilion's surf spot, then a right turn around a buoy just off the beach, and a last sprint along the shoreline to a finish line between the end of the beach pavilion and a buoy offshore. Rodney started the race then ran to his car and sped down to Ho'okipa for the finish.

Laird and Kanoa pulled the entire field from the start and I slipped in behind. These two magnificent specimens of premier paddling conditioning battled each other going out of the bay and through the left turn out into the wind and swell. I easily kept a quiet pace behind them, letting them use up some, if not most, of their considerable energy. My strategy was to hang back until the end, then dash ahead on my faster board. It seemed like a good plan at first, but as I followed, I began to think about something else.

I had surfed with these two since they were kids and watched as they grew into men. There was a sense of savagery in both of them, a primitiveness that set them apart from the rest. It was more than sheer strength, though both were stronger than anyone else I knew in an almost inhuman way. It was that light that I had seen many times in both their eyes, a crazy shining that was the first indication that something explosive was occurring within their bodies, their minds, and, maybe, their souls. It was a scary light.

I could hear them both grunting as they exerted themselves to the maximum, each trying to gain an edge. Finally, Laird pulled ahead, and it was at that point that I threw my initial game plan out the window. If I waited until the end, no matter how much faster my board was, their minds were not going to let me win. They would dredge up some superhuman reserve and I'd be swept away.

Bill Boyum, his son Cyrus, and me paddling the Maliko run on some prototype paddleboards I made. Photo: Erik Aeder

Giving myself some sea room so Kanoa wouldn't grab me as I went by, I slowly increased my pace and inched up behind him. I waited until I caught a good glide and went by Kanoa in hurry, getting some distance right away so he wouldn't have time to think about what was happening. With him behind, I concentrated on Laird up ahead, and using the same tactic, I went around him as well. I figured I'd better build as much of a lead as I could while I was out in the wind and bumps, and steadily stroked away from the two of them. By the time I reached the corner of Ho'okipa and made my left turn, a glance back showed me that I had about a hundred yards on Laird, a sizable and, I thought, comfortable lead.

Rounding the point into the smooth water out of the wind, I could hear the cheering from the beach. There was always a big crowd at these surf contests, with all the different age groups as well as their parents and friends, and everyone was yelling as I came in toward shore. I made the right turn around the buoy and the crowd was screaming, I thought they were all cheering for me, so I waved a couple of times as I began the last leg of the course.

Right about then I felt a premonition, a little tickling in my inner senses that maybe something was behind me. Looking over my shoulder, I saw Laird less than a board length behind and charging like a mad bull, the whitewater boiling around him. With a startled yelp, I kicked it into gear and my Waterman took off like a jet. I could feel the Laird presence right on my tail even more than I heard his splashing and the yelling from the beach. Now I knew what all that noise from the Pavilion was: They weren't cheering for me, they were screaming at the beast crawling up my rear. I managed to beat Laird by less than half a board length.

As soon as we crossed the finish line, Laird paddled up and said, "Lemme see that board." We swapped boards, and he paddled off to give my Waterman a try. I never got my board back; I never even saw it again. Several months later, the phone ringing in the wee hours of the morning awakened me. It was a collect call from Laird somewhere in France. He called to say he had my board, had just paddled from Sardinia to Italy, and was planning to paddle the English Channel next. He did paddle that channel, but that is another story. And I did hear about my Waterman years later: It ended up in Biarritz and started a paddleboard-racing group of Frenchmen. Keep paddling.

Top　Laird Hamilton and Buzzy Kerbox in Dover, England, still in their wetsuits and carrying the boards they used to paddle across the channel from Calais in France. Photo: Buzzy Kerbox collection

Bottom　Buzzy and Laird on the beach at Calais, France, getting some advice from a local about which way to go to get to England. Photo: Buzzy Kerbox collection

The Gorge

Anyone who enjoys downwind standup paddleboard runs usually found on the ocean—places like the Moloka'i Channel between Moloka'i and O'ahu, the run between Hawai'i Kai and Waikiki, Maliko Gulch to Kahului, Maui to Moloka'i Pailolo channel, the Na Pali coast of Kaua'i—might be surprised to know that one of the best runs can be found far from the ocean on a river: the Columbia River.

The Columbia River has a lot of history. It's the same one Lewis and Clark followed on the last leg of their transcontinental expedition 200 years ago. Now it forms a natural border between the states of Oregon and Washington. Just at the base of the north face of Mount Hood and on the banks of the Columbia sits the town of Hood River. In the 1980s, Hood River became well known among windsurfers as a great venue for their sport. Kite surfing blossomed in the 1990s, and another decade later, along came an unlikely sporting endeavor that also took to the strong winds so prevalent in the spring, summer, and fall seasons: standup paddling.

It might seem that ideal conditions for standup paddling include little or no wind, but on the contrary, with a specialized downwind board, there is nothing like a run on water with a strong tailwind and the swells and waves formed by the blowing wind. This is a form of surfing where no territorial imperatives exist, everyone has all the space they need, and in today's crowded world, that sort of surfing experience is increasingly difficult to find.

Waves of this type are very close interval, consistent, moving fast, and not for the faint of heart when the wind gusts hit forty miles per hour. Steve Gates at the Big Winds shop and Naish standup paddleboards get together every August to put on a two-day event, and this year the wind conditions couldn't have been better. On Saturday, the wind was light, making for an excellent round-the-buoys course race. Early Sunday, the wind kicked in like gangbusters, and it was game on for the downwind event.

The course from Viento State Park to the Hood River Event Site in town is about eight miles. The paddlers run upstream against the current that helps to create the waves. With the winds averaging thirty-plus, it was going to be a wild ride. The start of

Standup paddling on a specialized downwind board
in good conditions is equally as satisfying as a good
day of surfing perfect waves. Photo: Dana Edmunds

any elite race is always an awesome sight. Perhaps the most inspiring part is the stroke rate the top racers generate while trying to pull ahead. I get tired just watching the blur of the paddles and thinking of the heart rates and oxygen depletion the paddlers must be experiencing. In no time, the elite field was gone and the open paddlers began to line up for their start.

The start in any type of racing is always critical. In a standup paddleboard race, the racers' boards and paddles bang and knock into each other, and this first moment is pure mayhem. The idea is to get a quick start and jump ahead of the field. Of course, everyone else is attempting to do the same thing and pandemonium generally ensues. Sometimes the boards are so close together one is not able to even put one's paddle into the water. One person will fall into the next, and it can be like dominoes. I usually try to get between two people I know so at least we won't try to foul each other, though just about anything goes in a start.

We all stood next to our boards, waist deep, watching Steve, who would signal the start. I had my headphones on, but I saw Steve yell and everyone moved. I still can't believe my luck, but I pushed off, jumped first to my knees … and caught a wave. That put me just ahead of the two boards to either side of me. When I put my paddle in for the first stroke, I caught another wave and again I surged ahead. There were over a hundred paddlers shoulder to shoulder, board to board, and just like that I was a couple of board lengths ahead.

"Baby Please Don't Go" by Them was blasting through my headphones, and I couldn't believe my good fortune. Someone from the right was angling toward me, and at the last moment I switched my paddle to the left so it wouldn't get trapped between the boards, J-stroked hard to stay left, and braced for the impact. The boards bumped, he went down, and I was away. Another stroke, another wave, I was in clear water and able to paddle strong and clean. I had the kind of start everyone dreams of.

Let's be clear. I'm not a racer: I'm a guy who paddles in races. I come because I like to hang out and rub shoulders with all the real racers, but I just got the start of a lifetime. A fast start and a fast run is the nature of this venue: the Gorge rocks.

Equipment is a key part in this type of paddling. The wind waves are not steep and seldom break, and some finesse is required not only to catch the waves but also to stay riding on them as long as possible. Something one never should do in a race is to try anything new; however, I just got my first production sample of a new fourteen-foot board I shaped and I was dying to give it a shot. When I saw the forecast for the strong wind, I wavered a bit, thinking a more familiar board might be prudent, but the more I stared at the shape of my new board, the better it looked. Every time I paddled it in the local river, I felt how stable and forgiving it was. In rough conditions, these two traits are a premium, especially in a river where the waves come from all sides, current eddies come into play, and the short interval buries the nose into the wave ahead almost before one can react.

On this new board I had shaped a displacement bow feeding into a planing hull with a slight concave amidships. The advantage of a displacement hull is that it requires less effort to move. A planing hull works best when riding a wave, but before one can ride that wave, one needs to catch it first. The concave adds stability when paddling in a parallel stance. The outline plan shape is also distinct. Most race boards feature a narrow, sharp nose, wide point amidships or behind center, and a lot of curve in the tail to compensate for the lack of wideness up front. My board looked more like a 1970s outline with a wider nose, centered wide point, and straighter lines out the back half of the template.

My design theory goes back to my single fins at the Pipeline, in contrast to the more modern thruster shapes that favor the narrow nose and more hips in the tail. I always felt the narrow nose took away paddling to increase a quicker turning ability when up and riding. Just like at the Pipeline, in the open ocean, or river wind swell, my prime concern was catching the wave rather than performance once the wave was caught. The secret of successful downwind paddling is letting the waves do most of the work, but you have to catch them first. Downwind running is its own kind of animal; in the right conditions and on the right equipment, it sure makes distance paddling fun and exciting.

I got into this kind of ocean-swell paddling on a prone board in the 1980s and built a lot of boards to maximize the catch and glide. The first thing we learned on the prone paddleboards was that we weren't able to paddle fast enough to catch swells that seldom broke, or even got steep. Utilizing a full displacement hull shape—round-bottomed like a sailboat—we were able to use the push of the swell combined with a coordinated paddle stroke to catch the bumps. Riding them became a problem because the round bottom was like lying on a log; it just wanted to roll over at speed. Creating some drag with a foot or an arm outstretched like an outrigger gave some stability, but to the uninitiated, these boards were very difficult to keep upright even in flat water. Paddling them with power and at speed took a lot of getting used to.

The modern prone paddleboard has evolved into a shape similar to the standup boards; stability is paramount because the option of knee paddling is essential for long distances. Standing with a paddle offers more leverage and speed than lying down, or kneeling, and paddling with the hands. A surfski or an OC-1 are the most efficient single-man craft for paddling downwind, but riding a standup is a lot of fun because it is so similar to board surfing.

My pretty little start was just a matter of that displacement bow taking advantage of the push of the swell and having the board start to go on its own. Most of the other race designs use variations of planing hull shapes and need some horsepower to get up on a plane. In the confusion of a mass start, it is difficult to get clean, full-power strokes when everyone is so close together.

I knew there were a lot of strong paddlers in the field. I had paddled with a few of the guys before, and they were fast and experienced on this course. But anything can, and usually does, happen at the start. So just like that, in the first minute of the race, there were only about six people ahead of me.

The glides were one after the other. It's hard to imagine that waves would come in sets on a river, but just like in the ocean, that's how it was. When one came, it was certain there would be several more behind it. The tail of the board would lift, the surfer would give a couple of quick strokes to connect, make a swift shift from a parallel stance into a surf stance, take the rapid drop into the trough, maybe take another step back to keep the nose from going under, maybe moving all the way back to the tail to keep the nose up, and as the trough began to flatten and fill up, take another few steps forward, combined with some hard paddling to try to bridge the gap and use the speed to transfer into the wave ahead. Sometimes the board would plane across the flat, climb over the wave in front, and drop down another one. Back in my prone paddling days, we used to call this railroading. Other times the jump back forward would be too late and the wave would get away.

The way I designed the nose, if I wasn't quick enough and the nose did bury into the back of the wave, the board would stall, slowing down and letting the wave catch up again. Other board designs use a lot of nose kick to keep from pearl diving, but too much rocker can push water and be slow. Some boards use a variation of a displacement hull, like on a fishing trawler, with a pronounced vee in the nose to split the water; this can track one way while the paddler is expecting to go the other. On all the race boards in heavy downwind conditions, one needs to be quick and light on his feet. My round-bottom nose would bury but still lift; the deep vee on the deck would let any water coming over the top drain quickly away to the side. As long as I didn't get thrown off balance forward, I would just wait for the tail to lift again and reconnect with the wave.

In a way, this is one of the most subtle forms of wave riding. Only by becoming sensitized to this light push and glide can one put together long, connected rides. At times, a gust of wind would try to blow the paddle out of my hands as I reached for another stroke. I had to keep a firm grip with my lower hand on the return, or the wind would turn my blade before I could get it back into the water and I would miss my stroke. On some of the bigger waves, the down angle of the drop would be pretty steep, and I found myself standing on the tail with a lot of board ahead of me. Yet from the tail, I could turn easily and aim for the tallest point of the bump in front.

Generally the peak of each succeeding wave would line up, but without a look behind, the only way to gauge the biggest part of the wave I was riding was by watching the wave ahead. In the open ocean, the swells come from either side, sometimes going left and other times going right. In the river, this effect was more pronounced. One moment I would be heading to the Washington side and the next toward Oregon. The difficulty was not getting to the back of the board, where I could steer, quickly enough, because while I was being pushed hard to the left, suddenly another swell from the opposite side would sneak in and try to roll me over. If I did it right, I would be on the tail, turn back right, and be going the other way. My track zigged and zagged from one side to the other, never running in a straight line.

The other great thing about a course like this is that there really isn't all that much paddling involved—just a couple of quick strokes here, a few there, a lot of footwork, back and forth to trim the board, using the speed from the wave to keep the board in the swell and the glides long.

About a month before, while recovering from a broken heel, I came up and went for a downwind run with Steve and his gang. I was on a prone board, since I wasn't able to stand up without the aid of crutches. My board, a twelve-foot—state of the art in 1980—hollow, superlight shape, had me feeling pretty confident about having a good

run. The water level was high, so there was a strong current, but the wind was blowing hard, and as we drove down to the launch, we could easily see the corduroy-like lines of waves in the river.

We shoved off and right away I began to connect some glides. Before standup, this is how we used to do it, and it was great back then. But lying down is not comfortable, and my two hands do not come close to the area of a paddle blade. The standup boards walked away. If I stopped paddling at all, the current took me backward. After a while, I remembered why I never went on the prone boards anymore once we started to standup paddle. To make a long story short, a couple of hours later I finally made it to the finish site. It took me twice as long as it would have on my standup paddleboard. My wife had my crutches ready for me at the water's edge. As she grabbed my board, concern was written all over her face because of how long the paddle had taken me. I told her I hoped to never do this paddle on my belly again.

Back at the race, the course and conditions were great, which was a good thing because I had not done much paddling before the event. Had some hard work been required, I would have choked. I got in ahead of most of my friends, had time to catch my breath, and watch them come into the finish. Almost all told me about the rough conditions dumping them off their boards repeatedly. I smiled, thinking about how stable my board had felt throughout the entire run. I love everything about that new board, from the shape to the cool-looking paint job. I had already toweled it dry, put it back into the bag, and had it strapped on to the car.

From now on, I plan to keep closer tabs on the Gorge wind forecasts because any run even remotely like this one we just enjoyed is guaranteed to be memorable. Like surfing, no two sessions are quite alike, but that is one of the big attractions: You just never know what's going to happen. As in life, no matter what gets thrown in your path, it always seems to work best to just keep paddling.

Top and Bottom   A fourteen-foot board
will catch almost every ripple that comes by.
Photos: Dana Edmunds

vi. JUST FOR FUN

Rory Russell and I debate how to best tie our boards on the rack.
The last thing we wanted was to arrive at wherever we were
going to find our surfboards gone, a common occurrence in the
days before specialized surfboard racks. Photo: Art Brewer

The Country

No one said North Shore in the early 1970s. The Country was what we called North Oʻahu. It was a sleepy, quiet place where the roosters crowed at first light and the roads were always empty. I can remember trying to hitchhike one time and standing out on Kam Highway for about an hour without a single car coming by in either direction. Finally, the public bus came, and I paid my quarter for the long ride back to Town. That's what we called Honolulu.

Craig Sugihara got the name for his surf shop, Town & Country Surf Designs, by combining the two because he was in Pearl City, midway between town and the country. He was kind of an inland surf shop in our way of thinking back then, although how that could be on a small island like Oʻahu shows how provincial we were. Actually, he was in the best place—close to ʻEwa Beach, not far from the south shore, a little farther to Makaha, and a lot closer than our shop was to the Country. And there were a lot of surfers around there who wanted surfboards. Craig made a good business, which he still has today.

Maybe the distance made it seem more idyllic, but everything in life seemed to slow down once you got to the Country. At first we were always driving out through Pearl City since we lived in town, but later on Wayne Santos and I got a great house in Kahaluʻu, just past Kaneʻohe. From there we would drive the back way around the east side, through Hauʻula and Laʻie, and approach the Country from the other end. The countdown would begin every time we passed through Kahuku. Going by Kawela Bay, we would hold our breath until we got our first glimpse of the day's surf. If the waves weren't too big, our first check would be down the old dairy road to Velzyland. We never knew who owned that property, but they apparently didn't mind that we parked there.

The parking lot—if the hau bush clearing at the end of the winding dirt road could be called that—offered an outstanding view of the lefts. If the tide was high enough and the surf inviting, we could paddle straight out from there. If not, we would walk down the beach to paddle out the channel by the rights. We spent a lot of time surfing Velzyland.

If V-land wasn't doing it, we would go right to Sunset, which was the main spot back then. BK was the man there, so if we saw his car, we didn't have to check anything else; we'd just take our boards off the racks and paddle out. If 'Big Roy' Mesker was with us, he would insist we go check Haleʻiwa. I didn't mind that because we could stop at the Pipeline for a look on the way. Santos was regular foot and hated the place, but goofy-foot Roy would paddle out with me if it looked good, but only after we took the long drive down to Haleʻiwa first. Checking the surf was a big part of the program.

If the Pipe was good, Haleʻiwa was usually good too; both worked on a west swell. So we would get a quick surf there since all of us loved Haleʻiwa's great rights and fun lefts.

After surfing we would make a quick stop at the IGA supermarket for some food and head back up the coast. I would have to badger Wayne and Roy to stop again at the Pipeline; it was a ritual with us. They both wanted Sunset and I wanted Pipe, but because we were eating by then, there was no rush, so we would pull over and park on the side of Kam Highway. This was long before the hau bushes were cleared and the Sunset Elementary School built. There was no traffic so we could park where we liked. We would go by Billy Hamilton's house; he would usually be working on a surfboard under

Rory came in farther down the beach from us but didn't see his board anywhere toward the beach park where normally a lost board would wash in.

the banyan tree. He would ask about the surf we had seen, we would talk story for a bit, and if he wasn't too busy, together we would walk out to the beach to look at the waves.

There was a coconut tree grove on the slope in front of his yard that made a shady spot to check the surf. Billy was renting from old man Nonaka, who used to come out once in a while and talk to us about the old days. He owned another place a few doors down but lived in town. Years later, after Billy had gone to Kaua'i, I would buy the property from Mr. Nonaka, but that would be in the distant future.

The Pipeline is seldom picture perfect. Those days are rare. More often there were some pretty good-looking waves mixed in with a lot of rough ones. That was what I looked for. Billy, because he lived there, also had the same eye for Pipe. We weren't looking at the whole picture, just the few waves we wanted to see. Big Roy and 'Wayne the Pain' never saw it that way; they only had Sunset on their minds.

Overall, Sunset would usually be better, just because there would be more ride-able waves and bigger sets. But I liked the Pipeline. More times than not, I would lose out and we would surf Sunset. Sometimes, if I knew the swell was going to be west for a few days, I would stay out there with friends. Then I could hit the Pipeline early in the morning.

One morning at Pipeline there were good waves and not a lot of guys in the lineup. Rory came out. He was always happy and loud, but he was a pig when it came to waves. With those long arms and big hands, he was a strong paddler who could and would take off in front of anyone.

We tried to ride the tube together, but he always rode a little too low on the wave so there wasn't much room. I seemed to be able to ride a little higher on the wall, so when I was in front, we would often both make it. But he was usually in front of me—as was just about everyone else—so more times than not, I would get snuffed by the lip. That's what happened this time, and I had to swim in after my board. I caught a pretty good bodysurf wave all the way in to shore.

I saw a little towheaded kid running after my board as it washed up the beach. I knew who it was right away. It was Billy's stepson. Although they might not have shared the same blood, the boy was Billy's son in every other way there was. I guess you could say this kid was rambunctious, but I generally preferred another term: brat. His name was Laird and he must have been about five or six years old then.

Laird saw me coming in and dragged my board back and gave it to me. "What's happening?" I asked.

"Oh nothing, just playing on the beach," he answered.

As we walked back down the beach, I noticed he had excavated a pretty big hole in the sand. "What's that for?" I asked him.

"Oh nothing, just a hole I dug," he said, but I noticed a little glint of mischief in his eyes.

Laird has the most unusual eyes—they are a cat-like gold and very expressive. I knew he was up to something and being in no rush, I decided to sit down with him and enjoy whatever he had in mind. We lay in that beautiful Pipeline sand, lobbing sand balls into the waves with Laird still industriously digging his hole deeper.

Rory took off late, ate it, and lost his board. I was watching the board bounce in the whitewater when I sensed Laird's eyes on me. I turned to him. He had a questioning look on his face but didn't say a word. I looked at the big hole he had dug, looked back at the board washing in, and it dawned on me. I smiled and vaguely nodded.

That was all he was waiting for. Laird exploded out of that hole, ran down the beach, grabbed Rory's board as it washed up, and dragged it back to his hole. I jumped right in and helped him bury the board.

The boy was smart; he had dug his hole just high enough on the beach where only the biggest surges reached. Right after we got the board covered, a wave washed in and smoothed out the digging marks in the sand. No one could even tell it was there. We both sat down, put innocent expressions on our faces, and waited for Rory to swim to the beach.

Rory came in farther down the beach from us but didn't see his board anywhere toward the beach park where normally a lost board would wash in. Assuming it must have come straight in, he started walking back toward us. Looking toward Off the Wall, he didn't see anything in that direction either.

"Hey, did you guys see my surfboard?" he asked us. Laird had his face buried in the sand, but I could see he was trembling with laughter.

"What color is it?" I asked trying to keep a straight face.

"It's a brand-new red one," said Rory.

There was absolutely no one else on the entire beach except us, but I nudged Laird, saying, "Didn't we see some scruffy, hippie-looking guy with a red board down by Off the Wall?"

Top   Photo: Jeff Divine

Bottom   I am hanging by a prayer and the slightest pressure on my inside rail on a beautiful, trade-wind-combed face. Photo: Steve Wilkings

Laird put his head up long enough to nod affirmatively, then plunged back down. His whole body was shaking, but he was trying not to laugh out loud. I thought Rory had to notice something, but he had this look of anguish on his face and immediately started screaming, "That fu@#er just stole my board, where did you see him?"

"I thought I saw him running up toward the right of way down there," I pointed toward Off the Wall.

Rory took off running, his long legs churning the sand. Laird pulled his face out of the sand, and we both started cracking up.

"Look at him go," I giggled.

We watched Rory run all the way to the right of way, a good distance in the soft sand. We watched him frantically run up the path and disappear toward Ke Nui road. A few moments later he reappeared and ran down the beach, literally running in circles. Next he ran back toward us. His face was bright red and he was huffing and puffing. He was literally running around in circles.

"You sure you saw him over there?" he gasped, "God, Shipley is going to kill me if I lose that new board. I just got it yesterday."

"Maybe he was by the beach park. Jeez, we weren't really paying attention," I said.

"By the park, you sure?" Rory was panting hard.

"Yeah, maybe over there," I pointed vaguely toward the park.

Rory took off running in that direction. We were about to bust a gut. Rory was running around in more circles up in the park. There was no one to ask about his lost board. Finally, we saw him slowly heading back down the beach, his head hung low in total desolation. If I knew Rory, he was probably crying by then.

"Uh-oh, Laird, look at that," I pointed to where the wave action had uncovered one end of the board we had buried. "I think we better get out of here," I told him.

Laird scampered off toward his house and I picked up my board. Rory was getting closer as I jumped back in the water and paddled out. About halfway out, I heard a loud, "YOU FU@#ERS!"

I knew Rory had found his board. I guess he was too tired from all that running around to paddle back out. I told the guys in the lineup what Laird and I had done to 'Bonzo Doggy-Hoggy-Froggy.' Everyone had a good laugh, and then we enjoyed a great session without Rory hogging the waves.

The

Money

Motive

Fitz and I knew the surf was going to be big, but until we started down the hill past Wahiawa we had no idea it would be gigantic. From that panorama, the ocean looked like wide wale corduroy: thick lines stacked up all the way to the horizon. After a few moments of shocked silence, little or no breathing, and intense staring, we also noticed lines that looked darker and thicker. We assumed those were the sets. As if the waves in between weren't big enough.

It was huge, as big as we ever had seen it while still clean. I remembered bigger waves back in 1969, but that was all storm surf. What we were seeing was clean, perfect, and enormous. We had an early report that they were going to run the contest at Waimea. It was obvious as we drove by Haleʻiwa with waves breaking almost across the channel that nowhere else could hold a swell of this magnitude.

It was Thanksgiving Day, 1974, and the North Shore had a long tradition of supplying a good swell on the third Thursday of each November. This, however, was almost ridiculous. Terry Fitzgerald, an Australian surfer who had earned a solid reputation among the elite Hawaiʻi winter crew, and I were both feeling the butterflies as we passed by Laniakea and Chun's Reef showing nothing but whitewater as far out as we could see. The ʻehukai in the air made it seem like there was a fog, but it was just the mist from the waves.

As we pulled over on the side of the road that overlooks the Bay, we were greeted by a beautiful set. Waimea was as perfect as we had ever seen it. The lines were wrapping around the point and peeling into the bay. There were a group of guys scrambling in the lineup, and several turned to paddle for one of the bigger waves. Two caught it, stood up, and began taking the long drop. It looked like Jose Angel and Mike Miller, two longtime veterans of Waimea. Their experience showed as they made the drop successfully and bottom turned together to race the wall. What took our breath away was how high above their heads the wave towered. It was a solid twenty-five-foot wave and without a drop of water out of place. As they rode their way out into the channel, Fitz and I finally started breathing again. We looked at each other, and I wondered if my eyes were as big and round as his were.

"Jesus Christ!" I said, "Are we ready for THIS?" Fitzzy slowly shook his head.

"I don't know, but we might as well get down there and see what's going on with everyone else," he replied glumly.

We drove down and parked in the lot. We walked over to where we could see Freddie Hemmings animatedly talking to a crowd of the guys. They, like Fitz and I, had made it through the preliminary heats run earlier that week in more reasonable waves at Sunset Beach. We were all here to surf the semifinal heats and hopefully make our way into the finals of the Smirnoff Professional Surfing Contest.

As I looked around and saw guys like Peter Townend, Mark Warren, Jimmy Lucas, Barry Kanaiaupuni, Larry Bertlemann, and others whom I knew had never even surfed Waimea before, let alone at this size, I began to understand what was making Freddie boil. He had promoted this event for the past several years, and here was this great-big, beautiful swell at Waimea Bay that would make unbelievable press for his sponsor, but the surfers didn't want to go out because it was too big. Fred was livid.

Reno Abellira taking the drop on a winning wave,
while I shove hard and pray my board makes it over
the top. Photo: Steve Wilkings

"What do you mean this surf isn't any good for a contest … it's great," he screamed.

He started to peel off his shirt, "I'll paddle out there myself and show you guys how good it is."

In his time, Fred Hemmings had been one of the top big-wave chargers in Hawai'i with lots of days in at spots like Makaha, Laniakea, Sunset Beach, and Waimea. Having gone to high school with Fred, where he was the captain of the football team, I figured he just might borrow a board off someone and paddle out to make his point.

Just then the sun climbed over the hills behind Waimea, and it was as though a whole new light was shone on the subject. The beach where we were standing had been in the shadow of the hills. Suddenly it was lit up and warm. The whole mood seemed to change. The waves were really good, and the regular Waimea guys, including Jose, Eddie Aikau, Peter Cole, Ricky Grigg, and Kimo Hollinger all were getting fantastic rides. It looked spectacular from the beach.

"The contest is ON," Fred announced.

Everyone went, if somewhat reluctantly, to get ready. Generally before contests, a lot of guys would get to the beach early to have time for a practice session to gauge the waves. That day at Waimea not one of the contestants paddled out before his heat. Everyone was going in cold, and for quite a few of them, it would be their first time out at the break. Even guys like Hakman and Reno, who had surfed many times before at Waimea, were a little nervous.

I was in the second heat and began to wax my board even before they called the first heat. I probably waxed that thing for half an hour, going through several bars of wax in the process. It was my first time out on this new 8'10", and if I was going to have any problems with it, lack of wax was not going to be one of them.

People who surf Waimea a lot have said that over the years it's changed, that sand has filled up the bay. Years later I would go down there to watch, and it seemed that once the waves were twenty-five feet or so, they would close out the Bay completely. On that Turkey Day of '74, I don't remember one wave closing out. Maybe it was just a very clean swell, but as it came time for my heat to hit the water, I jumped in at the corner and paddled out without getting my hair wet.

When big surf is clean and perfect like it was that day, from the elevated vantage of the beach, it has a tendency to look smaller. Once I was in the channel paddling out the full size of the waves was more evident, and it was a chilling sight. The size was unusually consistent at eighteen to twenty feet, the sets regular and frequent.

The tubes were probably the most astonishing thing about the waves that day. It was so top-to-bottom that sitting there in the safety of the channel watching, I didn't think there was a way to catch one, stand up, and make the drop on such a hollow wave. The tubes were completely round and looked like the Pipeline except two to three times bigger. The caverns were so enormous that several city buses stacked on top of each other would have fit inside.

As if to make the point of how difficult it was to drop-in, I watched Larry Bertlemann get pitched and take the worst wipeout I have ever seen. It made me sick to

my stomach just seeing the beating he took. On the very next wave, Jimmy Lucas did the same thing. He free-fell from the top through twenty feet of space. Then the thick curl just pounded him deep and held him down for much too long. Both surfers came up, swam in, and didn't return. I couldn't fault either for deciding to quit after the pummeling they took. Finally the heat ended, and we paddled into the lineup to try our luck.

Being seasoned veterans of many surf contests, our initial apprehensions were soon overcome by the heat of battle, especially since we were surfing for the biggest purse in the short history of professional surf contests. Reno and I paddled out together to join the Waimea regulars, who had decided to stay out in the lineup without interfering with the contestants.

Freddie had tried to get them to clear the water, but the intensity of the situation, the size of the waves, and the fact that it was one of the best days in the history of Waimea was just too explosive. Fred wisely backed off and let the guys stay out in the water. Most of the contest surfers were unfamiliar with the break and didn't even want the set waves so everything worked out.

The regulars were sitting farther outside and much deeper than any of us wanted to, so Reno and I took a position closer to the channel and just inside. With our insides boiling, we tried to appear calm as we waited for the first waves.

With a clean swell like this, the wave interval was widely spaced and very regular. We spotted a set coming in and paddled a few strokes outside mostly out of nervousness since we were already in the right spot. Reno went for the first good one and I got ready for the second.

It was as perfect a wave as I had ever seen at Waimea. Jose, Peter, and Ricky all shouted encouragement as I paddled hard for it. I caught it pretty easily and made the drop. I turned at the bottom and held my line toward the channel. It was no big deal and that really surprised me. I cut back a few times and weaved in alongside the channel, milking the wave even though the critical part was over. I felt more confident as I took the easy paddle back out.

Bud Browne was swimming out at the edge of the impact zone filming from the water. He and I were good friends. He saw me, smiled, and said, "Nice wave."

Bud was known as the 'Barracuda' because he moved like one through the water. He was sixty years old, but I didn't have a second thought about him being out here in these giant waves. Later on that day, he would find himself caught inside by a big set and take the pounding of his life. Afterward he would comment in his usual deadpan way, "I'm getting too old for this." That would be the last time he shot from the water at the Bay.

I got back to the lineup and asked Reno how his wave was.

"Good," he said. "But we need to catch bigger ones."

Oh boy, I thought, I guess that is what a guy has to do to win. A few more sets came. They were about the same size as the previous ones, and we both got a few more rides. Finally what looked like a bigger set approached and we both got ready for it. This time I went for the first one, but it was a lot bigger than my first wave, and it jacked up so fast I barely had time to hit the brakes and pull back. I managed to keep myself from getting sucked over, but when I turned around and saw the next one I almost had a heart attack.

In front of me was the biggest wave I had ever seen in my life, and I was not in a good spot to avoid it. Reno was paddling hard to catch it and I was paddling even harder to avoid it. He was paddling down as I paddled up, as we passed we looked right into each other's eyes. Reno stood up and I could see the thick lip right behind him. I was pretty far up the face, but there was no way I was going to paddle through the top of the wave, it was already throwing out. I got off my board and shoved it as hard as I could straight up through the lip.

It was an enormous wave, but desperation must have worked in my favor. I saw my board penetrate the top of the wave just before I dove under and swam through to the other side. I was never so happy to see my red gun waiting for me. There were only these two waves in the set so I had time to calm my rapidly beating heart and catch my breath.

Reno paddled back and had this really intense look in his eye. I knew without asking that it was a result of the huge wave he had just caught. The big sets were a solid five to six feet bigger than the regular eighteen- to twenty-foot waves. The next set we saw looked even bigger than that. Reno and I watched as all the regulars who were a little further outside and deeper than us all moved out as the set approached. We looked at each other and without a word, lay down, and started paddling hard for the outside.

When we paddled over the top of the waves in front, we saw that this was a huge set. The first wave stood up outside of us and it was at least ten feet bigger than the largest ones we'd seen so far. No one wanted these waves, and because everyone saw them coming, we started paddling outside early and no one got caught. But the sensation of paddling over a wave this big left a feeling down in the pit of my stomach that I had never felt before. I guess it had to do with the thought of what one of these waves could do to me if I got caught inside. Everyone, including the Waimea regulars, just got out of the way of that set and let the waves roll through unchallenged.

They were the biggest waves that Reno and I had ever seen up close. Even now I remember the look that he had in his eyes. I realized that he really wanted to catch one of those waves. I understood that that's what we needed to do if we wanted to win this surf contest, but I wondered if I had it in me to launch myself into something that big.

We had a few moments to think about it, but soon we could see the next set coming our way, and it looked like another giant one. We both took a few deep breaths and got ready for it. It was big, not quite as big as the one we just paddled over, but much bigger than the waves we had caught so far. The first one was perfect, and I saw Reno wanted to make a move for it. I paddled over the top to see what was behind while he stroked hard to catch the wave and was gone.

The next wave was considerably bigger than anything I had ever ridden, but I was in position, it was clean, and I didn't give it a second thought. I turned and paddled as hard as I could. I felt the wave lift, I had it, I was in early, and I leaped to my feet. I crouched down feeling the board start to drop. I was stoked, everything looked and felt good as I began my descent.

The next thing I knew, the bottom dropped out of the wave and I free-fell into space. "Oh shit!" That good feeling I had a moment before was long gone and I knew I was in deep trouble. I fell about a third of the way down the wave still standing on my surfboard—at least ten or twelve feet. The first thing to touch the wave again was the nose of my board. It buried and flipped me off headfirst. That turned out to be a good thing because I had enough momentum built up that I managed to penetrate into the face of the wave instead of skipping off and ending up down in the pit.

I couldn't believe how lucky I was to dive through the wave and come out the back. What looked like the worst wipeout of my career ended up as nothing. I was behind the wave, safe and sound. I took a few deep breaths before swimming in after my board. The next heat was paddling out in the channel. When I swam by, they all looked at me and asked how I survived getting pitched by that set wave. I laughed and told them it was no big deal. They just shook their heads and paddled by, trying to prepare themselves should the same thing happen to them.

When I got to the beach, Grubby Clark was waiting for me with my surfboard. "What did you do that for?" he asked.

Everyone around saw me get pitched on one of the biggest waves and assumed the wipeout was horrendous. I didn't tell them how lucky I was to dive through the wave.

Grubby turned around and announced, "It was the money motive—the money motive made him do it. Nothing else could have made him try to catch that wave."

I didn't advance through the heat but actually that was a relief. Reno made the finals, continued his strong performance, and went on to win the event.

Afterward we left the beach and went to eat a big Thanksgiving dinner. All the while, Grubby was telling anyone who would listen: "The money motive made him do it."

The Best Surfer

in the Flesh

Being the best surfer in the world never had meaning for me. On my own, likely I never would have conceived of such a thought. I set goals to improve my surfing, but apart from a passing fancy, being the best seemed frivolously unrealistic.

There were other surfers who I thought might have deserved to be called that. I also knew that my experience was limited, and there was little likelihood that even the great surfers of my time could be gathered together for a determination. Moreover, all of this says nothing about the ambiguity of any standard of review. Judging surfers is a slippery slope and ultimately subjective. What the heck identifies a good surfer? We surfers think we know. "Don't fall off the surfboard," we can say with confidence. None of this, however, precluded me from having surf heroes.

I began to surf in contests where the object was to choose the best surfer. Right away I understood that such anointings were transient. Like bubbles of a breaking wave, those moments passed quickly. The next day, everything would start again from the beginning. Nobody would be "the best" anymore.

I discovered yoga when I was about nineteen years old. It provided me with some answers. I learned that winning at something is nothing when compared to mastering it. I applied this insight to surf contests, and was less disappointed when I didn't win. By expecting less, I suffered less.

Thus armed with a little yogic understanding as protection for fragile feelings, I walked my career as a surfing persona down some interesting paths. If the measure of surfing was based upon the sum total of competition results, my surfing stunk. I traveled to the world surfing venues, competed in the events, and most often finished at the bottom of the order. My few good finishes were in a contest with just five other guys at a spot where I was the only one who surfed there on a regular basis.

As it turned out, not only did this particular contest grow into a premier event, but overnight the spot became the most photographed wave in the world of surfing. Surf magazines and movies dominated that world.

Photographs and films of me surfing at this place called the Pipeline permeated that period of the commercial surf media. With that, I came to be recognized as a surfing star—what in the 1970s we called a "name." I thought it was a bunch of hogwash.

I also had a friend who was, I thought, a much better surfer than I was. Every time we saw another picture of me somewhere, he rolled his eyes, sighed disgustedly, and called me a kook. The truth of it was, he was right to a certain extent. But having few or no expectations, I was able to accept the fame or the criticism, and take what came with a sense of humor.

One time on a trip to Australia, I was performing poorly as usual in the pro surfing events there. Nevertheless, because I was known as 'Mr. Pipeline' to folks who had never heard of Jock Sutherland or the late Butch Van Artsdalen, I was interviewed by a surf journalist.

We spoke of many things. My view of the world was esoteric to him. Yoga, meditation, and Eastern philosophies were not widely known at that time in the surfing world. His pragmatic worldview was based primarily on facts and results. We might have shared a belief in the physics of atoms and molecules forming waves to ride, but our polar

opposite perceptions of life could have provided rich fodder for German philosophers. Finally, he asked me who I thought was the best surfer in the world.

I answered that it wasn't really something that mattered in the grand scheme of things. After all, I suggested, weren't we all the best that we could be in everything we did or tried to do? No, he wasn't interested in that. In his view, the best surfer in the world at this point in time was a person who could be named.

I saw where he was headed. The World Champion surfer of the time happened to be an Australian. Australians can be fiercely nationalistic. They love nothing better than to pound their chests when there is something to be proud of, and even sometimes when there isn't. I could see he wasn't going to take any other kind of answer.

"OK," I said, "the best surfer who ever lived was a guy named Tommy Zahn."

"Oh bloody hell, who is this Tommy Zahn?" asked the exasperated journalist. "I've never even heard of him."

Tom Zahn was a surfer from back in the 1950s who was a great paddler. Paddling was at that time a bigger deal than actual wave riding, at least in part because a paddleboard race was something that had a clearly defined winner. Tom Zahn came to Hawai'i, trained with the great Tom Blake, and went on to beat the indomitable George Downing in the prestigious Diamond Head race. Zahn later went on to become the Chief Lifeguard of the L.A. County beaches. He was also a very good-looking guy with a terrific build.

This journalist was well known for his expertise on the statistics of modern surfing. I would have wagered he could name the top five finishers in every single major surfing event spanning the five years preceding my interview. He was a bit heated on account of having been snagged on something about surfing he didn't know.

"What did this Tommy Zahn do that was so bloody great?" he spit out.

I lost my straight face during the delivery, much as I had gassed those surfing contests Down Under.

"He slept with Marilyn Monroe: How can anyone top that?"

With no wetsuit or crowd, Tommy Zahn slides across a slick-looking Rincon wall on a Joe Quigg shape that was ahead of its time. Photo: Joe Quigg collection

A Saturday

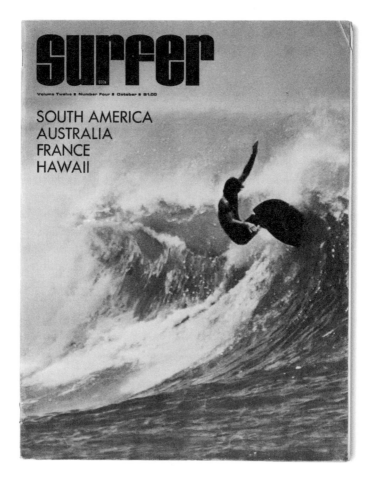

at
Ala Moana

The year was 1971. Wayne Santos and I both shaped surfboards for the brand-new Lightning Bolt Surf Shop, which Jack Shipley and I, with a little help from Wayne, had just opened two summers before on Kapiolani Boulevard. The shop was selling surfboards almost as fast as we could make them, so Wayne and I had all the work we wanted. But the truth was that we really didn't want to work and would take any excuse, like surf, to do something else.

Wayne was one of the best surfers I knew. We surfed Ala Moana in the summer, the Country in the winter, and lived together in a little house out past Kane'ohe in Kahalu'u on the east side of the island.

The surfing industry, a generous description of the business of surfing at that time, was mostly in California. Several years earlier, surfboard designs had begun to undergo a tremendous upheaval, and what would later become known as the shortboard revolution was in full swing. Any revolution is all about change, and only for this reason could a bunch of dropouts like Jack, Wayne, and me have any chance of success with a surf shop business.

During the preceding decade, almost all surfboard manufacturing took place in Southern California. The big brands like Hobie, Greg Noll, Bing, Hansen, Dewey Weber, Gordon & Smith, Jacobs, and others based in California built and sold a lot of boards during that first surfing boom. Except for a few local builders like Inter-Island and Surfboards Hawai'i, neither of which lasted out the 1960s, most of the surfboards in Hawai'i came from California.

By 1969, surfboard shapes were evolving at a pace so rapid, it was only the surfers on the beach riding the new boards that were able to keep up. So it was that many of the boards began to be shaped and glassed in the backyards and garages of these surfers and, almost overnight, an underground industry was born. Hawai'i, with all its waves winter, spring, summer, and fall, became a focal point for design innovation and suddenly found itself at the forefront of this new wave of surfboard making.

My own entry into the business began when I invested fifteen dollars in some resin and fiberglass, stripped the glass off my old longboard, reshaped the blank, glassed it, and headed down to our local spot to see how it went. That surfboard, at 7'6" in length, rode like the wind ... at least in my mind. When I paddled in and climbed up into the Ala Wai Harbor parking lot, there was a gang of all my surf buddies waiting to take a closer look at my very, for the spring of 1968, short board. One of them had eighty dollars cash in hand and extended it my way, I handed over the dripping board, and just like that, I was in the surfboard business.

Pretty much anyone with some craftsman skills, or even just a gleam in their eyes, was doing exactly the same thing. Some may have had a little experience working in surf shops; or, like me, they repaired dings, a much smaller step into actually building an entire surfboard. Most just winged it, asked a lot of questions, or did the trial-and-error method and discovered that making a rideable surfboard wasn't that difficult. It wasn't long before almost all surfers wanted boards just like those they saw ripping apart the waves at their local spot but couldn't find in any of the existing surf shops, which relied on the big mainland manufacturers for their inventory.

Much of this board building was happening in garages or little hole-in-the-wall operations where the neighbors didn't complain about the stink of resin or the piles of garbage. Our Lightning Bolt shop was just the showroom where Jack sold the boards. Wayne and I shaped anywhere we could. Our friend Wylie Artman rented a rundown dump behind Seagull Lake in Hale'iwa with a small garage and some plywood additions, which we turned into a shaping room and glass shop. That was fine during the winter when the surf was good out there, but when spring came and Ala Moana began to break, we had to come up with something closer to Town.

I found a little industrial space behind the fire station in Kaka'ako, where we built three shaping stalls and still had space enough for glassing if necessary. By then, there were other glassers who would come by, pick up the shaped blanks, and deliver them back to Shipley at the shop when they were done. This was a much better arrangement since Wayne and I could concentrate on our shaping, but mostly because it allowed us more time to surf.

Having a whole stable of board builders working for our shop created a competitive atmosphere where everyone was constantly raising the quality of their work. Looking back on that time, the level of the creativity in the shapes, tint and opaque laminations, pin line and lightning bolt color work, and polishing reached an unprecedented height never before seen in surfboard building. The boards were works of art, but at the same time totally functional, and therefore highly coveted surf vehicles. Hence, they flew out the door. Surfers from California, the East Coast, Australia, Japan, and the rest of the world couldn't wait to get to our shop to buy a surfboard.

Just five minutes from the shop were Ala Moana, Kaisers Bowl, Rockpiles, and the parking lot at the small boat harbor. There was our home away from home. Actually, at that point in our lives, it was Home, and where we would be most of the daylight hours during the spring, summer, and early fall. The south swells coming from the Roaring Forties latitude in the Southern Hemisphere focused on that little stretch of coastline, and we wouldn't dream of being anywhere else except there to meet them.

There were many other excellent breaks within sight, but Ala Moana was the crème de la crème of them all. The long, fast-breaking left was a challenging wave at any size from two to ten feet, and most of the best surfers found their way there, if not daily then, at least when the south swell pumped. The best of it was when the surf was big enough for the Bowl to break, which we would call Pole Sets at Ala Moana.

In the early 1950s, the City and County dredged the natural channel to create a safe access for the growing little yacht harbor. In doing so, they also made two natural surf spots much better. Across from Ala Moana to the west was Garbage Hole, called that because all the debris from the boat moorage and the Ala Wai Canal flowed out on that side of the channel. It was a bowling, hollow little right, which Wayne Miyata made famous in Bruce Brown's *Endless Summer*. But the Magic Island project got underway not long after Hawai'i became a state and buried Garbage Hole under a landfill. Ala Moana was unaffected and actually gained a perfect viewing area from the new park across the channel.

Needless to say, the lineup at Ala Moana was very crowded whenever the waves were good, and even on the less good, small days during the south shore surf season. It was here that the most progressive surfing went down on a regular basis and, with it, the progression of the shortboard shape for smaller waves. On any given day during the summer at Ala Moana, one would find the best surfers doing the most advanced surfing on state-of-the-art equipment.

A thing to note was that there were a lot of great surfers all the time at Ala Moana, not any one particular standout. Conrad Cunha and Sammy Lee were older and well respected, and Donald Takayama or David Nuuhiwa might show up for a day or two from California, but overall, it was everyone's show.

If someone felt he deserved more than he was getting, he would just have to suck it up. There were too many others of equal, if not more talent, on the next wave or the one after that … or more than likely, on the same one Mr. Hotshot thought should be his. Even when the contest came around, whoever won knew that he was the lucky one for just that day, and the next day the lineup would be level again.

This was the natural order of things, and while egos might have gotten out of hand, that happened mostly in the parking lot and hardly ever in the lineup. At Ala Mo's, it was always about the wave more than the surfers, and the high level of the surfing was expected given the quality of the surf.

The arrival of a significant swell could have several effects. Usually, everyone would show up and the lineup would be even more crowded. Sometimes, however, a new swell would open up a variety of other spots and have the effect of dispersing the crowd to the different breaks along the South Shore.

It was a Saturday morning when I drove into the parking lot and noticed it was almost empty except for a few of the boat owners' cars. I was surprised to see a nice set roll through the Bowl and no one on any of the waves. But I didn't think much of it as I changed into my surf trunks, unstrapped my board, waxed it up, and headed out.

In the mid-1960s, another break wall had been added to create more moorings for boats, so we would paddle across the slip, between the boats, and climb over the rocks. From the outside break wall was a better view of the wave, and again I was surprised as another set came through the lineup without anyone on a wave.

On a five- to eight-foot day like this, the first waves of a set would start from the middle lineup and peel through several tricky sections; if one was skilled enough, or lucky, these waves would offer a long, fast ride. The bigger waves later in the set would invariably shift over toward the channel to create the Pole Sets that set Ala Moana apart from most of the other summertime surf breaks. A good wave at the Bowl was a punchy, thrilling, deep, and hollow tube that would spit a fortunate rider out with his hair still combed.

There was a steel pole about eighteen inches in diameter anchored into the reef that marked the east edge of the channel for the boats coming and going from the yacht harbor. The position of the pole was almost exactly where the big waves stood up, so it also marked a perfect place to wait for the sets. Most of the summertime South Shore waves around Waikiki were on the gentle side when compared with similar size waves out in the Country, but the Bowl at Ala Moana packed a wallop and could rough up a surfer, pin him on the bottom, and give him a good scare.

After seeing the size of the waves, I just paddled out and sat by the pole to wait for the next set. Glancing around, I saw a couple of surfers up toward Rockpile and more at Kaisers, but here, the lineup was empty. There was always an early-morning crew, guys who worked the late shifts at the restaurants and nightspots in Waikiki and came straight from work to the beach, but maybe they had come and gone, as it was already midmorning. Looking the other way, I could see a few guys down by Big Rights and Tennis Courts in front of the Ala Moana Park. I thought I saw someone with a tripod set up on the break wall at Magic Island, but a set was coming so I didn't have the time to be sure.

Any day at Ala Moana with an empty lineup is too good to be true, but on a day with sets in the Bowl, it was crazy. I figured Wayne and our other surf partner, Big Roy Mesker, would show up soon, but no one came. It really was a fine swell, the sets pumped, and I had my pick of any wave I wanted. Every time I rode a wave in, I'd look in the parking lot, actually hoping some of my pals would come out.

Being a weekend, the harbor was busy, and the boats going out the channel offered some great entertainment. It seemed that every time a boat tried to breach the channel entrance a set would roll through. On the biggest waves, the channel would actually close out and break all the way across. It certainly wasn't a top-to-bottom wave like the Bowl, but there was a lot of whitewater. If the boats mistimed it, which they almost always did, there were some tense moments as they crashed up through the soup and slammed down on the other side of the wave.

After several hours of having the whole place to myself, a couple of guys paddled out. I was glad for the company even if they didn't last long, losing their boards, and taking the long swim in. With a good swell, the rip would run along the break wall, so unless one swam in quickly, the lost board would get taken down toward the channel and eventually right back out. I never did it, but I always thought one could just swim over to the channel and wait for a lost board to come back around.

Wayne and Big Roy never did show up that day, and even though I wasn't the kind of person to rub it in when they missed something, I wondered why they weren't there and would be asking. After all, at that point in our lives, surf was the central focus of what we did every day. The buzz of not having to jockey around for waves wore off and was replaced, as strange as it seems, by a slight melancholy of not being able to share this beautiful day with my friends.

Don't get me wrong: When a good set approached, I would focus on it completely and, except for the task of putting myself together with that wave, no other thoughts crossed my mind. Pole Sets Ala Moana was serious surfing, and a surfer needs to give it his or her complete attention, or be ready to pay some serious dues. That kind of intense surfing takes it out of a person, but a good ride puts the energy right back in.

There is a give and take going while surfing. Burning up the juice by paddling hard to catch waves, surviving horrendous wipeouts, swimming in after a lost board—all that effort makes surfing one of the most strenuous sports. Then the thrill of a good turn, a difficult but successfully executed tube section, a flowing cutback reversing direction back into the power, the end of a long ride, paddling back out watching a big set rolling in—all these pour the energy back in, easing any fatigue. The back and forth between the body and mind, one using up the gas, the other refilling it, is like a tally on a ledger. Inevitably, the gas tank is being emptied a little faster than it can be filled. It is a combination of several factors, the waves and the stoke, balanced against the time spent doing it. Eventually the gas tank goes dry, and it's time to go in.

Later that fall, Wayne decided to accompany me on one of my increasingly more frequent mainland business trips. I'm sure his interest had less to do with any actual business and more to do with the California girls. Wayne with his shoulder-length hair, broad shoulders, and piercing eyes was one of those guys that women swoon over. Both Wayne and I had been born and raised in Honolulu and, in comparison, California was like the center of civilization or, at least, some sort of imagined Babylon. We parked our rental car on a side street in downtown Huntington Beach, and I took him on a small tour, starting on the pier. Watching the surfers from above on either the north or south side has always has been a great show, and we spent the better part of an hour looking at the waves, the surfers, and the people on the pier.

Later we walked up Main Street to George's Surf Shop where a local surfer girl named Jan ran a great juice-and-sandwich bar. As we walked into the shop, there was a copy of the latest *Surfer* magazine, which Californians would have long before anyone in Hawai'i. Wayne looked at the cover and muttered, "Who's that f@#%*n kook?" And there I was, just like Dr. Hook sang, right there on "The Cover of the Rolling Stone."

I was in total shock, and I'm pretty sure Wayne was too. No one in our group had ever dreamed we would make a cover shot. We opened the mag, and there was a feature on Ala Moana by John Severson. I remembered the day and seeing the guy on Magic Island with the tripod.

Wayne was still muttering about the feature just showing a bunch of kooks, and I felt bad that there were no shots of him or Big Roy since both of them surfed better than I did. I reminded Wayne that it was the Saturday they both had missed, he with a toothache and Roy with a modeling job, but I could see it still rankled him.

As we looked at the cover again, I added, "Well, I ate shit right after that picture. You can see I'm catching my rail." That mollified him somewhat, along with my offering to pay for lunch.

As he put the mag back on the shelf, I heard one last, muffled, "Kook!"

Get It While You Can

The surf was up. Even though he wanted to get some work done at the blank warehouse, we conned 'Grubby' into going surfing with us. Rory and I squeezed him in between us in the cab of my pickup, and we cruised down to the parking lot at Ala Moana.

It was full-on Pole Sets and we could hardly wait to get out there. Grubby was pretty game and followed us out between the parked boats, over the outside break wall, and out into the lineup at the Bowl. Actually, he had done quite a bit of surfing at Ala Moana long before Rory was even a gleam in his father's eye and while I was probably going through my terrible twos.

Back in the early 1950s, Grubby had come over to Hawai'i and had gotten a job from Tom Blake reglassing and repairing a bunch of old paddleboards and surfboards. It was to be his first job in the surfboard industry. In a way, I guess we owe Tom Blake a debt of gratitude for not only his own contributions but more so for the tremendous contributions Clark Foam has made to the modern surfboard. Grubby might not have become interested in surfboards without that first job from Blake.

I remember a snapshot that Bud Browne had pinned up on the wall of the little room above a garage where he lived in Costa Mesa. It was of a skinny guy on a surfboard with a small gaff-rigged sail that was operated from a prone position. The photo's caption read, "Gordon Clark sailing at Ala Moana." It was taken during that first trip to Hawai'i. Grubby was definitely ahead of the windsurfing craze that would hit thirty years later, which he would also play a hand in developing.

But today it was a solid south swell, the waves were pumping, and Rory and I had only one thing on our minds. So we sat up in the lineup and waited for the first set to come our way.

The Bowl at Ala Moana is no easy wave; in fact it can be a lurching, sucking out, vicious devil that can hold a surfer underwater for a lot longer than is healthy. It was all that today, made worse by the slightly onshore Kona wind that often accompanied the arrival of a big south swell. The pushing wind made the already fast-breaking wave break even faster. Poor Grubby with his favorite 9'4" named 'Baby' was having a hell of a time. Baby was just a little too long for the quick takeoffs. Grubby and Baby kept getting stuck in the lip as the wave lurched up right next to the pole.

Gordon 'Grubby' Clark at the Clark Foam
factory in the 1970s. Photo: Bev Morgan

The pole is a navigation aid to boaters, marking the edge of the channel. It also works for surfers, defining the takeoff zone on big south swells. On most of his waves, even before he could get to his feet, Grubby was thrown over the falls and into the washing machine wring cycle. But he kept swimming in, retrieving his board, paddling out, and going for it again and again. Rory and I kept looking at each other, both cringing every time Grubby took another beating, and wondering if maybe we had really screwed up making him come out here with us. The Kona winds were making a mess of the waves anyway, and after about an hour, we all decided to call it quits, go in, and look somewhere else.

Back in the truck, we thought we would go take a look at Diamond Head, as the surface conditions would be less windy up there. From the cliff lookout there is a great view of the surf from Black Point all the way down to Tongs.

As soon as we pulled up, we could see a pretty good set rolling through at Brown's, and Grubby immediately said, "That's our spot! I went out with you guys at your place, now you have come out to mine."

Well, we couldn't argue with that and, besides, that set didn't look too bad. So we drove down by Black Point, parked in front of my friend F. William Littlejohn's house, and walked down the road to the beach.

The paddle, although a long way out, was easy and pretty scenic as well, with all the beautiful homes that line the beachfront. Doris Duke's famous mansion is perched on the Diamond Head side of Black Point, with a spectacular view of the ocean and all the surf spots in front. There is a pretty good view of her sprawling home when looking in from out in the water.

Brown's is a great wave but needs a big south swell before it will begin to break, as it is a deep-water spot. On the right swell, it can be reminiscent of a south shore Sunset Beach peak at ten to twelve feet. On a few occasions in the past, I had found myself caught inside a stacked-up set, wishing I were back on the beach instead of in the path of the thick steamroller about to mow me down. Brown's could be heavy and very scary because the deep water meant long hold-downs after a wipeout.

Grubby had not waited for us at all but just left us paddling slowly out on our shortboards while he blazed straight toward the peak. As we got to the lineup, we

Grubby at Kawaihae Harbor on the Big Island. Photo: John Russell watched him ride a pretty nice wave past us. He gave us the sign as he went by, arm up and middle finger extended.

The next wave looked good, and both Rory and I paddled hard to catch it. With our little boards, we just weren't moving fast enough, the wave wasn't steep enough, and the swell rolled by underneath us. We tried for the next smaller wave and the same thing happened; we just couldn't get into the wave. We paddled back outside and joined Grubby who was going on about how great the waves were. We hadn't caught any yet so we didn't have anything to add. Another set loomed up on the outside, and all three of us paddled for what looked like the biggest wave. Again Rory and I were denied, while Grubby easily caught the wave and rode off for another great ride.

"What are we doing wrong?" I asked Rory, who just shrugged since he couldn't figure it out either. Grubby paddled back from his wave, beaming, and told us what a good wave he just rode. He proceeded out to his lineup position way outside, while Rory and I moved further inside thinking we could catch the waves there. The next set came, Grubby stroked right into the best wave and we floundered once again.

As he paddled back by us, Grubby yelled out, "Hey, what are you guys doing? Catch some waves, they're really good."

We both muttered something not fit to print that just made Grubby giggle. After all he was the only one catching any waves, and here we were, two supposedly hot-shot surfers, and we couldn't even catch a wave. Rory and I tried everything we could think of, but the waves were just getting harder to catch. I did finally manage to catch one wave, stand up, and ride for about twenty feet before my board just bogged out and the wave rolled on without me. Rory was red in the face with frustration and I probably was about the same. Meanwhile, Grubby was catching everything he paddled for, and getting long, gliding rides all the way in.

Finally, after about an hour of complete and total exasperation on our part and some pretty good surfing from Grubby, he announced, as he paddled by us into yet another wave that we couldn't catch, "I'm tired, I'm going in. I'll see you guys on the beach." Well, we couldn't go in without catching a wave, so Rory and I stayed out there for another thirty minutes struggling and flailing, until at last we had no choice but to surrender.

"I think we are going to have to paddle back to the beach, I can't catch a god-damn wave to save my life," I whined to Rory.

He just looked at me with anguish written all over his face. Both of us had been completely humiliated by the surf out at Brown's. The worst part was that it had been witnessed by Grubby who, we knew, would never let us live it down. So with our tails between our legs, we started the long paddle back in to the beach.

Walking up the beach, Grubby was nowhere to be seen. We didn't particularly want to see him anyway since we knew the ribbing we were going to get from him. All of a sudden, as we approached the right-of-way up from the beach, we heard him say, "Hey you guys, up here."

Looking around we saw Grubby sitting on the veranda of the beautiful beach-front home we had walked by a thousand times going surfing here at Black Point. It was an immaculate white colonial style home surrounded by a manicured green lawn

Rory went into complete and total shock. His jaw almost hit the table as he watched Grubby chew up the huge hunk of cheese.

looking straight out at the ocean. It was just across the right-of-way from Doris Duke's mansion and, while not as opulent or as large, this home was just as elegant and regal in an understated way.

Grubby was sitting there with an older couple, and they invited the two of us to come in. Rory and I were dripping wet in our surf trunks, surfboards under our arms, sunburned, unshaven, and feeling a little bedraggled after our episode out in the surf. The wrought iron gate swung open and Grubby waved us in. There was an elegantly dressed older gentleman with him, welcoming us into his home.

"Dr. Stevens, this is Gerry Lopez and Rory Russell, two of the best surfers in Hawai'i. You might have heard of them, although they aren't as famous as your ex-son-in-law was; neither of them have made the cover of *Sports Illustrated* yet. You guys, this is Phil Edwards's first wife's father," Grubby said by way of introduction.

We walked through the gate and vine-covered arbor onto the veranda, where we were introduced to an equally elegant Mrs. Stevens. She kindly asked us to please sit down and join them. Would we like something to drink, she asked. But we were both in such shock to be inside a home like this that she had to ask us a second time. Rory asked for a Coca-Cola, and I think I asked if she had any juice.

She brought our drinks and offered us some cheese and crackers that were already sitting on the table. I noticed that my orange juice glass was solid crystal; I hoped in my nervousness and dripping-wet condition that I wouldn't drop it. Grubby, of course, was completely at ease with the Stevens and they were with him; it was obvious that they were old friends. Grubby went on to explain how he had been the best man at their first daughter Heidi's wedding to Phil Edwards. Meanwhile, I couldn't help noticing Rory hungrily eyeing the cheese and crackers.

Sitting on a fine china plate with a sterling silver cheese knife was a big ball of some fancy soft cheese covered in crushed nuts and surrounded by tiny gourmet crackers. I knew Rory, who dearly loved to eat, was dying of hunger because we hadn't eaten all day. I guess Mrs. Stevens noticed as well, since she pushed the plate toward Rory and suggested he try the cheese.

Rory needed no further urging as he put a little dab of cheese on one of the crackers and popped it into his mouth. I prayed that he would chew with his mouth closed for once and wouldn't spray the table or the Stevens with chewed food. He was on his best behavior and even stuck his little finger out when he took a sip of his Coca-Cola. The conversation went on around Rory while he attempted to be discreet, continuing to dab the cheese on the little crackers and put them into his mouth.

The size of the crackers, the small amount of cheese they would hold, and the newfound manners, all forced Rory to eat at a moderate pace. I was kind of laughing to myself because I knew he was barely scratching the surface of his eternally insatiable hunger. He would have liked to devour the whole ball of cheese and could easily have done it in a couple of bites. The surroundings, however, dictated a higher degree of etiquette and he was able to restrain himself.

Grubby must have been paying attention to Rory's predicament. He suddenly reached across the table and pulled the plate toward himself. Taking up the knife while still carrying on his conversation with Dr. and Mrs. Stevens, he started to cut into the ball of cheese—all of this under the close scrutiny of Rory who was aghast that the cheese plate was now out of his control.

Turning his attention to Rory, Grubby proceeded to slice the softball-sized chunk of cheese in half. To Rory's complete horror, Grubby took half the ball, put it on one of the tiny little crackers and somehow managed to stuff the whole thing into his mouth. Rory went into complete and total shock. His jaw almost hit the table as he watched Grubby chew up the huge hunk of cheese.

I bit a hole in my lip to keep from laughing out loud when Grubby looked Rory right in the eye and said, "Get it while you can, kid."

I thought Rory would faint on the spot; the look on his face was one neither Grubby nor I will ever forget. For anyone else, it would have been as if the Dalai Lama himself had made a life-changing personal pronouncement.

"Get it while you can, kid," would change Rory's life, liberty, and pursuit of happiness for all time. Grubby would continue to issue choice one-liners, with his wry sense of humor, perfectly timed delivery, and profound implications, to everyone who ever crossed his path. Most would go over the heads or below the belts, but perhaps none would have such a lasting effect as the one that day to Rory.

A Good Deal

Walter Hoffman on an epic wave at Padang Padang, Bali, before this awesome wave was known to the surfing world. Photo: Don Marsh

After I returned from my first trip to the beautiful island of Bali, I thought I had been to heaven. The surf was perfect. It was consistent and made up mostly of long, hollow lefts, just the way I like them. The lifestyle was idyllic, languid and slow moving, the best way to live. The people were gracious, happy, and inspirational—they made me want to be like them. Prices were outrageously inexpensive. A comfortable bungalow, three good meals per day, transport by bemo or motorbike, plus batik, woodcarving, or other local handmade gifts for friends and family back home cost almost nothing. It was a heavenly vacation.

At home in Hawai'i afterward, thinking about it all at a distance provided necessary perspective. It was even better than I had thought it was while I was there. I couldn't wait to go back to Bali. I told my close friends about it, and my genuine enthusiasm was quite persuasive.

I knew that my friend Walter Hoffman spent a lot of time near the area anyway. His business was fabric and he traveled the world, Asia in particular, in search of new materials and new sources. He questioned me thoroughly. Apart from the surf reports, I think the part that made the biggest impression on him was how inexpensive it all was. Walter, even though a very successful and astute businessman, was notoriously tight and dearly loved to find or make that elusive "good deal." The Bali "deal" in the mid-1970s couldn't have been better.

Two years after I first toured Bali, Walter and OP Sportswear President Jim Jenks were traveling through Australia researching surf fashion and setting up new accounts. Australia always has been a leading locale for sport/lifestyle fashion and at that time was home to some of the most forward-thinking surf companies like Quiksilver and Billabong. Most of the stuff made or worn down in Oz was several years ahead of anything in the U.S. and a good indicator of what was going to be happening soon on the world's beaches. Walter mentioned to Jenks what I had told him about Indonesia. They planned to visit China and Japan next anyway, so they decided they could stop off for a few days in Bali.

Walter found the most inexpensive way to get there. True to form, Walter's steerage-class itinerary involved a milk run out of Sydney, up through Darwin, to Timor, and then on to Bali.

Darwin, Australia, is one of the most humid places in that entire huge country. The flies are so bad that the Aussies always joke that one has to drink his beer through clenched teeth to strain out the insects. Jimmy Jenks was sweating profusely while they waited through the layover, nervously eyeing the decrepit-looking twin-engine prop plane they were soon to board for the next leg of their journey.

Walter, with a patience born of many years spent waiting for waves, not only was unfazed but even felt a tiny bit triumphant about the money he was saving by coming this roundabout way. Quantas Airways had a flight direct from Sydney to Denpasar, Bali, but it cost twice as much. Twice as much! Finally, the flight was called and everyone boarded.

Australia and Indonesia are actually very close. From Darwin to Timor is only about 400 miles, so the flight was not long despite the slow, old airplane. As their flight made the approach into Dili, East Timor, both noticed what looked like fires burning in the hills around the capital city. Landing, the plane taxied up to an antique terminal, and everyone was invited to deplane.

Outside, they felt concussions of distant explosions and heard what sounded like gunfire. Jim looked at an oblivious Walter for explanation but got nothing except a smile and an offhand remark.

"Isn't this bitchin'?" commented Walter as they walked.

Beyond the terminal they saw groves of swaying coconut trees and beyond those were rolling hills of dense jungle. It was pretty nice, except for the smoke, flames, and mildly unsettling noises arising from the distant dark.

A thin young man in a white shirt greeted them and beckoned the whole group to where he waited behind a small table. He stood next to a shorter man in a fancy military uniform with a chest full of medals and mirrored aviator sunglasses.

The young man spoke English and, speaking for the soldier in charge, asked everyone to show their passports and medical cards. Entering Indonesia back then required a visa and an up-to-date medical card as proof of a number of mandatory vaccinations. Everyone had the proper stamps on his card except Walter who, in his search for the cheapest flight, had found one that neglected to tell him a yellow fever vaccine was needed to get into Indonesia. Of course traveling through Asia did require cholera and smallpox shots in those days and, since Walter did that often, he was current on those, but yellow fever was uncommon.

Jenks on the other hand had gotten everything just in case, and his card easily passed the inspection. The boy in the white shirt had detained Walter, explaining that entry was refused and he would have to wait several days in Timor for the flight to return, at which time he would be sent back to Australia. Meanwhile, the other passengers were already reboarding the airplane, whose engines were still running. Jenks noticed the delay with Walter and the immigration officials. He lingered to see what the problem was.

"What's the deal?" demanded Walter, his face turning red.

Patiently the boy explained a second time. The military man behind obviously didn't speak any English but just stood there, looking somewhat formidable behind his mirrored shades.

Jenks recognized the problem immediately and made a good suggestion to Walter. "Maybe ask the guy if some money will take care of it," Jim suggested quietly.

The translator picked up on it right away and with a quick glance around to see if the coast was clear, nodded his head in agreement that this was indeed the way to solve the problem.

"Well, how much will it take?" Walter asked the lad.

Again glancing around somewhat furtively, the kid said something in Indonesian to the military man who returned a quick, one syllable answer.

In a quiet voice, the youngster told Walter and Jenks, "Fifty dollars will fix everything. This is the only immigration check; from here on the flight is domestic, nobody else will look at your documents."

"Fifty dollars!" Walter bellowed. His loud voice and angry tone made the boy wince. He had hoped not to attract any attention to this definitely illegal transaction.

"That's too much. Ask him if he will take ten." Walter felt he was on familiar ground negotiating price.

At this point in the story as related to me by Walter several months after the fact, I was shocked and shook my head in disbelief. I was familiar with the history of Timor.

Back in the twelfth century, Chinese travelers discovered huge forests of sandalwood and began trading in it. The Dutch and Portuguese came in the sixteenth century to set up colonies to further exploit the sandalwood trade. For almost 200 years, they fought over the island until a treaty in 1860 divided it between them. The Dutch took West Timor and Portuguese got the eastern half of the island. During World War II, the East Timorese fought with Australian commandos against the Japanese occupation: 50,000 of the Timorese were killed in the conflict. In 1949, West Timor became part of Indonesia when the Netherlands relinquished their colonies in the Dutch West Indies. In 1975, the Portuguese left East Timor after four centuries of rule. In the power vacuum during the decolonization and creation of the Democratic Republic of East Timor, the Indonesian Army invaded and annexed it.

The events in East Timor, small, remote, and poor, escaped international attention. At the time of Walter and Jenks's trip in the late summer (winter in the Southern Hemisphere) of 1976, East Timor was in the midst of a small but brutal war in which 200,000 East Timorese reportedly died. I couldn't believe that Walter would bargain over an insignificant amount of money in the midst of such a dangerous situation, and I told him so.

"Walter you're such a cheapskate, how could you do that?"

"Whaddya mean?" he answered in true Walter form, proud of having bested his adversary and come away with a good deal.

"He took the ten dollars!"

The Last Laugh

Some argue that snowboarding offers no tuberides, but flying through the air is almost as exciting. Photo: Kirk Devoll

We were pretty excited to be going down to Tavarua, Fiji, with our group for two wonderful weeks of just surfing. I mean that's all there is to do there on that little island, but what could be better. We had Laird, Darrick, my brother Victor, Bill Boyum, a few other guys I can't remember, and these two friends, Ken and Don, from Canada.

Ken Achenbach and Don Schwartz are two of the best snowboarders in the world for two reasons. First, they were born in the snow and have known it all their lives, and second, they got on snowboards when the snowboard first came out, so they have more time snowboarding than almost anyone else.

But what they wanted to do more than anything at this point in their lives was learn to surf. Oh, they had tried it lots of times, but they felt this trip would be their crowning glory because they had all of us there to get advice from. When they took off their shirts, they were so white from being in the mountains in Canada for such a long time that the first advice from everyone was to slather on tons of sunscreen.

We launched them out in the very inside break right in front of the island so they could work on their paddling and get the feel of their surfboards. 'Schwarty' is an extreme athlete no matter what sport, but Ken has had quite a bit more time on surfboards, so while both needed a lot of work on basic surfing technique, they were at about an even level. Their perseverance and natural skills paid off quickly, and in few days' time we all agreed that they were ready to get out to Cloudbreak and get some real waves—which they were very eager to do.

It was some nice small Cloudbreak, maybe four to five feet, but with an occasional six-foot set. Nothing really life-threatening but even small, Cloudbreak is still a powerful wave breaking over a very shallow and sharp reef. Ken and Don sat in the boat for almost an hour getting up their nerve by watching us all have a great time in the clean waves.

Finally, they figured nothing from nothing leaves nothing, so why not get out there and give it a try. They carefully paddled over to the lineup, which is easy from a boat in the channel; there aren't any breaking waves to paddle through. Once in the lineup, they felt more confident and started to paddle for waves. They each caught a few small ones and their confidence was growing in leaps and bounds.

Ken kept asking how big the waves were and we kept answering the same thing, "Small."

"Yeah, well how big is small?" he asked.

Laird told him, "There aren't any waves out here today that are over four feet."

"Well, four feet is only this big," said Ken spreading his hands about four feet apart. "You're telling me that wave isn't taller than this?" he asked, indicating his spread hands. A wave went by us that nobody wanted because it was so small, but it was definitely a lot taller than the spread of Ken's hands.

"No, that wave was only two feet," said Laird with a chuckle, and the rest of us all exchanged knowing looks.

"I can't figure out what kind of measurement you guys use for waves; how can you say that wave is only two feet—this is two feet," Ken said, bringing his hands in closer together.

A few minutes later a nice set rolled in, and Laird yelled for Ken to start paddling for one of the waves. Ken took a few moments to get into paddling position before he began to paddle. His arms were a blur as he paddled as hard as he could to get this wave that the Great Laird Hamilton had selected for him.

"How big is it, how big is it?" we heard Ken asking as he kept paddling. It was actually quite a nice wave and, surprisingly, quite a bit larger than any that had come in so far that day, maybe a good seven feet by our standards. But Laird wasn't going to tell Ken that.

"It's only four feet, keep paddling," Laird yelled back with a devilish smile on his face.

The wave jacked up even more as we watched Ken get caught in the lip and pitched headlong over the falls. He took quite a beating from that wave and all the rest behind it, getting washed in to the very inside Shish Kabob reef. Humiliated and beaten, he finally made it back out, but went straight to the boat and would have no more of the waves that day.

All that evening, he kept asking, "Were you sure that wave was only four feet? Right before I got launched into space, I could see how far it was to the bottom and it looked more like ten or twelve feet."

"Yes," we all answered, "It was barely four feet, maybe only three.

"Do you guys measure waves from the back or what?" Ken just kept shaking his head in disbelief. No matter what we said nor how many times we said it, he just couldn't believe that a four-foot wave could give him such a beating.

"Nobody in the world measures from the back," Laird disdainfully told Ken.

The waves wouldn't get any bigger for the rest of the trip, and just got smaller, much to our dismay. But that was just perfect for Ken and Don who continued to have a great time trying to improve their surfing skills without putting themselves in any scary situations. Here were these two mountain men, who had stood on top of the highest peaks, looked death in the face numerous times in severe avalanche conditions, gone down the steepest cliffs often in midair, and they were freaking out in four-foot surf. We teased them to no end.

Later that winter, we would all have the chance to meet again, but this time in a world more suited to the two Canadians. We met up at a place called Blue River in British Columbia, where Mike Wiegele runs the finest helicopter skiing operation in the world. With 3,000 square miles of mountainous terrain to ride in and some of the heaviest snowfall in North America, his operation is the biggest and most successful of any heli-ski operation.

Wiegele World caters to the very top end of skiing and snowboarding, with lavish accommodations, world-class gourmet dining, the most experienced mountain guides, and a fleet of first-class helicopters. Ken and Don are frequent visitors, and since that trip, Don has actually gone on to become one of Mike's top mountain guides. But this time we were all guests, and the mountain boys were eager to show the surfer boys a grand time.

The operation is pretty slick; the helicopter drops the group on top of one of the thousands of runs, and after it lifts off, the guide gathers the group, gives a brief description of what will be encountered on the run, and yells, "Follow me."

Each run is a new run over virgin, untracked snow, and down some of the best alpine terrain to be found anywhere. It's like perfect surf with no one out except your best friends.

So all day long we were flying down these mountainsides, in and out of the pine trees, over jumps made by fallen trees under the snow, wind cornices, or sometimes even small cliffs. Soon we were all looking for the next jump, which the guy up front would spot and stop to call out to everyone above that a good jump was ahead.

On one jump, Ken stopped and yelled back uphill that there was a great drop right below him. From above, where we all gathered, we could see the drop-off but couldn't see what was on the other side. It's somewhat intimidating to not know what lies on the other side. Occasionally there are big cliffs or trees in the landing. Having someone spotting the jump and calling it is always a little better. Going off anything blind, even if someone says it's OK, is always unnerving. But Ken was getting his camera out and telling us what a good jump this was. He threw snowballs about five feet apart and told us all to go together, me, Laird, and Darrick.

"Well, how big is it?" Laird asked.

"It's small, it's no sweat," Ken yelled back as he got his camera ready.

"Look, you guys start where you are, come flying down together, and all jump at the same time; Gerry you go to the left, Laird you go straight off, and Darrick go slightly right. It will be a great shot. Don't worry, it's all deep, soft powder on the landing."

"How far is the drop?" asked Darrick. I know he felt like I did about going off blind jumps.

"It's only four feet so get all the speed you can; otherwise you won't even get off the ground," said Ken. "Come on, I'll count back from three, then you guys start. OK?"

So we all looked at each other, and as Ken counted, we got ready.

"Three, two, one, go for it," he yelled.

On the count of "one" we all took off, blazing down toward the edge we could see and whatever was on the other side. As one we all went off the edge together. And as one, I'm sure we were all equally shocked to find not a four-foot drop but a twenty-foot-plus drop. And we all realized at the same time that we were going way too fast. And that we had been had by Ken. Not expecting such a long fall, none of us made the landing, and all of us landed in a heap in the deep powder below.

As we were digging ourselves out, Laird a little pissed off, shouted up to Ken, "Hey, I thought you said it was only four feet!"

We could hear Ken cracking up as he yelled back down to us, "We measure from the back here in Canada."

f. GALLERY

Prone paddleboarding was the first kind
of surfboard riding that went worldwide as
far back as the 1930s. Photo: Erik Aeder

Barry Kanaiaupuni, during the second Expression Session,
charging the Pipeline in true BK style—this was the first time
I ever saw him surf the break. Photo: Jeff Divine

Taking a break with Brian Seurat and Ricardo Pomar in the coolness of the
cave at Uluwatu after the morning surf session. We would wait in the shade for
the tide to change for the afternoon surf on the inside. Photo: Dana Edmunds

Previous spread   What one generally does at the
Pipeline ... is ride the tube. Photo: Jeff Hornbaker

Above   The tree house at G-Land was Spartan
accommodations, but we would have slept on the
beach to ride the waves there. Photo: Art Brewer

Right   Wayan, my board carrier at
Uluwatu. Photo: Dana Edmunds

Previous spread **Laird Hamilton on a massive wave at Peahi that dwarfs his 6'1" to the point where he looks positively tiny. Photo: Tom Servias**

Left Snowboarding is surfing without having to paddle—one turn after another, on waves of snow that hold still while you ride them. Photo: Andy Tullis

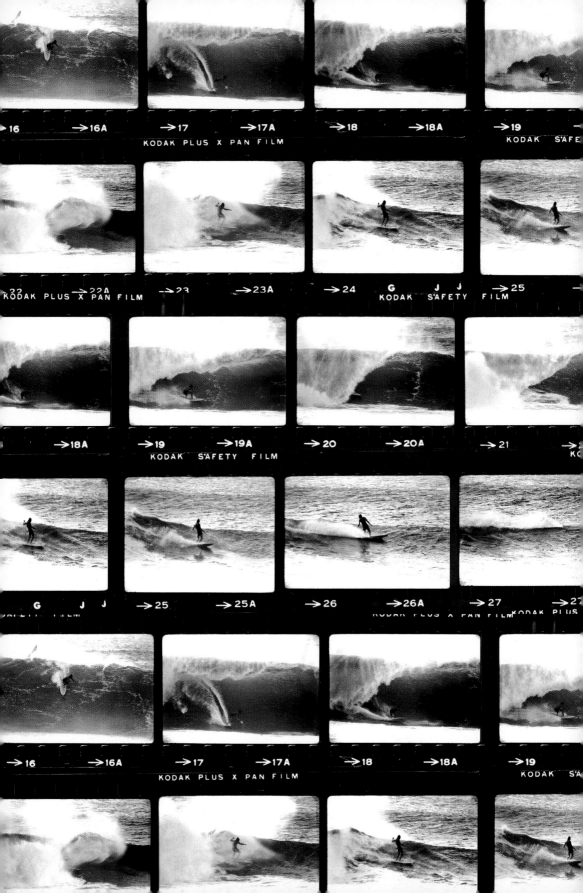

vii. FINALLY

The Expression Session was designed for the Pipeline,
but the first year there wasn't any good Pipe to be had.
The second year the Pipeline went off ... maybe it was
just making us pay our dues before giving us the goods.
Photo: Jeff Divine

The Coral Cruiser

The price of surfing the Pipeline on a regular basis came in a variety of forms. All of them are etched vividly in my memory. There were the psychological costs: dealing with the fears and anxiety induced by the most terrifying and powerful wave in the known surfing world. There were the physical costs inflicted on flesh, blood, sinew, bone, and muscle during wipeouts that were as certain a part of any session there as the paddle out into the fearsome lineup. The material costs of broken surfboards were, however, arguably the most painful and certainly the most frequent.

Throughout the winter seasons of 1969 through 1971, I'm sure I broke at least one board for every two times I surfed the place. I made all my own boards and most had some design flaw I wanted to improve upon, so breaking them wasn't so painful. But it did end my surfing for the day. I dragged the broken pieces into the shaping room, figured out how to make a better one, and by the next day I'd have a new board to try again.

If I thought the fin was working well, I'd salvage it off the broken board and use it on the next one. Surfboard materials were cheap and the waves uncrowded. Life more or less moved from one surfboard to the next at a slow and enjoyable pace. Those early days were a wonderful and exciting time to be a surfer and a shaper in the finest and most fertile surfing area in the world.

No two surfboards of that period looked alike. This was a function of unique design theories but also of the fact that, during the transition from longboards to short, no one knew what surfboards were supposed to look like or what worked best. Everything was in a state of transition, and there was no established norm.

The foam longboard era had been roughly a decade long. That period saw many innovations. Hobie Alter had the first signature model by Phil Edwards, who was considered to be the best surfer of the 1950s. The Yater Spoon was a favorite of noseriders at Rincon. In the South Bay, Greg Noll copied several features of Yater's noseriding design into his 'Da Cat' model marketed by the inimitable Miki Chapin Dora. Hap Jacobs sold the Donald Takayama model. The Morey 'Penetrator,' endorsed by John Peck, came and went. Rich Harbour Surfboards had a popular design in the Trestle Special. Further south Gordon & Smith featured shapes by Mike Hynson and Skip Frye. The Hawai'i shops making longboards, Inter-Island Surf Shop in Kaka'ako and Dick Brewer's Surfboards Hawai'i in Hale'iwa, for the most part made no radical departures from California design ideas.

But none of those boards were ready for Pipeline. That Pipeline was ridden on longboards at all—most notably by the late Butch Van Artsdalen, but also by Jock Sutherland, Jackie Eberle, Stanley 'Savage' Parks, and a handful of others—without numerous fatalities is astounding.

Everything began to change in the fall of 1967 when Dick Brewer returned from a hiatus in California, where he had been working for Bing Copeland creating his "Pipeliner" series. He showed up at Ala Moana with what looked like a child's surfboard he'd made for his team rider, Gary Chapman. Basically it was an 8'10" scaled-down Pipeliner, but it was a big step away from the longboard standard. Enter the shortboard.

A few months later, Brewer shaped the first mini-gun for me at his Lahaina Cannery shaping room on Maui. It was an 8'6" dream board that stood surfboard design on its head. This was a quantum leap toward the kind of surfing we dreamed about doing on the waves that our previous equipment just didn't allow.

Brewer got very busy after that, providing similar mini-guns for everyone else, and I got tired of waiting for boards from him. I began to build my own surfboards. When my attention turned toward the Pipeline, the whole process suddenly became more serious and focused. Surfing the Pipeline was no joking matter. Instant terror and severe injury were only one slip on a banana peel away.

At the Pipeline, the routine seemed pretty basic. A surfer caught the wave, hoped he made the incredibly steep takeoff, and turned left as quickly as possible before the whole wave crashed over to form a spinning tunnel. The surfer either made it out the end or, more often, he didn't.

We weren't short on desire. We knew where we wanted to be and what we had to do to get there. The technique to make the wave was to ride through the tunnel on a line that moderated between getting axed by the falling lip and getting sucked up the face and over the falls. Either of those was a horrifying thought and an even worse pummeling. There was a fine line between riding too low and riding too high. Finding that line was a key to survival in big Pipeline.

Another factor involved was that the tunnel was the fastest part of the wave. Early shortboards, like the clumsy longboards that preceded them, were notoriously unstable when subjected to sudden acceleration and high speeds. Surfboard lengths gradually stabilized enough that most surfers knew what size board fit their own styles and the waves they were attempting to ride. More subtle features such as outline templates, rail and bottom contours, and rocker curves were still evolving. Different designers had different ideas, and nearly every day there was a test flight in progress.

There was a day at Sunset Beach when Bob McTavish boldly attempted an off-the-lip on an extremely wide-tailed, deep vee-bottom Australian design. Much to the amusement—and horror—of seasoned Hawai'i surfers watching from the point, McTavish looked as though he was launched off a springboard from a tall building. To his credit, he paddled back out to try again but the results were similar. The powerful winter waves quickly revealed design limitations of the new equipment while showing little mercy to the test pilots.

One day on the drive home after another session at the Pipeline resulted in the usual broken board, I had an inspiration. In talking about design theory with other surfers, one of the ideas that seemed to hold merit was the concept of the "nine-inch tail." Nine inches, measured twelve inches up from the tail, was a very narrow tail. The few occasions it had been tried before were with experimental Waimea big-wave guns that were ten feet or more in length.

A tail that narrow would be difficult, if not impossible, to turn, but the waves of Waimea had not required much maneuvering. As I drove, I thought that a narrow tail might actually be an advantage at the Pipeline, where the wave was so steep, hollow, and fast. I had read that the steering on fast race cars was tighter than normal because at high speeds, loose steering could be dangerous. I figured the same theory applied to the Pipeline.

I got to the shaping room and drew an outline that included the nine-inch tail; it looked very narrow. I laid the blank on the floor and stood on it in where I would be as I took the drop at Pipeline. My back foot almost touched the outline. If my foot had been any further back, my toes and heel would have draped over either side. Despite that minor detail, I felt I was on the right track, even though the outline shape was different from any of my previous boards, or anyone else's for that matter.

A new energy flowed through me as I started running my Skil 100 electric planer up and down the blank, shaping it to match the vision I had in my mind. A flat to slightly concave bottom shape flowing into a slight vee out the tail worked best for me. The rocker was much less of a consideration at that time and was predetermined by the blank; basically, it was very flat.

I shaped turned-down rails from nose to tail, a result of experimentation Reno Abellira and I had done with Mike Hynson, a great surfer and shaper from La Jolla, California. Among many design ideas during the abrupt transition from the California foam longboards to the shortboards of the late 1960s and early 1970s, Hynson's low-rail theory was perhaps the single most significant breakthrough. Low rails were the linchpin that tied all the other design factors together to make the shortboard a truly functional direction for the future.

When the shaping was done, I put the board on the glassing rack, draped the fiberglass over it, and mixed up a batch of resin. My previous boards had been yellow tints, the smoothest color to laminate evenly, and the easiest to spot in rip currents when swimming after a board in the days before leashes. For this departure, however,

For me the best days were when there were only a few good waves mixed in with a lot of bad ones.

I wanted something unique. I added a dash of brown pigment into the yellow, stirred it up and poured it out on the fiberglass-shrouded blank. The color, depending on who was looking, was sort of a sad yellowy tan, but there was no turning back on the already catalyzed resin. I suppose in a generous mood one could call the color coral, but one might also have described it as baby-shit brown.

Back then I never gave much thought to a surfboard's lifespan, especially at the Pipeline. I figured if I didn't grow to like this color, the board probably wouldn't last long anyway. I finished up the lamination, stuck on the fin I had used on several previous boards, and put on the final hot coat so it would be ready to sand the next morning.

I was shaping at Surf Line Hawai'i, a shop owned by Fred Schwartz. Fred, although a tough taskmaster and shrewd retailer, was still a great boss. As long as I finished up my orders, I had an open schedule and, the best part, a constant supply of Clark Foam blanks to make myself a board anytime I had a new idea to try.

A phone call to the Country had confirmed that the swell was still running, so I went in early to sand my board and get out to the Pipe to try it. A fast way to get a new board done quickly was to do a sand finish. All showroom boards were glossed after sanding to make them shiny and more saleable. By foregoing the gloss coat I would have a less attractive and slightly weaker board, but I could ride it right away. I sanded the bottom, the fin lay-up, and just a little bit of the way up the deck. In a short time, I was ready to go.

Strapping down my new board on the roof racks of my VW Bug, I stepped back to eyeball the side profile. The rack level was a perfect setup for a clean side view of the shape. This look could tell a lot about how the board would ride before it ever got into the water. I liked what I saw and that image stayed in my mind as I began the drive out to the Country.

When I got to the Pipeline, the waves were decent but nothing spectacular. This was fine by me because the infrequent good waves were not enough to attract anyone else. The beach and lineup were empty, perfect for trying out an experimental shape. All shapes of the period were experiments, but my new board was a dramatic departure

Previous spread   Tail stalling the Coral Cruiser to set up the tube through the inside section at the Pipe during the 1971 Expression Session. Photo: Jeff Divine

from the general standard of the time. I didn't want to "make ass" in front of my friends if it didn't work; that had happened enough times already.

I already had a thing going with the Pipeline, a relationship with the break that went beyond the usual favorite surf spot connection. On certain days during the preceding few years, I felt the place was trying to communicate with me on some deep level. Most surfers regarded the Pipeline as a heavy duty "yang" surf spot because of the explosive nature of this powerful break. I felt differently and had already decided that the Pipeline was a "she." I loved her but was still trying to figure out if she loved me. If she did, it must have been tough love because I got my butt kicked on a regular basis.

But that was standard; everyone took a licking at the Pipe. For this reason, there were not a lot of guys who surfed there often. The Pipeline was one assault after another on minds, bodies, and wallets. It just plain wore guys out because there wasn't any question about whether or not a surfer was going to suffer a terrifying wipeout; it was only a matter of when.

One reason the wave is so hollow is because the reef is shallow. A good fall almost certainly resulted in hitting the bottom, but to eat it with the force of the lip pressing down was similar to a high-speed head-on collision in a thin-skinned convertible without seatbelts. A Peruvian surfer named Shige had been killed there a few years before, smashed headfirst into the bottom, crushing his skull.

I had fallen out of the top of a wave once, landing feet first and going down a lot deeper than I anticipated. Upon finally hitting bottom, I pushed off only to bang my head on coral. I had gone into one of the deep crevices and smashed into an overhang when I tried to resurface. It was impossible to see with the turbulence but I could feel the reef on all sides of me. For a moment I began to panic until the whitewater washed me up and out of the hole. I made it a point to dive the entire area between swells, study the bottom, and know what to expect next time.

The more I surfed it, the better I understood the many moods of the Pipeline. I found that those picture-perfect days when every wave was good were exceedingly rare, with some winter seasons not having even a single day like that. And when those great days did occur, the lineup was packed, as were the photographers on shore. Everyone hoped to strike it rich.

For me the best days were when there were only a few good waves mixed in with a lot of bad ones. The ugly waves would deter most surfers from even checking the surf for very long.

During the late 1960s and early 1970s, Sunset Beach was the main spot. The best surfers were found there, as were the biggest, most consistent waves. But there just weren't that many surfers back then, which is why the Pipeline could have good waves and nobody surfing.

That's how it was for my new surfboard's maiden voyage. I paddled out to a completely empty lineup and had my pick of any wave I wanted. I already knew which ones I liked. I had a lineup right in front of Warren Harlow's house and hung out over the boil from the big crack that I had once been stuffed inside. It was as though an "X" marked the spot for my takeoff point.

Without many bodies in the takeoff zone, I was free to range around. There were several different starting places further inside, depending on where the sets came. There were also several places to avoid where the waves broke too fast and too hollow to safely ride them. I liked my outside takeoff best of all; it was the most likely spot to get in easy and set up for a long tuberide through the bowl section.

A good-looking set approached and I got ready. I let the first wave go past. My theory was to take the biggest wave of the set so I wouldn't be kicking out of a smaller one, only to have the next one break outside of me. The third wave looked good, so I swung my board around to get into it.

It never took more than two or three good strokes of paddling to catch the waves I wanted at the Pipeline. If it took more than that, there was something wrong with the wave. The best waves were always very easy to catch. The bad ones were difficult. Too many times before I had kept paddling, thinking I had it, only to get hung up in the lip, drop into space, and freefall into the pit.

Falling out of the sky on the takeoff is never a good way to eat it at the Pipe. The water in front of the wave is being drawn into and up the face of the wave—this guarantees that the hapless surfer will be sucked back over a second time immersed in the powerful curl. That's how guys got really hurt, being driven into the shallow reef bottom in an uncontrolled body contortion, often as not headfirst.

My first wave, however, was an effortless takeoff. I leapt to my feet and began the steep descent. The board held the vertical line so easily that I was able to curve into an angle on the drop, instead of being forced to drive straight down. With plenty of speed and a good angle at the bottom, I cut a quick, easy turn to duck underneath the falling lip and entered the tube section on a perfect line.

At Pipeline there was always plenty of room in the tube, and that new board leapt across the bowl section, accelerating as it crossed the part of the wave that made the Pipeline so famous and challenging. I exited the tube in a spray of mist from the air compressed by the spinning tunnel. It literally blew me out of the tube, stinging my face and body like a thousand tiny needles.

Well, I thought as I rode out over the shoulder, the new board seemed to work fine. Or had that been just an easy wave, one of those "free rides" a surfer gets every once in a while?

I paddled back out wondering about that and returned to sit on my lineup spot to wait for a second try. While I waited, I got off the board to see how it sat on the water. Again I liked what I saw. Some surfboards are that way. I could look from any angle and the curves would flow together smoothly. I ducked underwater to look at the air bubble the board rested on, an indication of how much wetted surface the board would plane on. Reaching up to feel the rails, I ran my hands along both sides, as I held the board in place with my toes on the fin.

I climbed back aboard as another set approached. Picking the wave that looked best, I once again caught it without much effort. Just three strokes and I could feel the board lift as it connected with the wave's energy. It was a bigger wave with a steep face but the narrow tail held in firmly on the slide down. I was early at the bottom, ran out into the flat ahead of the wave, and banked a long bottom turn. As I came around, my direction parallel with the wall, I pressed down into a tail stall to allow the curl to get ahead. The tube rushed by and I lowered the nose back down, letting the board run again. It took off like a jet, and again I was amazed at the instant acceleration and positive control speeding through the tunnel.

Other boards before had felt squirrelly in that position, on the verge of spinning out. I moved slightly forward and into a tighter crouch when the tube funneled down toward the end. Like a cherry pit spit out with force, the wave shot me out into the daylight. I cruised with plenty of speed over the shoulder of the wave until I came to a stop.

Sitting back down, I knew I had something special in this surfboard. It seemed to fit the Pipeline wave like no other board before. It made everything easy, a total cruise. Right then a name popped into my mind, and from that moment on the board would be the Coral Cruiser.

Somehow the Coral Cruiser defied tradition and stayed in one piece. On an early morning with a clean west swell and glassy conditions, it revealed to me the biggest, most significant lesson about surfing the Pipeline and big, hollow waves in general. That morning I pulled into a long, unmakeable tube. For some reason, instead of bailing out like everyone did in that impossible situation, I stayed on my board until the wave closed down around me.

I really don't know what prompted me to keep riding until the end, but I was certainly surprised when I surfaced and found my surfboard right next to me instead of on its way in to the beach. I thought about what happened as I jumped on and paddled back out.

On the next wave, the section again closed down, and again the Coral Cruiser popped up beside me. A light bulb went on in my mind. I thought that if a tube was collapsing on itself, then there was no place for the surfboard to go. Once the force of the wave passed on, the board would resurface in the same place.

Furthermore, it might be safer to ride into the inner ending of the wave because the board slowed down or stopped altogether. Bailing out as soon as one realized there was no way to make a wave was a risky maneuver. At the Pipeline, the risks were magnified. It was downright dangerous, and after attempting this escape technique, many guys had been carried up the beach on their boards much the same as fallen warriors were carried on their shields from the battlefield. Tuberiding in 1970 was a somewhat new experience in the broad context of surfing.

Surfers had been getting inside the curls of waves since the beginning of surfing, but the equipment precluded anyone from riding the hollowest deep surfaces. There were several surfers who had figured out how to ride inside the Ala Moana bowl on the old longboards. Jackie Eberle and Jock Sutherland were skillful tuberiders as far as their equipment allowed. But for the general surfing public, a tuberide usually had been accidental and short. Surfing a big wave, especially one like the Pipeline, involves a great degree of uncertainty.

Mostly through the innate design characteristics of the Coral Cruiser, and not through any tremendous skill on my part, I had stumbled upon a discovery of significant magnitude in regard to riding inside the tube. The design of the Coral Cruiser was the result of a long process of trial and error, but the lightbulb moment I had was more in the nature of a divine revelation. I suddenly knew something that no one else had found out yet, or if they had, they weren't telling and certainly were not using this information to increase their success in riding the tube.

My confidence swelled with this realization. My surfboard had taught me a trick that, in the future, would save me many swims to the beach and probably a few to the emergency room. Everyone knows this stuff now, but back then, it was brand-new information that accelerated the learning curve dramatically.

The Coral Cruiser got complete validation during the 1971 Golden Breed Expression Session. This "non" event was the collaborative brainchild of Jeff Hakman, Duke Boyd, and Dick Graham. Created as a promotion for Golden Breed surfwear, affiliated with Hang Ten, it reflected the sentiments of most surfers of the period in that it wasn't a contest and there would be no winner. All the invitees would be paid the tidy sum of $200 for surfing twice in a free-flowing, noncompetitive format.

The idea was that this atmosphere would enhance creativity and a higher level of performance. The inaugural event had been held the winter before, but the surf had been uncooperative at the designated venue. The winter of 1971 was a different story, as the invited surfers gathered at 'Ehukai Beach Park on a grey morning that looked like rain. The gloomy weather was offset by a strong west swell that was too powerful for Sunset Beach, where second reef sets mauled the inside lineup.

At the Pipeline's Second Reef, booming sets stood up tall from an ocean laced with lines of swell. Most of the invitees were not regular surfers at the Pipe, and many had never surfed the outside lineup. There was an air of apprehension mixed with the excitement that the event was finally getting the surf its promoters had dreamed of. Massive sets rolled in without let up, causing discussions about the difficult paddle out, the horrendous drops, and gaping barrels. I was smiling because it was exactly the kind of surf in which the Coral Cruiser reveled in.

Finally, the first heat was called and the 1971 Expression Session got underway. Eddie Aikau and Barry Kanaiaupuni paddled out to the Pipeline for the first time I had ever seen them surf there. Both were fearless surfers in the prime of their careers, but backside at Second Reef Pipe was a formidable challenge. Collective winces went up from the beach as they bravely pulled into closeout sections that looked like tall buildings falling. Eddie ventured outside and picked off a beautiful peak on the Second Reef lineup.

A photo of his wave ran on the front page of the *Honolulu Advertiser* the following morning. I kept a copy for years until the newsprint eventually deteriorated to dust. It was my all-time favorite photo of the Pipeline.

Billy Hamilton, Sam Hawk, and Jackie Baxter in the next heat charged the hollow, difficult waves and put up a good showing. A skinny, young, fresh-faced Rory Russell got the best rides, crouching low and streaking through several long barrels.

Tom Stone and I were in the final heat of the day. It was still grey and cloudy, but the giant sets had tamed down and solid ten-foot sets focused on First Reef, the premier Pipeline lineup. Tom and I had grown up together surfing Ala Moana. We watched the

best tuberiders of the longboard period, Conrad Cunha and Sammy Lee, do their thing on thick, tubular Pole Set days when the south swell ran big. Of the entire field of invited surfers, we were the only two who surfed the Pipeline on a regular basis, and there was no apprehension on our part. We were totally pumped by the waves and couldn't wait to get into them.

Tommy, one of Mike Diffenderfer's team riders, had some beautiful boards by the master shaper. He preferred a sleek balsawood gun that had served him well during many sessions at the Pipe, and he was riding it that day. I had my trusty Coral Cruiser, a homemade surfboard that looked drab next to Tom's shiny gun. But I knew there was infinite magic contained within her lackluster exterior.

The waves were neither clean nor perfect. The swell was raw and a little unruly, but to Tom and me, it was still good Pipeline with plenty of tubes. Tom caught a wave, and then I caught one. Both gave up decent tuberides. Tommy got another while I waited through the few behind until a big, healthy wave rolled toward me.

I had to paddle out to it, and it lurched up suddenly, forcing me to spin quickly and take off late. The thick lip heaved just as I stood up, and I felt my board disconnect from the wave. It was a bad moment: Airdrops at the Pipeline have a scarily low rate of success. But the Coral Cruiser re-entered the water smoothly, allowing me to set my line and pull up cleanly into the tube. Out of the corner of my eye as I went over the ledge, I had seen Tom paddling out over the shoulder. He had a perfect ringside seat to my late drop. The thought that he had witnessed the heavy takeoff made me smile.

When I paddled back out, I could see he was shaking his head. With a rueful smile he asked, "How did you make that drop? I could see your whole fin not even touching the wave."

I laughed and gave all the credit to my surfboard. The Coral Cruiser, masked in her plain-Jane glass job, was the most efficient shape for riding the steep, hollow waves of the Pipeline. The next issue of *Surfer* magazine ran a cover shot of an inside tuberide from the session that day.

I got orders for the same shape as the Coral Cruiser, some of them from very good surfers whom I admired, and I gained quite a bit of confidence in my surfboard shaping. Two summers before, Jack Shipley, the head salesperson at Surf Line Hawai'i, and I had joined together to open a shop of our own just down the street. We called the new shop Lightning Bolt Surf Company. The brand and insignia would go on to become recognized by surfers everywhere. Eventually it would grow into an international licensing company, the first of its kind in the surf world.

The Coral Cruiser would stay intact, and at one point, I painted a small blue lightning bolt on her deck. Eventually, she would become relegated to the back of the pile, replaced by shiny, new bright-colored Lightning Bolt boards. She sadly sank into obscurity, left under a house somewhere and forgotten. When I did think of her and all she had done for me, it was too late. She was gone. But I'll never forget the magic, the excitement, and the many glorious moments when she was the best that ever was.

Jungle

Love

Surfing is whatever one wants to make of it. With the fluid stage and the cast of characters, anything goes is usually the rule ... actually there aren't any rules. This is what makes surfing so appealing. But in my almost fifty years of surfing, I've made a few rules for myself.

Lopez Rule #1: Surf to surf tomorrow, never surf like there's no tomorrow. Leave that to the young guys: Their bones are strong and heal quickly and they have more enthusiasm.

Lopez Rule #2: Pace yourself. This goes with a corollary: Sitting in the lineup is always better than sitting on the beach. When traveling around the world for surf, one may as well spend as much of the daylight hours as possible out in the surf.

Lopez Rule #3: Don't talk in the lineup unless you want to get caught inside. There is absolutely nothing worse than taking a ride around the horn for not paying attention.

Rules notwithstanding, there was one time I got really caught inside down at the surf camp in G-Land. What follows is a cautionary tale.

The surf was coming up. There were solid ten-foot sets. That is about the maximum size G-Land can hold. The waves don't get much taller there, only more powerful and more consistent. A great set started to come in. The lineup was crowded. Most of the guys were trying to play it safe. The first wave rolled in. I saw it was perfect, big, and no one was even looking at it. They were all looking at the rest of the set. Breaking Lopez Rule #4—never, ever, take the first wave of the set—I spun around and paddled into the sweet-looking first one.

The takeoff was very late. The lip was already pitching out down the line. I was riding a 7'4", giving me a lot of horsepower. Ducking under the heaving lip as I got to my feet was a tricky, delicate maneuver. Lightly setting an edge, I threaded a high line in front of a few guys paddling for their lives. Moderating this precarious course, I banked down the face slightly as the wave began to tube.

G-Land's best feature is that even when it's smaller, once the tube starts spinning, there's a lot of room to run a deep line. At this size, there was room enough to stand straight up, but I stayed crouched in the attack stance, racing for the daylight. The wave started from the main takeoff at Outside Moneytrees. In what seemed a blink of an eye, I had traveled a considerable distance down the line.

The next section at the Launching Pad loomed ahead. Looking out from inside the tunneling wave, the upcoming section had the appearance of wanting to break before I got there. If it was hollow enough, there was a chance to slip in the backdoor. From my position, it didn't look that way. We named this part of the wave the Launching Pad

Racing the fast and seemingly endless wall at G-Land was a lesson in how to be an efficient wave rider ... any mistake, and in a blink, it was all over. Photo: Art Brewer

because it was just that, a mushy, relatively speaking, easy launch into the run at Speed Reef, the inside and most hollow part of the main break. The Speedies section was easier to make if the ride started at the Launch Pad.

I was coming in behind the backdoor. To have it collapse on me would be roughly the equivalent of having a 400-pound gorilla jump off the roof right on my back while all his pals were waiting on the bottom with baseball bats. There is always a slight pause between sections of a wave. I took this opportunity to sweep down to the bottom. Turning there as hard as I could to square it off, I wanted to punch straight into and through the wave.

The 7'4" was as long a board as I would ever use here, stable on the open face but not able to make tight turns. My turn wasn't as perpendicular to the wave as I needed for penetrating through the face. Just then I noticed the section ahead was throwing out a lot more than the first time I looked at it. Now it seemed to have room to ride through, except I was already midway into a Hawaiian pullout.

It was too late for anything other than the thought to cross my mind. I punched into the wave face and knew instantly my board wasn't going to make it. On a clean pull out, I would have come through the back of the wave still standing on my board with time to paddle and escape the wave behind. By abandoning ship, I knew I was going to pay a price on the next wave. The wave I was riding was simply too big, too hollow, and too powerful for any gamble. My first priority was to save myself; the board was on its own.

Kicking off my stricken surfboard, I could feel the passing wave's suction, trying to pull me back into the turmoil where my board was headed. I swam hard, turning over, facing back toward where the leash began to pull.

The danger was enhanced by the big board and heavy-duty leash. A smaller leash might have snapped, ending the terror. Escape was not an option. I was firmly attached to all that was about to happen.

I flailed backward, trying to hold my ground. On the other end of the cord, my surfboard felt like a huge fish on the line about to pull me right off the boat. I couldn't even go up for air.

At last the power of the wave passed, enabling me to scramble to the surface and breathe. My surfboard was underwater, still within the wave's power, pulling me further inside. I gasped for some air, then hurried to duck under as the second wave of the set broke right on me.

Somehow this wave must have pitched completely over my submerged board. As I came up, I could feel the tension on my leash slacken. Breaking the surface, I saw my surfboard about thirty feet away on a seven-foot leash. The board came back fast. It flew through the air and plopped down right next to me with such good manners that without thinking I just jumped on and started stroking to evade the wave after and get back out.

The last conscious decision I made was when I foolishly decided to catch the first wave of the set. The drama was beginning to resemble those major tests in life: the ones where people don't even know they are being tested until waking up in the hospital, at the altar, or just lying on the ground. This was not an ultimate test, but neither was it a pop quiz.

A smaller leash might have snapped, ending the terror. Escape was not an option. I was firmly attached to all that was about to happen.

I was on my board, paddling hard, when I experienced a moment when everything at that precise point in time is absolutely clear. Clarity can be so startling that it transcends before and after. What I saw bearing down on me made me change my mind about what kind of test this was. Maybe it was going to be very close to that ultimate test, very close indeed.

In case the reader doesn't know what the ultimate test is, let me say that the ultimate test is whether or not one will be able to survive death. Is there something after? That question we spend our lives asking has yet to induce a reply.

No such question, big or small, was in my mind during my moment of clarity. What I did understand was that I was looking up at the biggest, meanest wave that I had ever seen at G-Land during the twenty-five years I had surfed there. In all candor, things could have been better. This wave was *Howard Huge*, Godzilla, and "The End" all rolled into one. It was bearing down on me with absolute and utter disdain.

Despair filled me like the smell of carrion on a hot day as I snuck a glance up the line. I saw other surfers in better positions than mine jumping ship, headed for the bottom in search of safety. The unfortunate jumpers seemed to fear even making eye contact with the energetic gorgon at the heart of this monster gathering before them. Panic was everywhere and I could feel its icy breath trying to envelop me. No one was even thinking about riding it, they just wanted to get away.

This was one of those pure moments that transcends the emotion of "I don't like it here." What looms is beyond the choice of "I don't want to be here." Reason can't form the words to say, "This is too crazy." If a person believes in destiny, and I do, then he has to believe that fate put him here in this moment to decide what is real for him.

If faith cradles him, he will subconsciously do the right thing. If he has no belief, he may perish. So there it was: infidel or true believer, choose one and make it fast. The sole function of consciousness at a time like this is to clear the parade ground, not intrude, step back, and listen to the band play.

I had been in similar spots before, but with better options. In those moments I was younger and usually in much better condition, so a thrashing wouldn't worry me much. In this fateful moment, at my age and with my strength much diminished, a set like this one could very well have been the end of me in my current mortal form. This I knew absolutely. I think ultimately that's what was so defining about this moment. I really thought I might drown, but I wasn't ready just yet.

To quell my mind and the ensuing panic, I put my head down and concentrated totally on paddling. I focused on each stroke and each breath. Knowing the sight of this monstrous wave alone would defeat me, I dared not look. Nearing the wave, I needed to glance up to get my bearings. Even knowing what to expect, seeing this wave rearing up before me was chilling. I could feel the panic rising like a tub full of cold water about to overflow. I am still not sure precisely what to believe about the moment that unfolded.

This wave was pitching. I was still about thirty to forty feet away. This was too far to make it, but this wave had a mind of its own. It pitched out, and out, and still further out. Picture a wave pitching out more than three times its height. It didn't seem real.

When I saw the lip suspended, I thought maybe this wave is trying to give me a chance. It would be a very slight one, but a chance nonetheless, if I could get underneath the lip. Later on, I would imagine that perhaps some force of my will had something to do with making this wave throw out in such an unexpected manner.

Even though the wave was still a long way off, I pushed down deep, concentrating on keeping my surfboard level. It had to be perfect or I was done. As I went underwater with the lip throwing overhead, the water being drawn up into the wave accelerated me with such force that I almost lost my grip on the rails. I hung on for my life and could feel when I entered the wave face.

My forward motion slowed dramatically as though the water of the wave itself was somehow denser than the remaining ocean. Then suddenly I wasn't going forward anymore. I hung suspended. The suction was so immense that I actually could hear it. I was in the bowels of the wave. Then it began to pull me backward with great force. I used what momentum I had, porpoise kicking like mad, even paddling with one arm underwater as I held on with the other.

I think the dynamics of having a big board with more flotation worked in my favor. Its buoyancy squirted me up, and I surfaced with my engines going at flank speed.

I looked at what was next. Like a slap in the face there was another bigger and meaner wave than the one I had just escaped. Cold fear washed over me as I forced myself to look away and concentrate on paddling. Turning my head to the side, again I made the mistake of looking up the line where panic-stricken surfers were abandoning ship in a fear-induced frenzy. If there was a time to call for Mama, this was it.

I put my head down, looking at the deck of my board, putting everything I had into each and every stroke. I knew I couldn't afford to waste anything. As I felt the wave loom up, I looked and again felt my entrails go icy cold. The wave appeared to be too far away for me to get successfully under it. But again this wave also pitched out beyond any understanding. As before, I knew that if my duck dive was anything less than perfect, I would be instantly sucked back into the blackness. Once into that nightmare, I would entertain scant likelihood of survival. Scratching for my life, I pushed under and kicked through for all I was worth.

Again the big board's momentum and buoyancy shot me out the other side like a Polaris missile firing. I had made it, or so I thought. But no, the wave behind was still yet more immense and bearing down on me as surely as a hungry shark that scents blood.

I put my head down and paddled like there was no tomorrow. My vision was narrowing down from overexertion and lack of oxygen. I was dimly aware of other surfers in the water, off their boards, not even trying to paddle before they were whisked away in a blur. I had the drill, but the physical reserves were spent. I was making the motions of paddling but without any power.

As I came up on the wave, feathering precariously and standing so tall, again a look at it was almost my undoing. My technique was being driven by something as near to instinct as a human can have. I pushed down into my duck dive. The wave exerted the enormity of its power. It was like a bear pulling at my feet trying to tear off my legs. I kicked harder.

Somehow I did it right and popped up again, believing this had to be finished. How many waves had that been? There couldn't be any more in the set—but there was. The ultimate King Kong was coming fast. I was beyond knowing or even caring if this was a bigger wave. It seemed huge, but my mind was as weary as my body. Could I go on? What if there were more after this one? I couldn't let go now. I knew I was finished if I did. I was depleted, exhausted, and my spirit was perilously close to broken.

Then from some faraway place in my mind came the thought that I had made it this far, much farther than I had first thought possible. Like a ray of hope, it seemed to galvanize me, my strokes felt smooth. Like many paddleboard events raced in the past, my whole world at this moment was stroke and trim, smooth out the frenzy, become wholly efficient.

I noticed I was suddenly calm. The thicket of my mind was clear. More power seemed to come back with each stroke. I made it. I wasn't through this wave or whatever was behind it, but in my mind I felt I had been put through the crucible. Upon finding I was not lacking, another force rose to the occasion. It was an ally I had been aware of but had found difficult to access. I felt I had single-handedly turned the tide in my favor not through any physical prowess, but rather by the simple technique of allowing my mind to work for me instead of for my defeat.

I duck-dived the next wave, and just like that it was over, the ocean was calm again on the other side, no more waves. The spirit of the place seemed different after, as if the energy spent on producing that set had drained its tank. The surface texture, the color, even the smell seemed like it had changed.

Maybe it was me who had changed as well. I paddled out and intersected my brother, Victor, who asked how my first wave was and did I see his second one. That was the wave that broke on my head when I was still trying to get my board back. I hadn't realized that anyone was riding it.

Victor said his wave was great and I told him mine was too. But I didn't have the energy to go into what came after that first wave just then. The moment was still

Top and Bottom   At G-Land, speed down the line was essential. But once up and running, there were moments where one could relax and go with the flow. Photos: Art Brewer

upon me. It seemed to linger and I liked the feeling, but I needed to examine it before I shared it with someone else.

Victor and I had ridden the only two waves of that set that anyone got. After the first two waves it had totally cleaned out the lineup. Where there had been thirty or more guys minutes before, now there was no one else but us as we paddled back out.

It was strange. I pondered all I had been through, and here was my brother going on about how great that set had looked to him. Victor was just paddling back out after his wave, oblivious as to how it had looked to me. It was as if he was on one side of a time warp and I was on the other, yet there we were, paddling side by side.

I felt that my moment of clarity was like a momentary glimpse of the Truth. The Truth is when things are as they are. I was caught inside and should have been pounded, perhaps even killed. Somehow the situation called on some inner power that pulled me through while everybody else was washed away.

Life is a series of moments. I came through that set to find that all moments are simultaneous but at the same time separate and unique. Victor's moments were not like mine. And as to the Truth, it is "What Is So." But after talking with Victor who told me about his own entirely different experience very nearby at the same time, I've decided that Truth may also, but not so obviously, be "So What!"

Seldom are there situations in our lives where there really are no choices. But that was my experience with the killer set at G-Land. There was no luxury to tarry thinking, weighing the whys and wherefores and so on. My actions and reactions had to be immediate.

The one choice I found was to believe that the tools and skills to handle the situation were already there. I didn't believe I was going to escape that set, but I was put into the situation where I had no choice but to try. Usually there is some choice of better or worse options, but in that instance there wasn't any choice. That's why it worked for me. No choosing, no deliberating, just do it.

There is a Taoist saying: The way to do is to be. Facing that monster set at G-Land, I did right because I was already right, once I got out of the way of myself. I didn't panic like the other surfers and allow myself to be swept along with the current. By abandoning the notion of a choice, I was in a place where my innate abilities and intrinsic wisdom were able to rise above my fears and expectations.

The inner self is a great place. It's closer than most people think and it is nearly perfect. When a person can find the way to access this wonderful state at will, there is no worry about being caught inside again. Surfing has an endless supply of lessons to teach us. Surf realization is about believing those lessons can, and should, be applied to life.

I've come to believe that surfing is as deep and meaningful as one wants to make it. At the same time, surfing is as shallow and light as pure fun can be. Do it for whatever reasons a person can want, but keep doing it.

The fifth and final Lopez Rule: The best surfer in the water is the guy having the most fun. I try to remember that one.

Above   The golden sunset and the
kids of Bali had the same thing in
common: beauty. Photo: Dana Edmunds

Next spread   While not all Pipe Masters events had
good waves on contest day, this one back in the 1970s
sure seemed to have one I enjoyed. Photo: Dan Merkel

Again I had survived and that was something
to relish after a day surfing the Pipeline.
Photo: Ralph Cipolla/Lost and Found Collection